Populism to Progressivism
in Alabama

POPULISM TO

PROGRESSIVISM

IN ALABAMA

BY SHELDON HACKNEY

PRINCETON, NEW JERSEY

PRINCETON UNIVERSITY PRESS

1969

Publication of this book has been aided by
the Whitney Darrow Publication Reserve Fund of
Princeton University Press.

Printed in the United States of America by
Princeton University Press, Princeton, New Jersey

++

ACKNOWLEDGMENT

++

I f many of the patterns and themes that emerge from the following study are familiar to the reader, that is a tribute to the many able scholars upon whose investigations of Populism, Progressivism, and the South I am building. I am particularly fortunate in writing about a state whose history has received the attention of an unusually large number of professional historians. I trust that the footnotes will adequately express my indebtedness to these predecessors. To C. Vann Woodward of Yale University, the foremost among them, I owe a debt that is both intellectual and personal. Influence is too weak a word to denote the role he played in this project from inception to realization, yet he constantly encouraged me to depart from well-worn paths, even from his own, and he always had the grace to allow me to make my own errors, as I undoubtedly have done. Arthur S. Link of Princeton University read the manuscript twice with a perceptive eye. Though he did not succeed in convincing me to alter it in all the ways he thought necessary, his criticisms improved the work tremendously.

The extent to which I have benefitted from the help of teachers, colleagues, and friends while completing this book has revived my belief in the existence of the community of scholars. I received valuable assistance from John M. Blum, George W. Pierson, Howard Lamar, Robert E. Lane, James M. McPherson, Duane Lockard, Martin Duberman, William S. McFeely, Lewis Gould,

ACKNOWLEDGMENT

Richard Jenson, and Peyton McCrary. The services rendered by Ray Arsenault went qualitatively and quantitatively beyond the requirements of his job as my research assistant. Archivists and librarians gave me almost unfailing cooperation. Milo Howard and Caroline Virginia Kennedy Jones of the Alabama Department of Archives and History, of which Mr. Howard is now the director, went out of their ways to make my task easier. Wilbur Helmbold, the librarian of Sanford University, was also especially accommodating. For all of this assistance, I am deeply grateful.

I also owe a debt of gratitude to a legion of unsuspecting friends and relatives who, from time to time, innocently asked me what I was doing. I hope that they learned as much from the monologue they got in response to this question as I learned in the process of trying to explain that Alabama actually had experienced reform movements in the past and that we could learn much from them that is relevant to contemporary problems.

To my wife, who will see the humor of being mentioned last, I owe much that can not be noted here. Nevertheless, my appreciation of her fund of understanding, her vitality, and her painfully proper sense of priorities should not go unrecorded.

SHELDON HACKNEY

Princeton
July 1968

CONTENTS

CONTENTS

viii

INTRODUCTION

E veryone is familiar with William Allen White's quip that Progressivism was simply Populism that had "shaved its whiskers, washed its shirt, put on a derby, and moved up into the middle class." Historians, finding it similarly natural and fruitful to compare Populism and Progressivism, have always noted large differences between the two. At the same time, however, they have agreed with the implication of White's jest that there was something basically similar in the two reform movements that occurred so close together in time and space. This study is centrally concerned with the nature of Populism and of Progressivism in Alabama and with the problem of the relationship between them.

The question of the continuity between Populism and Progressivism is a very subtle matter of emphases, involving such things as common leadership and constituency, similarity of programs, and shared rhetoric. Most historians of the American South probably think of Populism and Progressivism as sequential and complementary phenomena. In this view, one of the basic differences between the two political forces that fought entrenched big-business interests between 1890 and the First World War was temporal. They had the same enemy, professed the same program, used the same rhetoric—the big difference was that Populism was the ill-tempered, rural product of the depression in the 1890s and Progressivism was the more genial, urban, middle class child of prosperity after the turn of the century. In addition, in many ways the historians who deservedly are most influential in creating our image of the South have tended to sculpt Progressivism out of Populist materials. C. Vann Woodward characterizes Georgia Progressivism as "Populistic in ideology and heritage" and illustrates the nexus between the two movements with Tom Watson's muckraking efforts and with his alliance in 1906 with Hoke Smith that helped win Georgia for Progressivism. Speaking of the South in general, Professor Woodward explains part of the connection by noting that the collapse of the third party removed the stigma from reform and brought back into the ruling Democratic Party its alienated left wing. "Returning, the Populists brought along with them their ideological baggage, for which room had to be found."[1] Arthur Link, the scholar who first documented the existence of a Progressive movement in the South, also notes that "in the South and West the connection between Populism and Progressivism was fairly direct. In the West most Populists went into the Democratic party in 1896 and constituted the main part of Bryan's following in that region afterward. The process of assimilation was slower in the South, but the former Populists were by 1912 an important segment of a new progressive coalition vying for control of Democratic state organizations." Elsewhere Professor Link makes clear that much of the continuity between Populism and Progressivism was ideological but that Populism's conversion of "the great masses of farmers to this new philosophy, later called progressivism, made it a political force that could not long be ignored by the

[1] C. Vann Woodward, *Tom Watson, Agrarian Rebel*, New York, 1938, 366-368; and *Origins of the New South, 1877-1913*, Baton Rouge, 1951, 372.

two major parties."[2] Leaning on the work of such scholars as Woodward and Link, Richard Hofstadter's influential synthesis in his book, *The Age of Reform*, perpetuates the notion that "after 1900 Populism and Progressivism merge. . . ."[3]

In order to test the idea of continuity between Populism and Progressivism, and perhaps sharpen its meaning, we need to look closely at what happened to the Populists after 1896, a research design that has never been systematically exploited. While tracing Populist leadership and membership beyond the Populist era, we must also investigate the pre-1900 activities of the Progressives. In this way it may be that we can properly qualify the idea of temporal separation between the two movements and decide whether or not there were essential differences in their ideologies. Then we will be in a position to answer the question of whether Populism and Progressivism can more usefully be thought of as complementary assaults on a common enemy or as alternative strategies for different groups in the same situation.

It is of course impossible to compare two movements without considering their individual identities. Populism seems to have survived the deluge of criticism it suffered in the 1950s and the classic view of it is pretty much intact.[4] It is still thought of as a constructive, rational

[2] Arthur S. Link, *American Epoch: A History of the United States Since the 1890's*, 2nd edn., New York, 1966, 69, 10-11, and 8.

[3] Richard Hofstadter, *The Age of Reform: From Bryan to F.D.R.*, New York, 1955, 133-135.

[4] The classic work on Populism as a whole is John D. Hicks, *The Populist Revolt: A History of the Farmers' Alliance and the People's Party*, Minneapolis, 1931. The best guide to, and reply to, the critics of Populism is C. Vann Woodward, "The Populist Heritage and the Intellectual," *The Burden of Southern History*, Baton Rouge, 1960, 141-166. A more recent and less

movement motivated by economic self-interest, though not as a movement of crypto-socialist ideologues. Its defenders may concede that Populists were not always well informed and that their tactics were often ineffective, but they also believe that even though Populism was the last gasp of the yeoman-farmer tradition in America it was a heroic gasp that breathed new life into twentieth-century political reform. Now that the echoes from the shrill charge that Populism was a rural American version of Luddism have subsided, it may be time to make a closer examination of these charges than the critics that leveled them were willing to make.

Similarly, the realities of Progressivism should be closely questioned. If Progressivism was something more than an attempt on the part of the business community to solve its own internal problems through the use of governmental machinery, yet something less than an altruistic quest for social justice, exactly what was it and who was it and how did it get going?[5] Emerging out of the welter of interpretations of Progressivism, there is

placid encounter over the issue is Norman Pollack, "Fear of Man: Populism, Authoritarianism, and the Historian," and the replies thereto, all in *Agricultural History*, XXXIX, April 1965, 59-85. A sound refutation of the charge of Populist nativism is Walter T. K. Nugent, *The Tolerant Populists: Kansas, Populism and Nativism*, Chicago, 1963. The most recent pro-Populist statement from a scholar is Theodore Saloutos, "The Professors and the Populists," *Agricultural History*, XL, October 1966, 235-254.

[5] Gabriel Kolko, *The Triumph of Conservatism: A Reinterpretation of American History, 1900-1916*, New York, 1963. Harold U. Faulkner, *The Quest for Social Justice, 1898-1914*, New York, 1931. George Mowry, *The Era of Theodore Roosevelt, 1900-1912*, New York, 1958. Arthur S. Link, *Woodrow Wilson and the Progressive Era, 1910-1917*, New York, 1954. Samuel P. Hays, *The Response to Industrialism, 1885-1914*, Chicago, 1957. Robert H. Wiebe, *The Search for Order, 1877-1920*, New York, 1967.

apparent agreement on the existence of two basic types of Progressivism, with considerable overlap between the two.[6] One type was Eastern, urban, elitist, rational, fact-finding, environmentalist, more interested in extending government services to the business community than in political or social-justice reforms. Theodore Roosevelt was its hero. The other brand was Western, rural, democratic, emotional, conspiracy-minded, given to imputations of personal sin, more interested in enforcing competition than in regulating monopoly or oligopoly, and more interested in mechanical political reforms and legislation for social justice than in creating the conditions of business prosperity and growth. Its representative leader was William Jennings Bryan, or perhaps Robert LaFollette. C. Vann Woodward writes that "the Southern counterpart of a Northern progressivism developed nearly all traits familiar to the genus, but it was in no sense derivative. It was a pretty strictly indigenous growth, touched lightly here and there by cross-fertilization from the West."[7] Was Alabama an exception to this picture of southern Progressivism?

Precisely because this study is set in the South, matters of race must play a large part. This is inevitable, but not because Negroes wielded key political power. They did not. The period from 1890 to 1910 was the period during which the state created the system of segregation and disfranchisement which is only now being painfully disman-

[6] John Braeman, "Seven Profiles: Modernists and Traditionalists," *The Progressive Era: Liberal Renaissance or Liberal Failure?*, Arthur Mann, ed., New York, 1963, 82-93. Paul W. Glad, "Bryan and the Urban Progressives," *Mid-America*, XXXIX, July 1957, 169-179. Hofstadter, *Age of Reform*, 133. Mowry, *The Era of Theodore Roosevelt*, 54-57. Wiebe, *The Search for Order*, 176-181, and 166.

[7] Woodward, *Origins of the New South*, 371-374.

tled. A number of questions in this regard must be faced. Did the Populist attempt to attract Negro voters differ greatly from Democratic efforts along this line, and were the Populists successful? To the extent that Populists were accused of committing racial heresy, were their chances of victory hurt as much as some historians have suggested? In Alabama what social groups provided the pressure for Negro disfranchisement? What evidence is there to support the Woodward thesis as to the key role of legislation in *The Strange Career of Jim Crow*?[8] How did Negroes themselves react to Jim Crow legislation and disfranchisement, and how did the Progressives approach or use the problem of race?

Alabama provides a good laboratory in which to compare Populism and Progressivism in a revealing biracial context. The state also contained at the time a significant industrial sector in its economy based on coal, iron, lumber, and cotton. Focused almost totally outside the Black Belt,[9] investment in manufacturing enterprises rose from $9,668,008 in 1880 to $46,122,571 in 1890. Surviving the stagnant 1890s, the manufacturing capital in the state jumped from $60,166,000 to $173,180,000 between 1899 and 1909, while the value of products and the value added by manufacturing were doubling. During the same period, Alabama's annual mining production increased in value by 30.4 percent to rank tenth among the states in this index.[10] Such developments meant a

[8] C. Vann Woodward, *The Strange Career of Jim Crow*, 2nd rev. edn., New York, 1966.

[9] Throughout this work the term "Black Belt" refers to the crescent-shaped 12-county sector of rich farmlands stretching across the southern half of Alabama, in which the Negro percentage of the total male voting-age population in 1900 was greater than 60 percent. See Appendix I.

[10] U.S. Bureau of the Census, *Tenth Census of the United*

growth in urban population. The proportion of the population living in towns of 2,500 or more people climbed from 10.1 percent in 1890 to only 11.9 percent in 1900 and then leaped to include 17.3 percent of the total in 1910. Over the same period farm population dropped from 85.2 percent to 75 percent of the total, while the total grew from 1,513,401 to 2,138,093.[11] If in 1910 Alabama was still predominantly agricultural it also contained a significant variety of middle class urbanites and wage-earners, as well as farmers and other rural people. With the problems these men faced between 1890 and 1910 and with the interconnectedness of Populism, disfranchisement, and Progressivism, the following chapters are concerned.

States: 1880, Part I, 712. *Eleventh Census of the United States: 1890*, Part I, 67, Table I, Part II, cix; *Thirteenth Census of the United States: 1910, Manufactures*, IX, 29, and *Mines and Quarries*, XI, 318-319.

[11] U.S. Bureau of the Census, *Statistics for Alabama, Containing Statistics of Population, Agriculture, Manufactures and Mining for the State, Counties, Cities, and Other Divisions*, Washington, 1913. This is a convenient reprint of the "Supplement for Alabama" published in connection with the abstract of the *Thirteenth Census*.

Populism to Progressivism
in Alabama

Who Were the Populists?

To embrace Populism in the 1890s was an act of defiance. A man could not thereby increase his social prestige, for the Democrats constantly taunted Populists with the accusation that they were not quite respectable. No one voted Populist from habit, for the People's Party was new. Men who voted Populist were frequently plagued by social ostracism, loss of financial credit, and sometimes physical intimidation. If the charges of the white Democrats were true, Populists were guilty of treason to party, race, region, and sacred Jeffersonian principles. Yet 115,000 Alabamians, virtually half of the voting population, cast their ballots for the People's Party candidate for governor in 1892.

Obviously these were unusual times. The deepening two-decade decline in the price of farm goods, the growing incidence of farm tenantry and debt, the migration of people to new farm lands and new industrial towns in north and southeast Alabama in the 1880s, the intense competition of rural Southerners for the low-wage jobs in the lumber industry, in mining, and in the new cotton mills, the tremors of financial panic that were felt in the South in 1891 and 1892 following the fall of the House of Baring in November 1890, the spreading blight of industrial collapse that by 1893 was a full-scale national

3

depression—all these disruptive forces coalesced to create the crisis that gave rise to Populism.

As intense as the dislocations were, they did not make a third-party political revolt inevitable. When disaster strikes a well-integrated community, the result is likely to be an increase rather than a decrease in social solidarity and altruistic identification with the community.[1] When a crisis occurs in a poorly integrated society it may well lead to conflict across the fault lines of previously existing social stress. This was the case in the 1890s. Outside the South, Populism was most successful in newly settled states. Within Alabama, Populism flourished in those areas that experienced significant immigration in the post-bellum period and where traditional animosities toward the dominant social and political groups in the state were concentrated. This suggests that Populism was the product of people whose social position and relationships did not link them securely to their society. Even in areas susceptible to such disorganization, however, there were divisions that can only be explained by knowing who the Populists were and how they came to be Populists.

Firm evidence about the identity of the Populists was not available until they began to vote, but one clue to their origin lay in the ambitions of Reuben F. Kolb. Furthermore, the contrast between the careers of Kolb and

[1] Robert E. L. Faris, *Social Disorganization*, New York, 1948, 44-46. Bernard Berelson and Gary A. Steiner, *Human Behavior: An Inventory of Scientific Findings*, New York, 1964, 620-625, 629. Allen Barton, *Social Organization Under Stress: A Sociological Review of Disaster Studies*, Washington, D.C., 1963. The best definition of the concept of social disorganization is provided by Robert K. Merton in Robert K. Merton and Robert A. Nisbet, eds., *Contemporary Social Problems*, 2nd edn., New York, 1966, 800-805. See also Reece McGee, *Social Disorganization in America*, San Francisco, 1962.

his chief antagonist, Thomas Goode Jones, is instructive. Kolb was the leading Populist and perhaps the most successful Alabama farmer of his time.[2] Raised by his grandfather, who was the brother of Governor John Gill Shorter, and graduated from the University of North Carolina in 1859, Kolb entered adulthood with all the advantages that a prominent Alabama family could give a son. Nevertheless, his success story was real.

What would have been the normal course of Kolb's life as a planter and merchant in Barbour County was interrupted by secession and the Civil War. As the youngest member of Alabama's secession convention, Kolb voted for secession and shortly thereafter entered the service of the Confederate States of America as a sergeant. Later he raised his own company of troops, Kolb's Battery, fought through the war and emerged in 1865 with a captain's commission and an honorable record. Family, place, breeding, education, service to the Lost Cause—Kolb's future should have been secure.

Unfortunately the world which gave genteel attributes their meaning was seriously disjointed. Kolb returned from the war to find his family fortune in ruins. Like most other farmers in the deep South, he planted his large farm almost entirely in cotton, and until the war-starved market was satiated things went well. Cotton prices hit a post-1865 peak of 17.9 cents per pound in 1871 but then began to decline. By 1878 the price per pound was 8.59 cents. It fluctuated near this level through

[2] Information about Kolb's life has been gleaned primarily from three sources: Charles G. Summersell, "A Life of Reuben F. Kolb," unpub. master's thesis, University of Alabama, 1930; Luther Lister Hill, "Reuben Kolb and the Populist Revolt in Alabama," unpub. senior thesis, Princeton University, 1957; William W. Rogers, "Agrarianism in Alabama, 1865-1896," unpub. Ph.D. diss., University of North Carolina, 1959.

1890, while local and world production surged ahead. At this price level, farmers were squeezed between the high cost of land, mechanization, and credit on the one hand, and declining farm prices and deflating money values on the other. When the price of cotton reached a low of 5.73 cents in 1898, the estimated cost of production was 7 cents per pound.[3] "This of course could bring but one result," Kolb later wrote, "disaster."[4] Through the years of Reconstruction, Kolb searched for ways to avoid personal disaster. He tried the grocery business, managed an "opera house" in Eufaula for a time, and even sought appointment as postmaster. Nothing succeeded.

Eventually Kolb found success in his watermelon patch. He began to experiment and soon developed his own strain of melon, the "Kolb Gem," whose popularity spread. Orders mounted until Kolb was primarily growing and shipping seed. As his cash returns rose, he also learned to grow foodstuffs for his own farm rather than buying his supplies. Modernization usually means specialization, but Kolb and other agricultural reformers were convinced that diversification was the southern farmer's road to the future. "There is, nor can be but one outcome to the all cotton idea," thought Kolb. It meant "disaster not only to the pocketbook, but to the land as well."[5]

Kolb's experience made him an apostle of scientific

[3] U.S. Bureau of the Census, *Historical Statistics of the United States: Colonial Times to 1957*, Washington, D.C., 1960, Series K-303. William W. Rogers, "Reuben F. Kolb: Agricultural Leader of the New South," *Agricultural History*, XXXII, April 1958, 109-119.

[4] Kolb to John W. DuBose, July 7, 1888, DuBose Papers, Alabama Department of Archives and History (hereafter abbreviated "ADAH").

[5] *Ibid.*

agriculture and his success made him a leading agricultural spokesman. In 1887 he served as president of the National Farmers Congress at Chicago and was reelected when the meeting was held in Montgomery in 1889. When Governor Thomas Seay appointed him Commissioner of Agriculture in 1887,[6] Kolb used his position to further his dream of making agriculture in Alabama modern and capable of competing in national and world markets. Through farmers' institutes, all-day meetings held throughout the state, Commissioner Kolb spread the knowledge that was coming out of the growing experimental farm system.

It soon became evident that Kolb wished to do *well* as well as do good, for he had strong political ambitions. The institutes gave him the opportunity to meet and speak to thousands of Alabamians, an opportunity he exploited to the full. His department also flooded the state with agricultural bulletins, each of which bore the commissioner's name as well as useful information. Touring the Northwest in 1888 with an exhibit called "Alabama on Wheels," Kolb won additional publicity for himself, though he lured very few immigrants to Alabama. At this time he was already thinking of running for governor in 1890.[7]

Kolb's ambition and sympathies happened to coincide with those of the Farmers' Alliance. Following on the heels of rural discontent, the first lodge of the Alliance in Alabama was organized in Madison County, in the Tennessee valley of Alabama, in March 1887. The Agricultural Wheel, the other mass farm organization in Alabama, had entered the state in 1886, and in September 1887 helped to organize the Union Labor Party,

[6] Rogers, "Agrarianism in Alabama," Chapter 6, p. 125.
[7] *Ibid.*, 196-204.

which brought together laborers and farmers under the leadership of Republicans, old Greenbackers, and leaders of the Knights of Labor. But the tension between those who wanted the Wheel to go into politics and those who wanted it to stay out of politics rendered it ineffectual. When the two farm organizations merged in October 1889 the Wheel boasted 75,000 members, but many of these were also members of the Alliance, which claimed 3,000 lodges and 125,000 members.[8]

Few of the farmers who belonged to the Alliance were as successful as Kolb—but they wanted to be. Among the economic enterprises designed by the Alliance to aid farmers in their quest for success were cotton mills, fertilizer companies, bagging plants, warehouses, and even a bank. The largest undertaking was the Alabama State Exchange, a cooperative marketing and purchasing agency that enjoyed great popularity among the membership. The Alliance also planned a farm implement factory and a wagon works for the future. As practical as these attempts to accommodate to the changing times were, they enjoyed only brief success. Even before cooperative business proved a failure, however, the Alliance showed its interest in political activity.[9]

The disgruntled farmers began to look to politics as early as the Farmers' Alliance convention held in Auburn in August 1889. This convention approved the merger with the Wheel, voted to support what proved to be a successful boycott campaign against the jute-bagging trust, and ratified the constitution of the Southern Al-

[8] *Ibid.*, 227 and 247. William W. Rogers, "The Farmers' Alliance in Alabama," *The Alabama Review*, XV, January 1962, 9. John Bunyon Clark, *Populism in Alabama*, Auburn, Alabama, 1927, 74.

[9] Rogers, "Agrarianism in Alabama," Chapter 11, and "The Farmers' Alliance in Alabama," 17.

liance. Perhaps more important were the resolutions commending the efforts of Commissioner Kolb and condemning the criticisms of the Alliance voiced by the Montgomery *Advertiser*, the most influential newspaper in the state.

The *Advertiser* was opposed to the Alliance's economic boycott, as well as to Kolb's political ambitions. Its anxieties were not calmed by the informal poll of the convention showing that Kolb was the favorite of the delegates for the governorship in 1890, nor did the convention reassure the *Advertiser* when it named Kolb to head a committee of five to attend the national Alliance convention in St. Louis.

The action of the convention in St. Louis doubtless increased the *Advertiser*'s fears of a third force in state politics. The convention failed to unite the Northern and Southern Alliances, but the Southern Alliance adopted a set of "demands" which were endorsed by the Knights of Labor. These demands sounded the basic Populist trio of concerns—money, land, transportation. They called for various inflationary measures, legislation to eliminate large landholdings by aliens and railroads, and nationalization of the means of transportation. But these planks did not alarm the *Advertiser* as much as did two other acts of the convention.

The first bit of heresy in the *Advertiser*'s eyes was Dr. C. W. Macune's subtreasury plan, a commodity credit scheme to be backed by the federal government, which recalled the tobacco-warehouse-receipt currency of seventeenth-century Virginia at the same time that it looked forward to such legislation as the Warehouse Act of 1916. In essence the farmers were asking the federal government to rig the marketplace in their favor by providing credit, so that they could hold their products off the market until the price was right. Perhaps just as obnoxious to the *Advertiser* was the joint pledge made by the Southern Alliance and the Knights of Labor that they would "support for office only such men as can be depended upon to enact these principles into statute law uninfluenced by party caucus."[10] The *Advertiser* feared this was aimed at the South's one-party system.[11] The resulting controversy illustrated a key point.

The *Advertiser* and the New-South-railroad-industrial complex for which it spoke were not interested merely in maintaining Democratic Party solidarity. The party could always have maintained its unity by acquiescing in the leadership of the Alliance. But this would have disturbed the intricate system that controlled political rewards and guarded the interests of the Big Mule–Black Belt partnership.[12] Seen from within this established system of political obligations, Kolb was a threat for two reasons. Despite his disavowal of intentions to form a third party, Kolb was identified with forces within and without the state that were challenging party regulars. Alliance groups had already threatened to take over Bibb and Shelby Counties, for example. Despite Kolb's denial that he supported the St. Louis demands, and despite his efforts to keep his own appeals well within the accepted pattern, he was inevitably linked to leaders and groups that wanted to use politics to change existing conditions. When Kolb announced on December 22, 1889 that he

[10] John D. Hicks, *The Populist Revolt: A History of the Farmers' Alliance and the People's Party*, Minneapolis, 1931, 427.

[11] Montgomery *Advertiser*, December 26, 29, 1889.

[12] "Big Mule" is the colloquial term for the owners and managers of big business firms in Alabama. For "Black Belt" see note 9 in the Introduction. A graphic ethnological definition of the Black Belt appears in Appendix I.

would be a candidate for the Democratic nomination for governor, he presented himself as the best qualified leader of a classless community. In the succeeding campaign, however, some of his supporters talked of class conflict and radical reform. The Alliance was still led in 1890 by large planters, but it was clearly stirring up classes of men normally politically inactive—men who should defer to the leadership of those more qualified to rule.[13]

The *Advertiser* thought Thomas Goode Jones was more qualified to rule than Kolb. Both Kolb and Jones came from families of impeccable Southern pedigree, yet both had had to achieve individual success without the aid of family wealth. The contrasting ways in which they did so are significant. Where Kolb's achievements in the army, farming, and politics were the accomplishments of an individual operating outside of the system's established procedures for advancement, Jones had risen within the system.

Entering the Civil War in 1861 at the age of 17 as a cadet from the Virginia Military Institute, Jones quickly caught the attention of his superiors and was given a commission and the position of aide-de-camp on the staff of Gen. John B. Gordon of the Army of Northern Virginia. Skill as a staff officer advanced him to the rank of major by the end of the war. Jones returned to Montgomery and tried farming, then editing a Democratic newspaper, before turning to the practice of law as so many ambitious young men did. In 1870 he again managed to earn the patronage of his superiors and was appointed Reporter of the Decisions of the Alabama Supreme Court, a thoroughly Republican institution at the time. Jones served the Court until 1884 when he was

[13] Clark, *Populism in Alabama*, 92. Rogers, "Agrarianism in Alabama," 300.

elected to the state legislature. He was undoubtedly aided in his political career by his position at the Court and by his military career with the state militia, where he won a statewide reputation for ferocity on riot duty. In his second term in the legislature, 1886 to 1888, he was Speaker of the Alabama House of Representatives. By this time he had also followed his old commanding officer's example and joined the staff of the New South's economic high command, which in Alabama was the Louisville and Nashville Railroad (L & N).[14]

Jones was one of the L & N's two top representatives among an army of attorneys in the state in 1890. The other was his law partner, Jefferson Falkner. The alliance with the railroads was not an unnatural one for Jones. His father had been a pioneer railroad construction engineer in the South, and railroads remained important to Jones throughout his life. Joining with the president of the railroad in land speculation, lobbying with congressmen to intercede on the railroad's behalf before the Interstate Commerce Commission, distributing free railroad passes to probate judges and other officials, advising his superiors when to buy opposing newspapers and when to support friendly ones—Jones was completely identified with his railroad employers.[15]

[14] The best single source of information on Thomas Goode Jones is Henry S. Lynn, Jr., "Thomas Goode Jones and His Public Philosophy," unpub. senior thesis, Princeton University, 1966.

[15] Russell Houston to Jones, April 25, 1887; Jones to E. B. Stahlman, November 24, 1888, Jones Papers, ADAH. The opposing paper was the Montgomery *Dispatch* owned by D. S. Troy, an anti-railroad leader, political reformer, and businessman. Troy sold his equipment to Horace Hood who used it to print the Montgomery *Journal*, a consistently reform-minded and progressive paper throughout the period 1890 to 1910, with perhaps a lapse in 1904, just as the *Advertiser* was consistently anti-reform and pro-railroad.

12

The *Advertiser* was a friendly paper, and Jones appealed to the L & N for funds to keep it going. If it were forced to sell, he wrote, "it will do the Railroads and conservative progress immense harm."[16] Conservative progress was something Jones was certainly for, but he put as much emphasis on conservatism as on progress. In practice this meant the pursuit of industrialization by making the state as attractive as possible to outside investment capital. Such a policy was the logical one for an organization man involved with outside capitalists. Jones decided in November 1888 that he wanted to move up to the next slot on the organization chart: the governorship.[17]

The most important of the other three candidates for the governorship in 1890 was Joseph F. Johnston who in the future would serve as the rallying point for the budding Alabama Progressive movement. Though Johnston was born in North Carolina, he moved to Alabama before the Civil War and enlisted in the Confederate army as a private. Emerging in 1865 as a captain with some valuable wounds, Johnston decided not to return to what seemed a futureless northern Alabama and went instead to Selma, an old center of power in the Black Belt. In 1884, after 17 years as a successful attorney in Selma, Johnston left the stagnant Black Belt and moved to the "magic city" of Birmingham. There he quickly became a leading industrial promoter and president of the Alabama National Bank. Finding this unfulfilling, he began

[16] Jones to Eckstein Norton, December 31, 1888, Jones Papers, ADAH. The L & N was willing to subsidize friendly papers, one of which was undoubtedly the *Advertiser*. "Milton H. Smith Testifies Regarding Political Contributions," *Railway Age*, LXIV, March 1, 1918, 446.

[17] Jones to Governor Edward A. O'Neal, November 24, 1888, Jones Papers, ADAH.

in 1890 a search for political power. James F. Crook, who had won a reputation as a railroad regulator while serving with Walter L. Bragg on the Alabama Railroad Commission from 1881 to 1885, was also a candidate in 1890, as was William Richardson, a state court judge.

Kolb, realizing he was opposed by the established politicians, campaigned vigorously. Even though he was not the official candidate of the Alliance, just before the Democratic convention met, Kolb issued a circular letter to the Alliance. "Attend the convention," he implored, "help me and the delegates you have elected to defeat the unholy cliques and combinations now forming of plutocrats against the people."[18] Kolb the outsider was talking to all of the other outsiders in the state who felt alienated from the regular leadership of the party and the state.

The regular leadership recognized the threat. Speakers bombarded the delegates with anti-Kolb diatribes and the Democratic State Executive Committee rigged the convention against Kolb. Had he been given the seats in the convention that he contested, Kolb would have been close enough to a majority to lure other supporters to his cause. As it was, he lost the contests before the credentials committee, which had been packed by the Executive Committee, as well as on the floor. The first roll call on May 29, 1890 showed Kolb commanding the lead with 235 votes, just a few votes shy of the 264 needed. The other runners in the race stretched out behind him: Johnston, 104; Richardson, 88; Crook, 52; and Jones, 45. As the balloting continued in the evening of the 29th and through the 30th, the tension mounted, but the vote totals showed only marginal changes from one roll call

[18] Quoted in John W. DuBose, MSS *History*, Chapter 40, in the DuBose Papers, ADAH.

to the next. Characteristically, Kolb and his opponents found it impossible to compromise with each other.[19]

The deadlock was broken in a classic way. At 11 p.m. on the evening of May 30th, representatives of the four anti-Kolb candidates met in the Exchange Hotel in Montgomery. As a result of this meeting, future Progressives and agents of the railroad-backed wing of the party, the wing the Progressives later fought, cooperated to defeat a common enemy—incipient Populism. Jeff Falkner, the L & N's man in Alabama, represented his law partner, Jones. J. J. Willett of Anniston represented Crook. Willett found himself frequently on the opposite side of the counsel table from railroad attorneys. After 1900 he helped B. B. Comer in the anti-railroad campaign that precipitated the Progressive movement. Rufus N. Rhodes, owner-editor of the Birmingham *News* and also a future partisan of Comer Progressivism, stood in for Johnston. George Jones of Florence represented Richardson. These men had in common a desire to preserve the system from destruction at the hands of someone they viewed as essentially a threat to the established order of community leadership.

The meeting had all of the elements of the famed Wormely House conference of 1877, which was supposed to have provided a solution for the political impasse arising out of the Hayes-Tilden election. It was even more comparable to the real solution of that crisis. The genuine compromise of 1877 had been made possible by railroads,[20] the only force in national life strong enough to provide the motive for transcending political loyalties. The same was true of Alabama in 1890.

[19] Clark, *Populism in Alabama*, 104. Mobile *Register*, May 30, 1890.

[20] C. Vann Woodward, *Reunion and Reaction: The Compromise of 1877 and the End of Reconstruction*, Boston, 1951.

The real architect of the Exchange Hotel deal was Wiley C. Tunstall, Associate Railroad Commissioner.[21] Tunstall never held elective office, but he and his son, Alfred M. Tunstall, were among the small group of men who made the Democratic Party work.[22] A. M. Tunstall served in the Alabama House of Representatives from 1896 to 1907 and was Speaker in the sessions of 1901 and 1903. His father served on the Railroad Commission from 1885 to 1895. After an interregnum during Johnston's governorship, Wiley Tunstall was recalled to his post on the commission in 1901 when the right wing of the Democratic Party regained control of the state. Unsurprisingly, when Tunstall was reappointed to the Commission in 1891, the railroads were well pleased.[23]

At 7 a.m. on June 1, 1890, after an all-night session, Tunstall and the others at the meeting decided that Thomas Goode Jones should be the Democratic Party's nominee for governor in 1890. A survey of the field had revealed that Kolb was the second choice of enough of the Jones delegates to elect that dreaded interloper if Jones withdrew. Jones was the only anti-Kolb candidate who could win—for the simple reason that his delegates were not anti-Kolb.

Jones won the nomination on the first roll call of the fourth day of the convention, May 31, 1890. The tally showed Kolb with 246 and Jones with 277.[24] Kolb made

[21] Birmingham *Age-Herald*, January 28, 1891. Previous historians have overlooked this report and Tunstall's role in the deal, as well as his role in state politics in general. The report was made by Frank Julian, then a young reporter and later secretary of state under B. B. Comer, 1907-11, who knew state politics extremely well.

[22] *Ibid.*, February 11, 1891. This reports Tunstall's key role in getting the politically explosive redistricting bill passed.

[23] *Ibid.*, January 29, 1891.

[24] Mobile *Register*, June 1, 1890.

a conciliatory speech and promised to stump the state for Jones. And he did. Jones won the election on August 4 with customary ease by garnering 139,910 votes, to 42,440 for the Republican candidate, Ben L. Long. Though harmony reigned within the Democratic Party, orthodox politicians wondered just how long the more exuberant members of the chorus would restrain themselves.

As the Alliance drifted leftward during the closing months of 1890 and throughout 1891, it became evident that the Democratic Party in 1892 would be badly divided. Before the election of 1890 local Alliances and individuals were very hesitant to endorse the controversial subtreasury plan.[25] Democratic criticism of the scheme was concerted and withering.[26] After Jones' election in August 1890, however, the state convention of the Alliance adopted resolutions favoring the subtreasury and the whole set of St. Louis demands.[27] When the Southern Alliance approved a similar political program at Ocala, Florida in December 1890, local and district Alliances in Alabama began quickly endorsing the Ocala demands as their own.[28] At the same time, in Birmingham, a number of politicians and labor leaders formed a pro-Kolb political club, with their purpose to control Jefferson County politics in the next election.[29] That the Alliance contemplated violating the southern taboo against independent organizations engaging in partisan political activity was confirmed in February 1891 when the state

[25] Birmingham *Age-Herald*, July 27, September 9, 1890.
[26] Hicks, *Populist Revolt*, Chapter 7. Birmingham *Age-Herald*, July 3, August 6, 1890.
[27] *Ibid.*, August 6, 1890.
[28] Mobile *Register*, January 25, 30, 1891.
[29] Birmingham *Age-Herald*, October 26, November 1, 7, December 1, 2, 1890, January 17, February 17, 18, 1891.

president of the Alliance, Samuel M. Adams, returned from a meeting of Alliance leaders in Washington with a loyalty order. Adams instructed all primary Alliances in the state to cleanse their memberships of all men who were not actually farmers or who did not believe in the Ocala demands.[30]

Kolb announced his candidacy for the Democratic nomination for governor on July 21, 1891,[31] and Jones began his campaign on October 16.[32] The resulting contest for the nomination and then for governor was probably the most scurrilous on record in Alabama. Charges of fraud filled the air.[33] The Jones forces attacked Kolb for embracing socialistic, communistic, and un-Democratic ideas. Kolb men poured on the anti-monopoly and anti-machine rhetoric. The monster they attacked resided not only in Wall Street, but in Montgomery and numerous county courthouses across the state. Whether or not the antagonists were really getting across their point of view was problematical, for the discussion was quickly polarized. "Which side are you on?"[34] was the typical Kolbite query.

The discussion wasn't the only thing that was polarized. The governor's correspondence shows that Jones had the support of railroad, lumber, coal and iron interests, a large sampling of merchants and professional men, and,

[30] *Ibid.*, February 20, 1891. Rogers, "Agrarianism in Alabama," 327.

[31] Clark, *Populism in Alabama*, 118.

[32] *Ibid.*, 120. Charles G. Summersell, "The Alabama Governor's Race in 1892," *The Alabama Review*, VIII, January 1955, 9.

[33] *Ibid.* Rogers, "Agrarianism in Alabama," 349-350. Birmingham *Age-Herald*, May 3, 1891. Chappell Cory to Jones, September 8, 1891; Robert McKee to Jones, January 3, 1892, Jones Papers, ADAH.

[34] *Ozark Banner*, July 7, 1892.

of course, such influential politicians as Wiley Tunstall. Jones represented the existing economic, political, and social leadership and all those who identified themselves with it.

Governor Jones had certain other advantages. He used his influence with the railroads to reward political supporters with free railroad passes.[35] His supporters, in turn, used their control of the party machinery to set favorable ground rules for the contest, or to circumvent the rules when that became necessary.[36] Consequently, as the results of the county conventions and primaries began to accumulate in the spring of 1892, it was evident that Jones was leading in the race for convention delegates.

The primaries also revealed that the Black Belt support that Kolb had enjoyed in 1890 was melting away in 1892. As the Alliance moved to the left, the large planters obviously were falling away from it. Still, Kolb had the support of the Alliance in most counties.[37] Kolb's problem was what to do if he did not win the Democratic nomination. He was convinced Jones had captured many of the delegates fraudulently, but he could also be certain that at the convention he would lose the fight for the contested seats. Nevertheless, Kolb and the farm and labor organizations friendly to him continued to insist as late as May 1892 that they did not intend to form a

[35] Benjamin F. Riley to Jones, January 1, 1892; William J. Wood to Jones, January [?] 1892, Jones Papers, ADAH.

[36] Milford W. Howard to Jones, December 27, 1891; W. H. Lindale to Jones, January 7, 1892; Chappell Cory to Jones, April 1, 1892, Jones Papers, ADAH. Allen Jones, "A History of the Direct Primary in Alabama, 1840-1903," unpub. Ph.D. diss., University of Alabama, 1964, 206-208. Clark, *Populism in Alabama*, 125.

[37] Chappell Cory to Jones, September 8, 1891; Robert McKee to Jones, January 3, 1892, Jones Papers, ADAH.

third party.[38] This did not prevent Jones and his supporters from denouncing the third-party tendencies of Kolb and the Alliance. Some justification for Jones' charges was provided by events outside the state, as the movement to organize a national People's Party gathered momentum in early 1892.

The situation was made more complex in Alabama when a group of disgruntled Democrats led by Joseph C. Manning organized the People's Party in April 1892 at Ashland in Clay County.[39] Their call was answered by a few county Alliances and a few prominent Alliance leaders, but prior to the meeting of the state Democratic convention on June 8, their organization grew only slowly.

Kolb decided before the Democratic convention met that he would run for governor on an independent ticket if he did not win the Democratic nomination. He wrote to a political friend that if the Democratic thefts continued there would be two state conventions, just as there had been two county conventions in many counties, and he would "be the nominee of the simon pure Jeffersonian Democracy, and Jones the nominee of the machine Democracy."[40] His intention became public knowledge.[41] The Jones supporters had been saying all along that Kolb was not a loyal Democrat, and now they were proved right. But theirs was, after all, a self-fulfilling prophecy.

Attempts to negotiate a compromise settlement between the warring factions at the convention failed. As

[38] Rogers, "Agrarianism in Alabama," 328-335, 352-356.

[39] *Ibid.*, 352-356.

[40] Kolb to T. A. Street, April 22, 1892, Street Papers, University of Alabama Library; also quoted in Rogers, "Agrarianism in Alabama," 360 and in Jones, "A History of the Direct Primary in Alabama," 210.

[41] *Choctaw Advocate*, May 18, 1892; and Rogers, "Agrarianism in Alabama," 359-361.

a result, while the Democratic convention was nominating Jones on June 8th, the Kolb supporters met separately and organized the Jeffersonian Democrats. Until November 1894 the Jeffersonians maintained a technical distinction between themselves and the People's Party. Even though the two organizations maintained separate executive committees, however, they held joint conventions, nominated joint tickets, maintained joint campaign committees, and advocated a single platform. Clearly both organizations were Populists.[42]

The first electoral battle between the Populists and the Democrats was extremely bitter. The Democratic press pictured the Populists as rabble-rousing demagogues, if not actual anarchists, and praised Jones for the statesmanship of his businesslike administration. Without accepting the value judgments implied by the Democrats, the Populists agreed that the struggle was sharply dichotomized. To emphasize the "wool hat" versus "silk hat" nature of the battle, the precariously existing reform press served liberal portions of Democratic rhetoric. Torn between a desire for reform and a fear of disorder, many Alabamians were left with ambivalent feelings. Sam Will John, a leading Progressive politician, expressed to Robert McKee his regret that the Jeffersonians had left the Democratic Party. At the same time, he was very uncomfortable because it seemed to him that the most prominent men in the Democratic convention were those connected with organized capital.[43]

[42] Summersell, "Alabama Governor's Race in 1892," 15-18. Rogers, "Agrarianism in Alabama," 362-367. Clark, *Populism in Alabama*, 130-133. Jones, "A History of the Direct Primary in Alabama," 210-214. Kolb to Robert McKee, May 23, 1892, McKee Papers, ADAH. Chappell Cory to Jones, May 23, 1892, Jones Papers, ADAH.

[43] Sam Will John to McKee, June 14, 1892, McKee Papers, ADAH.

Despite the divided minds of such Progressives as Colonel John, the election on August 1, 1892 drew a record count of 243,037 ballots. It is difficult to say exactly how close this was to the actual turnout because of the unorthodox arithmetic of some of the canvassers. Anticipating this situation, Kolb had proposed to Jones during the campaign that they act jointly to insure a free ballot and a fair count. Robert McKee thought this was like the chicken who offered not to step on the horse's feet if the horse would not step on the chicken's.[44] Jones, who was always extremely sensitive about his personal honor, was indignant at the implication that some of the Democratic election officials might not diligently and impartially do their sworn duty.[45] The returns suggest that many Democratic officials interpreted their duty in terms other than those of their formal oath. Jones won the election by the slim margin of 11,435 votes. In the four Black Belt counties of Dallas, Wilcox, Montgomery, and Bullock, Jones polled over 83 percent of the vote. In these four counties alone his margin was 19,574. In fact, Jones lost only one of the 12 Black Belt counties, where he polled 45,454 votes. This gave him a margin of 27,210 votes, which Kolb could not overcome in the rest of the state.

There is little doubt that Kolb would have won in a fair election in 1892.[46] Even those contemporary ob-

[44] Piedmont *Inquirer*, July 7, 1894.

[45] Kolb to Jones, June 23, 1892, Jones Papers, ADAH. Rogers, "Agrarianism in Alabama," 371.

[46] Albert B. Moore, *History of Alabama*, Tuscaloosa, 1951, 624. Malcolm Cook McMillan, *Constitutional Development in Alabama, 1798-1901: A Study in Politics, the Negro, and Sectionalism*, "The James Sprunt Studies in History and Political Science," Vol. XXXVII, Chapel Hill, 1955, 228-229. Rogers, "Agrarianism in Alabama," 376-382. Clark, *Populism in Alabama*, 137n. Woodward, *Origins of the New South*, 262. For a

servers who were not antagonistic to the Democrats noted the massive fraud. "Excluding negro votes, or stuffed ballots, as you please," Robert McKee wrote to Willis Brewer, "their candidate unquestionably has a large majority."[47] Chappell Cory told Jones that 9 out of 10 people thought that he had won by fraud.[48] This bothered Jones's moral sensibilities, but he declined to do anything about it.

A closer look at the election returns, processed for analysis in Appendix II, sheds light on the question of who the Populists were. Jones ran extremely well in the towns and cities, but there was no particular relationship between the size of the town and the proportion of the vote that was Democratic.[49] Kolb captured enough votes in the cities to indicate the reality of his supposed support from wage-earners. In Jefferson County, contrary to what the mine owners assumed, the mining towns went strongly for Kolb. In Mobile Kolb carried one working class ward and ran strongly in three others.[50] Urban

---

lone dissent see Summersell, "Alabama Governor's Race in 1892."

[47] McKee to Brewer, August 7, 1892, McKee Papers, ADAH.
[48] Cory to Jones, August 14, 1892, Jones Papers, ADAH.
[49] See Appendix II, lines 24 and 25.
[50] Beat returns were culled from the following newspapers: Autauga County, *Prattville Progress*, August 12, 1892; Clarke County, *Clarke County Democrat*, August 10, 1892; Dale County, *The Southern Star*, August 10, 1892; Lowndes County, *The Citizens Examiner*, August 11, 1892; Marengo County, *The Linden Reporter*, August 5, 1892; Monroe County, *The Monroe Journal*, August 11, 1892; Morgan County, *The Alabama Enquirer*, August 11, 1892; Montgomery and Perry Counties, *The Weekly Advertiser*, August 9, 1892; Pike County, *The Troy Messenger*, August 11, 1892; Russell County, *The Russell Register*, August 6, 1892; Shelby County, *The Shelby Chronicle*, August 10, 1892; Jefferson County, the Birmingham *Age-Herald*,

labor's support of Populism became more formal in 1894 and 1896 when labor leaders joined the Populist campaign committee, and labor newspapers hawked the Populist ticket, but the votes were there as early as 1892.[51] Less than 2 percent of the Alabama population was foreign-born, but that portion, small as it was, was concentrated among the miners and industrial workers. The fact of Populism's firm alliance with miners and laborers adds another small bit of evidence to the refutation of the charge of Populist prejudice against ethnic minorities.

Historians have also argued about who the white Republicans were and whether or not their relationship with the Populists was unnatural.[52] The Republican organization did not run a state ticket in 1892, and advised its following to vote Populist. The great need for honest elections was the most obvious common denominator. Cooperation between Populists and Republicans followed a complex pattern among the various counties and from one election to the next, but the lack of correlation between the Republican vote in 1888 and the Populist votes in 1892, 1894, and 1896 in the nonurban counties outside the Black Belt indicates that white Republicans cast their votes much as their neighbors in the general

---

August 6, 1892; Tuscaloosa County, the Tuscaloosa *Gazette*, August 18, 1892; Mobile County, the Mobile *Register*, August 7, 1892; Escambia County, *The Standard Gauge*, August [?] 1892; Calhoun County, *The Weekly Times*, August 4, 1892.

[51] *The People's Weekly Tribune*, May 27, 1896.

[52] Woodward, *Origins of the New South*, 258, 276 and Hicks, *The Populist Revolt*, 391-392, see fusion as an unwise expedient. V. O. Key, *Southern Politics in State and Nation*, New York, 1949, 284, sees fusion as not entirely a marriage of convenience. See also Allen Trelease, "Who Were the Scalawags?" *Journal of Southern History*, XXIX, November 1963, 445-468.

population did.[58] In fact, the significant positive correlation between Populist vote and the Republican vote in 1902 indicates that Populism was the recruiting ground for Republicanism rather than vice versa.

TABLE 1

The Relationships among Populism, Population Growth Rate, and Farm Tenancy in 30 Counties outside the Black Belt with No Significant Urban Population*

	A	B	C	D	E	F	G
a. Populist percent of county vote, 1892	1.00						
b. Populist percent of county vote, 1894	.62	1.00					
c. Pop. growth rate, 1875-1890	−.10	−.01	1.00				
d. Pop. growth rate, 1890-1900	−.10	−.07	.22	1.00			
e. Proportion farms not operated by owners, 1890	.13	.05	−.49	−.41	1.00		
f. Proportion farms not operated by owners, 1900	.48	.33	−.43	−.42	.78	1.00	
g. Increase in farm tenancy, 1890-1900	.58	.41	.01	−.25	.15	.65	1.00

* Coefficients of Correlation computed from ranks by Spearman's footrule.

As the data in Appendix II imply, there were some complex relationships at work, but the single most powerful predictor of Populism in a county was the rate at which farm tenantry increased in the county during the decade of the 1890s. Among the 30 nonurban counties outside the Black Belt, which are the counties in which voting results were relatively undistorted by either the machinations of Black Belt political bosses or by con-

[58] See Appendix II.

25

centrations of the growing urban middle class, there was a significant tendency for the Populist vote to increase in direct proportion to the decrease in the percentage of owner-operated farms in a county. The significant positive correlation between the Populist vote and the value of farmland is probably accounted for by the fact that the best land generally drifted into the hands of large landowners and was worked by tenants of some description. Every indication is that Populism drew heavily from the ranks of small farmers who were uncomfortably close to, or had been pushed beyond, the margin between yeomanry and tenantry. Curiously, however, as Table 1 shows, there is no correlation between the Populist vote and the level of farm tenantry in 1890. If farmers who were forced from the ranks of ownership after 1890 had a strong proclivity for Populism, it is hard to understand why those who skidded downward in the 1880s or before would not also tend to vote Populist.

The explanation of this anomaly is that low position in the social order and downward mobility were not the only forces making for Populism. Geographic mobility may also loosen social bonds and prepare men for alienation from the existing social order. The relationship between mobility and Populism is not immediately apparent in the data in Table 1 and Appendix II, for a simple reason. While both tenantry and mobility predisposed men toward Populism, the two forces were usually operating at cross purposes, as the inverse correlation between them indicates. In 9 of the 30 counties they operated in the same direction and the result was almost invariably predictable. The five counties that experienced high population growth rates between 1875 and 1890, and had a high proportion of tenantry in 1890, produced high rates of Populist voting in 1892 and 1894. Similarly there were four counties with low growth rates and low proportions of tenantry; they displayed low levels of Populist voting. Only two counties, Winston and Randolph, produced more Populist votes than their low rates of population growth and of farm tenantry would justify. Winston County's long and colorful history of dissent includes opposition to the Civil War and support for Radical Reconstruction. Presumably well-organized white Republicanism might account for Randolph County's deviance from the pattern. The fact that the population growth rate and the level of farm tenantry were inversely related in the remaining 19 counties made for a much more random performance in the elections of 1892 and 1894. There were 9 counties in which the Populist vote varied with the population growth rate, rather than with tenantry, and 10 counties, where the reverse was true. These 19 counties also contained the cases of radical shifts in the Populist percentage of the vote from one election to the next. Consequently it is safe to say that alienation from the Democratic Party was fed to a slight extent by traditional animosities, but much more importantly by geographic mobility, low social status, and downward social movement.

The nature of the Populist leadership also reveals the disorganizing role played by low social position and mobility. The common denominator among the upper echelon of Populist leaders was restless aspiration linked to experience with failure. This was true of Albert Taylor Goodwyn, Milford W. Howard, W. H. Skaggs, George F. Gaither, A. P. Longshore, Frank Baltzell, and Colonel James M. Whitehead, for instance.[54] The restless, search-

[54] Rogers, "Agrarianism in Alabama," 397. Moore, *History of Alabama*, 529-530. *The People's Weekly Tribune*, June 18, 1896.

ing temperament of the leading Populists is illustrated in the career of Grattan B. Crowe. After growing up in rural Perry and Bibb Counties, and without formal training, Crowe began to practice medicine in Brierfield, an iron ore-mining town. When Brierfield collapsed in 1889 Crowe took the opportunity to go abroad to Edinburgh to learn his trade. Returning to Alabama in the early 1890s he became an ardent Populist and the foremost advocate of the use of violence to combat Democratic electoral fraud. After his humiliating defeat in 1900 as the Populist candidate for governor, Crowe returned to Europe again in search of the key to success. He studied geology. Back in Alabama he gained some practical mining experience, then in 1904 put together with borrowed money a coal mining operation that finally brought financial rewards and political inactivity.

Populist leadership at a lower level was recruited from social strata below that of comparable Democratic leaders. The origins of the Populist legislators in 1894, for instance, contrasted sharply with that of their Democratic colleagues. The best biographical reference work for Alabama history before 1920 is the *History of Alabama and Dictionary of Alabama Biography*. This was compiled by the archivist, Thomas M. Owen, who was the son-in-law of Sen. John H. Bankhead and a man who valued the ideals of the genteel tradition. Only 9 of the 35 Populists in the House of Representatives are to be found in Owen's dictionary, while 36 of the 65 Democrats are found there. This disparity leads one to suspect that at least in the eyes of "the better element" the Populists were "nobodies," as some historians have charged. Among the 36 listed Democrats only 3 were classed as "farmers" and 5 as "planters." But 5 of the 9 Populists were listed as "farmers" and only one as a "planter."

There was also one Populist physician, one businessman, and one real estate agent. Lawyers predominate among the nonagricultural Democrats. Eighteen of the 36 Democrats were either lawyers or judges. There were also three physicians, three civil engineers, one building contractor, one merchant, one banker, and one newspaper editor. None of the Populists were college graduates, and only one had connections with important relatives. The Democratic ranks were dotted with at least 14 college men, with numerous powerful connections. Data on the Civil War service of the members of the legislature are more available than other kind of information. As Table 2 shows, the higher percentage of Democrats who served as officers tends to support the impression given by the other biographical data. Populist leaders were not from the lower class, but they started from considerably further down the social ladder than did comparable Democrats.[55]

The analysis of biographical data and election returns

TABLE 2

Military Record of Members of the 1894 Legislature (percent)

	Democrat (N=64)	*Populist (N=33)*
Officer	28	9
Enlisted	40	48
No record	31	42

[55] The data in Table 2 was compiled from information kindly supplied by Mrs. Gloria Rutledge in the division of military service records of the Alabama Department of Archives and History. The best indications are that at lower levels of political organization the leadership is generally representative of its following in social characteristics. See Seymour Martin Lipset, *Political Man: The Social Bases of Politics*, Garden City, N.Y., 1959, 306ff.

supports the picture the Populists had of themselves. Joseph C. Manning, the founder of the People's Party in Alabama, divided society into two classes: the "better classes" and the "ordinary folk."[56] Most Populists were proud of the fact that they found support among the latter group. One Jeffersonian Democratic editor was a little more selective when he described the party membership as "the plain farmers, the country store keepers, the skilled mechanics and the workmen in the iron mills, the country doctors, preachers and lawyers. . . ."[57] More typical, however, were the Populists who saw themselves as the majority of the common people, "the great mass of the people among the farmers, the laboring men, miners and mechanics of the state. . . ."[58] In 1894 the Kolbites of Jefferson County nominated a ticket that was consciously shaped to represent the party: "one farmer, one railroad man [wage-earner], one mechanic, one lawyer and two miners."[59] No matter how the terms they used to describe themselves differed, and though they were not derived from the lowest classes, Populists were drawn from a distinctly lower level of society on the average than were their Democratic neighbors.

Populists were only tenuously connected to society by economic function, by personal relationships, by stable community membership, by political participation, or by psychological identification with the South's distinctive myths. Recruited heavily from among the downwardly mobile and geographically transient, they were vulnerable to feelings of powerlessness. They were largely super-

[56] Joseph C. Manning, *The Fadeout of Populism, Presenting, in Connection, the Political Combat Between the Pot and the Kettle*, New York, 1928, 101.
[57] *Choctaw Alliance*, April 25, 1894.
[58] *Troy Jeffersonian*, August 17, 1894.
[59] Mobile *Register*, May 30, 1894.

30

fluous farmers or ineffectively organized workers who were not linked to influential Alabamians by kinship or close association. They tended to come from isolated areas, from areas experiencing extraordinary influxes of population, and from areas with increasingly large concentrations of tenant farmers. In any case, their opportunity for the sort of psychological integration with the state's social system that developed from long-term personal interaction was limited. Populists also tended to come from the ranks and regions of Alabama life where the Old South, the Lost Cause, and the New South were myths with very little resonance. Given their position in the social structure, it would have been pathological for them to insist on conformity to the existing order. Those Alabamians who emphasized loyalty to the Democratic Party were expressing the need felt by well-organized sectors of the community for social solidarity and stability in a time of crisis. Populists were men who chose to resist the disorganizing forces in their lives by joining a protest movement.

Race or Reason?

Because the existing order against which the Southern Populists revolted had been erected at the end
of Reconstruction on the foundation of white supremacy,
the political debate of the 1890s frequently concerned
race relations. Some historians have suggested that the
failure of Populism was caused by the inability of whites
to put economic questions ahead of racial prejudice.[1]
Stated differently, this argument implies that a crucial
number of white men who were sympathetic to the appeal
of Populism voted Democratic because a Populist victory
seemed to them to threaten the status of the whites who
were dominant in Southern life. In view of the fact that
the differences between Populists and Democrats on matters of race were confined to a very narrow range,[2] this

[1] Hicks, *Populist Revolt*, 251-253, 391-392, 410. Wood-
ward, *Origins of the New South*, 254, 372. Woodward, *Strange
Career of Jim Crow*, 62, 80-81. Hofstadter, *The Age of Reform*,
New York, 1955, 61. Clark, *Populism in Alabama*, 180. Horace
Mann Bond, *Negro Education in Alabama, A Study in Cotton
and Steel*, Washington, D.C., 1939, 132.

[2] Paul Lewinson, *Race, Class and Party: A History of Negro
Suffrage and White Politics in the South*, New York, 1932, 79.
Woodward, *Origins of the New South*, 256-258. Elsewhere
Woodward classifies the Populist approach to race relations as
an "advanced brand of racial justice," Woodward, ed., *A South-
ern Prophecy, The Prosperity of the South Dependent Upon the
Elevation of the Negro*, by Lewis Harvie Blair, Boston, 1964,
xlv.

is an interpretation that deserves a close reexamination.

Any reexamination of the role of the Negro in the 1890s must begin with the realization that Negroes were still politically active and potentially powerful. The Alabama Republican Party, to which most Negroes belonged, emerged from Reconstruction in 1875 split into two major groups. As whites deserted the party and as newspaper support declined in the 1870s and through the 1880s, the party remained divided, with the two factions coming to represent the struggle between Negro and white Republicans for control of the party. The prize was recognition by the Republican National Committee and the harvest of political appointments that inevitably followed. In general, the white faction, led after 1888 by Dr. Robert A. Moseley, Jr., enjoyed supremacy within the party and received the major share of the patronage.[3] Moseley's position as state Republican boss was challenged from 1890 to 1896 by a rising Negro politician, William Stevens, who pressed for a greater role for Negroes within the party's high command.

In 1892 the Republican factional strife broke out into open warfare. Pro-Stevens Negroes captured most of the Republican county committees, yet could not gain dominance at the state level. They bolted the Moseley convention and sent an unsuccessful rival delegation to the Republican national convention, but did not run a state ticket. In conformity with previous practice and with the blessings of the National Committee, the Moseley faction, which can be thought of as the "lily whites" even though it included some Negroes, favored cooperation with independent parties in general and with the Popu-

[3] Allen J. Going, *Bourbon Democracy in Alabama, 1874-1890*, University, Ala., 1951, 49-52. Rogers. "Agrarianism in Alabama," 110-113, 360.

lists in particular. Instead of offering a state ticket in 1892, it recommended that Republicans vote for Kolb.[4]

While Kolb and Peyton G. Bowman were appealing explicitly and openly for Negro Republican votes in speeches throughout the state, Stevens avoided entanglement with the Populists, declaring that he doubted their promises of political equality.[5] In the fall, after the state elections, Moseley reached an agreement with the Populists. He would advise Republicans to vote for the Populist presidential electors on the condition that the Populist electors would vote for Benjamin Harrison if he had a chance to win and Weaver did not. Stevens, however, supported a straight Republican ticket which included Negro candidates for Congress in three districts. Of the 232,000 votes cast in November the Republican electors received approximately 9,000, or 4 percent of the vote.[6]

The picture becomes somewhat clearer in 1894 when the Moseley wing of the Republican Party endorsed the Populist ticket and Kolb made a widely publicized trip north to collect funds from appreciative Republicans.[7] After failing in an attempted reconciliation with the Moseley group, and after being physically chased from the 1894 Populist convention by an angry mob of whites, Stevens endorsed William C. Oates, the Democratic gubernatorial nominee.[8] The evidence suggests that many other local Negro politicians, teachers, lawyers, ministers, and editors followed Stevens' example.[9] Entrenched Negro leaders

[4] Joseph Matt Brittain, "Negro Suffrage and Politics in Alabama Since 1870," unpub. ph.d. diss., Indiana University, 1958, 81-100.

[5] Montgomery *Advertiser*, October 25, 1892.

[6] Brittain, "Negro Suffrage and Politics in Alabama," 101-108.

[7] Rogers, "Agrarianism in Alabama," 471-473.

[8] Brittain, "Negro Suffrage," 109-110.

[9] *Ibid.* Also see the circular put out by a Negro Republican

may have feared the effect of biracial politics on their position in the Negro community; they argued that acknowledging the fact of white supremacy and cooperating with the Democrats would bring racial peace.[10] In addition, in 1894 Negroes may have been alienated from the Populists because of the violence directed against Negro strikebreakers in the mineral district and Populist support of the strikers.[11]

In order to discredit Stevens, the lily-white Republicans held a convention in which half of the delegates were Negro and placed one Negro on the state executive committee. The convention then voted not to run a statewide Republican ticket. Instead, the Republicans urged the Negro voters in the Black Belt counties not to register or vote so their ballots could not be stolen by the Democrats.[12] However sought, by fair means or foul, Negro votes were considered essential by all parties.

The Democrats pressed their campaign for Negro votes with the utmost vigor. Negro Democrats were soon operating an Afro-American Democratic League in an effort to wean Negro voters away from the Republican Party. Prominent Negroes gave their names and prestige to the Democratic Party. The Democratic State Executive Committee sent Negro speakers into the field and had leading white politicians addressing Negro audiences in conciliatory tones.[13] This direct approach was important enough

---

named Locke in July 1892; and Z. T. Dunn to Jones, July 22, 1892, Jones Papers, ADAH.

[10] William C. Oates to John Tyler Morgan, March 12, 1896, Morgan Papers, Library of Congress.

[11] Robert David Ward and William Warren Rogers, *Labor Revolt in Alabama: The Great Strike of 1894*, University, Ala., 1965, 126.

[12] Brittain, "Negro Suffrage," 110.

[13] *Ibid.*, 88, 102.

that a distinguished supporter of Governor Jones in 1892 got very upset when former Governor Watts spoke in Pike County in southeastern Alabama, and was so indiscreet as to indulge in a diatribe against all of the Democratic Party's devils: "the Alliance, Kolbites, Carpetbaggers, Scalawags, Greenbackers, Republicans and negroes." To lump them all together insulted both the Alliance men and the Negroes who were present and whose honest votes the local Democrats had been seeking.[14]

Legitimate support for the Democrats from some sections of the Negro community did not preclude Democratic use of more direct methods. There were cases of Negro convicts who showed sudden Democratic political leanings and received pardons and the removal of disabilities in time for the next election.[15] Money was a more common currency. A Jones supporter asked the governor to "send me at Crawford Ala. a little money to be used among the floating (negro) vote,"[16] and one of the arguments for disfranchisement at the constitutional convention in 1901 was that Negro votes were getting too expensive in Randolph County.[17] Nor was fraud ineffective. In the Black Belt there was a magical process by which Negroes who walked into the polling place to vote Republican, plus those who stayed at home, and even a few who were dead, were all counted in the Democratic column.[18]

[14] Joel D. Murphree to Jones, July 14, 1892, Jones Papers, ADAH.

[15] Brittain, "Negro Suffrage," 88.

[16] J. C. Brooks to Jones, July 16, 1892, Jones Papers, ADAH.

[17] *Official Proceedings of the Constitutional Convention of the State of Alabama*, May 21st, 1901 to September 3rd, 1901, Wetumpka, Ala., 1941, III, 2,876.

[18] The flavor of the electoral mores of Alabama and the South

Populists therefore could favor Negro disfranchisement for reasons of self-interest, but they knew that any disfranchisement sponsored by the Democrats would purge the voting rolls of poor-white Populists as well as Negroes. Their suspicion in this regard was confirmed in the legislative session of 1892-93, when the Democrats passed the Sayre election law. This law made the process of qualifying to vote very complicated, and opened ample new opportunities for fraud and manipulation. Among other things, it transferred the appointment of election officials from the probate judges to the governor and made it much more difficult for illiterate men to mark their ballots correctly. The Populists responded to the situation by consistently opposing disfranchisement. Populists needed Negro votes, but lacked the money or the power to get enough of them. Therefore, with considerable ambivalence, they appealed in rational terms to Negro self-interest.

In the same platform of 1892 in which the Populists proposed a white primary, they made a bid for Negro votes by including Negroes within the protection of their goal of a "free ballot and a fair count." The platform stated: "We favor the protection of the colored race in their political rights, and should afford them encouragement and aid in the attainment of a higher civilization and citizenship, so that through the means of kindness, a better understanding and more satisfactory condition may exist between the races."[19]

The Populists were also willing to use limited eco-

---

can be otained from Chester H. Rowell, *An Historical and Legal Digest of All the Contested Election Cases in the House of Representatives of the United States from the First to the Fifty-Sixth Congress, 1789-1901*, Washington, D.C., 1901.

[19] Rogers, "Agrarianism in Alabama," 367.

nomic inducements to attract Negro voters.[20] As one Populist leader admitted later, some of these economic inducements were in the form of direct voter subsidies. This practice helped to bid the price of a vote up to $1, which was equal to two days wages for a field hand.[21] A less irregular indication of Populist intentions in this area was given by their willingness to vote against bills to make more stringent the laws punishing predominantly Negro tenant farmers in the Black Belt who frequently broke their work contracts.[22] It was on this point that the Populists diverged most markedly from Democratic practices.

Democrats in the Black Belt had other reasons to feel uneasy about the stability of their society. The Negro Farmers' Alliance, which did exist in Alabama, though weakly, was strongest in the Black Belt. The white Farmers' Alliance helped to organize the Negro Alliance as a segregated and subservient auxiliary that was intended to follow the policy set by the white Alliance. A national official of the white Alliance in 1889 estimated that 50,000 Negroes were affiliated with 1,600 local Negro Alliances in Alabama (compared to an estimated 125,000 in the white Alliances), but these were primarily in isolated units in the Black Belt. There was a convention in January 1890 attended by Kolb and Terence Powderly of the Consolidated Colored State Alliance, but there is no evidence that an effective statewide organization ever existed.[23] No common economic program was adopted; the Negro Alliance Exchange in Mobile was

[20] *The Choctaw Alliance*, April 21, June 2, 1896. The *Ozark Banner*, April 30, 1896. The Randolph *Toiler*, July 24, 1896.

[21] F. H. Lathrop to J. H. Bingham, October 18, 1900, O. D. Street Papers, University of Alabama Library.

[22] Alabama, *House Journal, 1894*, 287-288, 577.

[23] Brittain, "Negro Suffrage and Politics in Alabama," 92.

never big nor a success; the Opelika *State Alliance Banner* was the single newspaper of the Negro Alliance; and cooperation with the white Alliance in the state was never very real.[24] Even so, perhaps this minimal degree of organization is enough to account for the heavy Populist vote from Lowndes County, where white newspapers had reported the Negro Alliance to be particularly active.

Whether by direct purchase or rational appeal, the Populists made a major effort to secure Negro votes. In 1896 *The People's Weekly Tribune* featured letters from Negroes who responded favorably to Populist invitations.[25] The probate judge of Tuscaloosa County wrote to Jones that the reason Tuscaloosa went to Kolb in 1892 was, "the Alliance people worked up the Negro vote against us."[26] Similarly, Joel D. Murphree reported to Jones in 1892 that the "Kolb Klan" was working hard and with some success among the Negro voters of Pike County.[27] Macon County, where Tuskegee Institute is located, actually recorded 63 percent of its votes in 1892 for Kolb and the Populists.

Nevertheless, the evidence summarized in Appendix II shows that for all their effort the Populists remained considerably less successful in capturing Negro votes than were their opponents. In the rural counties outside the Black Belt there was no significant relationship between Negro population and the Populist vote, which suggests that Negroes in these counties divided their votes very much as did the population at large. But in

[24] William W. Rogers, "The Negro Alliance in Alabama," *The Journal of Negro History*, XLV (January 1960), 38-44.

[25] *The People's Weekly Tribune*, March 19, 1896. The Randolph *Toiler*, July 17, 1896.

[26] William G. Cochrane to Thomas Goode Jones, August 8, 1892, Jones Papers, ADAH.

[27] Murphree to Jones, July 14, 1892, Jones Papers, ADAH.

those counties containing urban centers there was a noticeable tendency for the Democratic vote to vary in direct proportion to the Negro percentage of the population. The major explanation of Democratic success, however, was the artificial near monopoly of votes the party enjoyed in the Black Belt.

While competing with the Populists for Negro votes, the Democrats also had to keep white voters loyal. White supremacy, the battle cry of the Redeemer regimes established at the downfall of Reconstruction, promised to be the most powerful myth the Democrats could use to reinforce existing relationships. In resorting to white supremacy Democratic orators revealed anxieties about political, economic, and social relations; it was impossible to determine which fear was the most genuine. "The cry is raised by democratic papers that Alabama is threatened with negro rule," wrote one Populist editor. Then he pointed out that "this statement is made in the face of the fact that there is not a negro running for office in Alabama as the nominee of either of the two parties with full tickets in the field. The negroes are not asking for office. They want justice. They want the right to work for the betterment of their race. We don't fear negro domination."[28]

Concern for the existing economic arrangement was revealed in the frequently voiced folk-proverb, "when you educate a negro you spoil a good field hand," a chestnut which was vouched for by the Montgomery *Advertiser*.[29] Senator John Tyler Morgan attempted to reinforce the blurred frontiers of social relationships by urging Southerners to "resist any movement, social or political that will promote the unwelcome intrusion of the negro race

[28] *Ozark Banner*, July 16, 1896.
[29] Montgomery *Advertiser*, April 2, 1901.

into the white family circle."[30] Similar comments noting
and advocating a wider breach between the races were
common in the period 1890 to 1910.

The situation was further confused by the fact that politicians who advocated great changes in other areas of life
were in the forefront of the race-baiting, almost as if they
were trying to compensate for their urge to change political, economic, and social arrangements. W. H. Denson,
consistently aligned with the progressive wing of the
Democratic Party, delivered a good example of the
sho-'nuff, ring-tailed, rip-snortin' stump speech in the
1890 campaign. He attacked the Republican candidate,
Ben M. Long, for his willingness to "hob nob with niggers." "Mr. Long says that he endorses the plan of race
amalgamation and miscegenation set forth in the Lodge
bill," cried Denson, referring to a proposed measure
which sought to authorize federal court supervision of
federal elections when requested by a portion of the
electorate. He continued:

THEY WANT TO REPEAL OUR LAWS AGAINST THE IN-
TER-MARRIAGE OF THE RACES. THEY WANT TO FORCE
OUR CHILDREN AND THE NEGRO CHILDREN INTO THE
SAME SCHOOL ROOM. THESE ARE THE PRINCIPLES IN-
DORSED BY MR. LONG. THE WHITE PEOPLE OF THE
SOUTH DO NOT WANT ANY SUCH. (NO! NO! CHEERS)

WE HAVE NOT TIME TO TRADE HORSES CROSSING
THE STREAM, ALL THE WHITE VOTERS MUST UNITE.
WE MUST NOT HAVE ANY FUSSING AND QUARRELING
IN THE MIDST OF A CAMPAIGN. NO MATTER WHAT
ORGANIZATION YOU BELONG TO, YOU OWE AN AL-
LEGIANCE TO THE DEMOCRACY OF THE SOUTH. THOSE
WHO ARE AGAINST US ARE TRAITORS TO OUR INSTITU-

[30] Mobile *Register*, September 7, 1890.

TIONS AND OUR RELIGION. LONG AND THE NIGGERS ARE TRAITORS TO OUR WIVES AND DAUGHTERS. THE MAN WHO VOTES FOR BEN LONG IS A TRAITOR, A SCOUNDREL AND AN OUTLAW AGAINST THE BEST INTERESTS OF OUR SOCIETY AND AGAINST THE GOD WHO GAVE HIM LIFE! (APPLAUSE) WE DON'T WANT ANY BUSHWHACKERS. WE MUST BE UNITED. CALL MEN BY THEIR NAMES. WE DO NOT WANT ANY NAMBY PAMBY ACTION, BUT A STRAIGHT-OUT DENUNCIATION OF ALL WHO ARE IN FAVOR OF PULLING DOWN OUR SOCIETY AND OUR RELIGION! IF YOU SPLIT AT THIS TIME YOU WILL MAKE WAY FOR LONG AND HIS NIGGERS. IT IS NO TIME TO GROWL AND WHINE ABOUT THE NOMINATION. I ASK YOU, IF YOU DON'T LIKE IT WHAT ARE YOU GOING TO DO ABOUT IT? WE MUST MAINTAIN WHITE SUPREMACY IN THE SOUTH. NO COMPROMISE WILL BE PERMITTED. OUR VERY RELIGION IS AT STAKE. THIS IS NO CHILD'S PLAY. I WANT TO BRING UP A ROUSING MAJORITY ON ELECTION DAY SO THAT THE REPUBLICAN PARTY WILL KNOW THAT WE MEAN BUSINESS AND NEVER INTEND TO GIVE UP THE SHIP.

WE ARE DOING ALL RIGHT IN THE SOUTH. ALL WE WANT IS TO BE LET ALONE. THEY MUST KEEP THEIR FINGERS OUT OF OUR PIE OR WE WILL STICK THEM SURE.[31]

Typically Denson's defense of the Southern way of life embraced sex, religion, and business, equating the very existence of society with the solidarity of white Democrats. There is considerable evidence suggesting that Democrats felt the social order was threatened more by the lower class than by the outcastes. While the Mobile

[31] Birmingham *Age-Herald*, July 27, 1890.

42

Register and Montgomery *Advertiser* led the Democratic attack on the Populists for threatening the one-party system, both papers approved of right-wing independent movements in Alabama and in other states when such movements were directed against a Democratic Party that had been captured by the forces of reform. It is also significant that Kolb lost his support in the Black Belt after the Alliance began to activate men with political and economic grievances, but before it was clear that Kolb would not be able to capture the Democratic Party and thus avoid the threat to race relations involved in breaking with the white man's party. It was not racial orthodoxy that was uppermost in the minds of the Black Belt planters.

Whether it was a prime mover or a derivative force, racial tension was on the increase in the 1890s. Negroes were being forced out of roles they had filled in the 1880s.[32] In 1891 and 92 the lynching rate hit its all-time peak—24 Negroes were murdered by mobs in each year in Alabama. Race relations were certainly in flux, and the most conspicuous example before 1901 of the use of law to define, solidify, and make uniform the Negro's subordinate position in Alabama life was the passage of Alabama's first Jim Crow law in 1891.

On December 14, 1890 the Birmingham *Age-Herald* reported that there was a bill pending in the House of Representatives, sponsored by the representative from Mobile, which provided for the segregation of the races on railroads. Negro leaders issued a call for a convention to meet in February to formulate a position for Alabama

[32] Woodward, *Strange Career of Jim Crow*, 104-105, and "The Case of the Louisiana Traveler," in John A. Garraty, ed., *Quarrels That Have Shaped the Constitution*, New York, 1964, 145-158.

Negroes. On January 19, 1891 the paper explained the background of the situation:

Some months ago, it is said, the daughter of Rev. C. O. Boothe, an educated and wealthy negro of northern Alabama, was refused admittance into the first-class car on the Louisville and Nashville railroad between this city and Decatur; whereupon she had to go into what the colored people call the 'Jim Crow car,' divided by a partition, one side of which is for smoking going one way and for colored people returning. They claim that white men are allowed to come into the part occupied by the colored people and smoke, use profane and improper language, drink whiskey and do as they please. The colored people of Louisiana have organized an Equal Rights Association, for the purpose of carrying the railroads into courts when colored people are refused such accommodations as are given the whites. It is said that the same course will be taken by the colored people of this state, at Montgomery, on the 3rd of February; when a conference, called by some of the leading colored men in the state, will convene to adopt some course for the colored people of the state to pursue. It is said that ten colored lawyers of the state have been invited to be present to advise the best plan to be adopted and the course to pursue. The leaders of the movement, it is said, claim that the Central of Georgia and the East Tennessee, Virginia and Georgia railroads are the only ones in the state that give them accommodations equal to that of the whites. The leaders, some of them, claim that a series of law suits against the other roads, whether they prove successful or not, constitute the only means by which negroes may ever get their rights on the railroads. They insist that they don't want to mix with the whites.

44

On January 20, 1891 the Alabama House of Representatives passed H. 119, the "Separate But Equal Accommodation Bill."[33] Despite the rapid action on the bill the Negro conference met on February 3 and adopted resolutions against the division of school funds by race, in favor of better treatment of convicts, and for better transportation facilities.[34] But they did not have a chance to present their petition to the legislature, for the Senate quickly passed H. 119 on February 5.[35]

Even though the legislators made much of the bill's provision for "equal" facilities for Negroes, the wording of the act makes plain its primary purpose. It gave conductors the power to assign passengers to seats and it provided for fines of up to $100 for those refusing to sit with their race. The act also compelled railroads, with the specific exception of street railways, to provide separate cars for the two races or to partition the coaches. The act was clearly aimed solely at separating the races.

Significantly there was not a dissenting vote in either House, nor was there any discussion in the Senate and very little in the House of Representatives. In the House the bill's sponsor explained that it was patterned after the Mississippi law which had been tested in court and found constitutional. Samuel M. Adams, the floor leader of the Farmers' Alliance and later a prominent Populist, moved that the word "equal" be struck from the clause of the bill that required "separate but equal" facilities for Negroes. Several delegates spoke in paternalistic tones about the

[33] Alabama, *House Journal, 1890*, 370.

[34] Huntsville *Gazette*, February 14, 1891. White papers did not report this conference. Dividing school funds between white and Negro schools according to the proportion of taxes paid by each race would have drastically reduced money available for Negro schools.

[35] Alabama, *Senate Journal, 1890*, 512.

duty of white men to protect the rights of Negroes. They claimed that this bill would convince those skeptics in the North who somehow doubted that white Southerners had the best interest of the Negro race at heart. This bill, they claimed, would protect Negroes against unjust discrimination.[36] Another delegate explained to Adams the danger of adverse court action if the word "equal" were not in the law; Adams withdrew his motion to strike it out. As one reporter wrote, "when the bill was fully explained it was passed without opposition."[37]

Negroes were not similarly agreeable. The Huntsville *Gazette*, a Negro paper, disproving the contention of Southern whites that Negroes were happy with segregation, reacted to the Jim Crow law with indignation. Segregated seating was "A Shameful Injustice," it said, and asked, "can the state afford to legalize such barefaced robbery?"[38] But in the face of white solidarity and the absence of a militant organization, Negroes did nothing.

The unanimous vote on the Jim Crow seating bill of 1891 indicates that there probably were no significant differences between the Democrats and the Populists on race relations, and that, though there was great confusion at the time about just what the position of the Negroes in Alabama life should be, there was a nearly perfect consensus among whites on the conviction that the Negro position should be subordinate. The Populists frequently denied that they were advocating any form of social equality between the races and insisted that their actions were consistent with the doctrine of white supremacy.[39] In the negotiations with the Democrats at the state

[36] Montgomery *Advertiser*, January 21, 1891. Birmingham *Age-Herald*, January 21, February 3, 1891.

[37] Mobile *Register*, January 20, 1891.

[38] Huntsville *Gazette*, July 18, August 1, 8, 1891.

[39] Randolph *Toiler*, November 21, 1895.

Democratic convention in 1892, in their party platform of the same year, and frequently thereafter, the Populists suggested that their differences with the Democrats should be settled in an all-white primary. The Democrats declined to engage the Populists in a test of strength in an all-white primary for the obvious reason that in the contest for Negro votes, a contest in which there was very little difference in the tactics used by the two parties, the Democrats enjoyed an immense advantage because they controlled the electoral machinery.

THOUGH the Democrats, by one means or another, managed to be the chief beneficiary of Negro suffrage, they tried to energize Negrophobia and direct it against the Populists. It was true, as the Democrats charged, that Populism split the white vote, thus creating a situation in which Negro votes were very important. There was, however, no objective difference between the two parties on racial policy and there was no obvious necessity to assume that the Democrats should be the sole protector of white supremacy. In fact, thousands of ordinary white Alabamians voted Populist without abandoning their belief in white supremacy. If other white Alabamians insisted that Populism was a threat to white supremacy it was because they first perceived Populism as a threat to some other highly valued order of relationships and consequently refused to admit that the Populist Party was legitimate in any way. For those whose faith in the Democratic Party had been sufficiently challenged by its failures in social, political, and economic matters, there was no difficulty in seeing that the racial policy advocated and practiced by the Populists was no more and no less cynical than that of the Democrats.

Neither Revolution Nor Reform

The Populists wanted change. In countless platforms and campaign statements they gave evidence of their dream of a more abundant life for the common man. Whether this was to be achieved by old methods or new, whether by revolution or reform, was a matter of some importance.

The matter of most immediate importance, however, was to salvage some gain from the election of 1892. Fuming indignantly at the blatant vote frauds of August, Populists made plans to carry their fight to the legislature. Several tenderhearted Democrats urged Governor Jones to offer some compromise, but he followed the wishes of his more irreconcilable supporters. One newspaper, edited by future governor William Dorsey Jelks, rubbed salt into Populist wounds by saying that even if the charges of irregularities were correct there was nothing the Populists could do about it. Which was true. When the Populists presented their objections to the legislature they were easily turned aside because there was no contest law governing such a procedure. Populist efforts to enact such a statute in the 1892-93 session were similarly defeated.[1]

[1] Clark, *Populism in Alabama*, 140. Rogers, "Agrarianism in Alabama," 383-397. Chappell Cory to Thomas G. Jones, May 23, August 14, 1892; R. N. Murphy to Jones, September 29,

But neither defeat in the fall presidential and congressional elections nor failure in the legislature diminished Populist enthusiasm.[2] The growing economic disaster in 1893 spread misery, thus confirming the Populist analysis. By September 1893 Populist speakers were touring the state with the message that the only way to revive prosperity was to throw the plutocrats out of power the following August.

Reuben Kolb again led the Populist efforts to oust the "Fraudocrats" from power in 1894. The Jeffersonian Democrats and the People's Party of Alabama held concurrent and joint conventions in Birmingham on February 8, 1894. They adopted a common platform reflecting the inner tension of Populist thinking. The first two planks called for a free vote and a fair count and for a contest law for state elections. The next three planks repeated the usual calls for the free coinage of silver, for increasing circulating currency to $50 per capita, and for trimming the powers of the national banks. The platform also endorsed better education and a national graduated tax on all income above "the comforts and necessities of life." In addition, the platform made some specific proposals aimed at the labor vote.

The twelfth statement of the platform of 1894 was designed to refute Democratic charges that Populists were opposed to industry and to capital. It could just as well answer similar charges by some recent historians. "We favor the development of our material resources and the upbuilding of industrial enterprises," ran the pronouncement, "and to that end we invite the investment of capital,

---

1892; Jones Papers, ADAH. Alabama, *Senate Journal, 1892*, 187, 327, 367, 377-380, 387-391, 548, 698, 714.

[2] Clark, *Populism in Alabama*, 141-143. Mobile *Register*, September 18, 1892. *The Southern Republican*, September 23, 1892.

pledging the enactment of such laws as will afford encouragement and protection of all legitimate enterprises."[3]

If the platform blunted the thrust of Populist antimonopoly talk, the resolutions adopted by the convention blurred the image of Populism as a new political departure. These resolutions accused the democracy of deserting its old principles. To emphasize their allegiance to old ways, the Populists made their usual appeal for economy and "Jeffersonian simplicity in government."[4] "Our forces are not organized for the specific purpose of making any radical changes in our organic law," wrote the Populist candidate for governor in 1898. "We come with no new untried theories of government. We advocate no new doctrines and are promoting no novel measures."[5] Its aversion to novelty and its urge for change set up a tension within Populism itself.

Looking at Populist rhetoric alone, one might conclude that the most significant features of its ideology were a belief in the moral superiority of rural life, a call for various forms of monetary inflation, an intense antagonism toward organized wealth, a conspiracy theory of history, and a firm belief that the voice of the people is the voice of God.[6] The Populists did exhibit all these traits of thought, but they shared them with their most bitter enemies, the Democrats.

It was characteristic for the Populists to believe that there was something special about the man who worked on the land. Most Populists were farmers who actually walked behind the plow, and the notion of rural virtue has a long tradition in American thought. In fact, it was

[3] The Troy *Jeffersonian*, March 2, 1894.
[4] *Ibid.*
[5] *Randolph Toiler*, July 15, 1898.
[6] For a slightly different typology of Populist thinking see Hofstadter, *Age of Reform*, 62.

so natural for the Populists to believe in the agrarian myth that they seldom used it, whereas the Democrats put it to good use. Democratic papers alternately scolded farmers and praised farming. "Agriculture is a noble pursuit," said the *Advertiser* with premature satisfaction, "and so is politics, but when they are mixed they take on a doubtful character, and we are glad the farmers decided to keep them separate."[7] But Populists wanted more than ego-boosting flattery from city slickers. One thing they wanted was prosperity.

Keynesian economists operate on the theory that monetary inflation stimulates the economies of underdeveloped countries. Inflation was a rational policy for Southerners in the late nineteenth century, for the South was certainly an underdeveloped region. Southerners were not perspicacious Keynesians, however. They justified their inflationary views on rational grounds, to be sure, but primarily they wanted justice rather than development. For them, inflation was a principle of morality. It would benefit a morally superior class—the farmer. "If you make money by the use of money it is all for your good," commented the Troy *Jeffersonian* about currency contraction. "If you use property and labor to earn money, it is all against you."[8]

Whatever the motive, almost all Alabamians were inflationists to some degree. "I am for free silver," Democratic Congressman J. E. Cobb wrote, "and anything else reasonable that promises relief to the people."[9] Both of Alabama's United States senators had long been ad-

---

[7] Montgomery *Advertiser*, February 3, 1887, as quoted in Rogers, "Agrarianism in Alabama," 159. For similar expressions see the Birmingham *Age-Herald*, September 3, 30, 1890; and the Mobile *Register*, June 30, 1894.

[8] July 20, 1894.

[9] Cobb to Robert McKee, February 22, 1892, McKee Papers, ADAH.

vocates of free silver. Governor Jones, while praising Grover Cleveland and fending off the president's critics within the state, at the same time was imploring the President to sponsor a reform of the banking system to allow state banks to issue banknotes and thus provide for the reasonable increase in the amount of currency, which was the real desire of the silver men.[10] Jones was the foremost sound-money politician in the state. In the campaign for the Democratic nomination in 1894, the issue of silver coinage threatened to split the Democratic party again. Happily the convention found an ingenious formula for reconciling the two factions. "While there are differences of opinion among us in matters of detail," read the platform, "we all believe in the free coinage of silver, whenever it can be done consistently with the maintenance of a sound and safe currency."[11]

Silver was frequently connected with a conspiracy theory and with antagonism toward trusts and monopolies. This was particularly true of Southerners who were marked with the scars of defeat and economic dependency. Even William Calvin Oates, the candidate of the gold wing of the Democratic Party, and one of the two Alabama representatives out of nine who voted in favor of the repeal of the Sherman Silver Purchase Act, told his audiences in 1894 that the money power had the "federal government by the leg." Of course, he blamed this on the Republicans.[12] E. L. Russell, vice president of the Mobile and Ohio Railroad and Joseph F. John-

---

[10] Thomas G. Jones to Grover Cleveland, November 14, 1893, Cleveland Papers, Library of Congress (microfilm). Oates and Jones both implored Cleveland, to no avail, not to veto the seignorage bill, because it would hurt Oates in the gubernatorial campaign of 1894. Thomas G. Jones to Hilary Herbert, March 23, 1894, Cleveland Papers.

[11] Mobile *Register*, May 24, July 19, 1894.

[12] *Ibid.*, May 29, 1894.

ston's campaign manager in 1894, took the same position.

Democratic Congressman George Cruikshank, an advocate of silver coinage, gave vent to his feelings of persecution and pessimism and his suspicions of conspiracy in a letter to John W. DuBose. "I grow daily more distressed at the condition of the South," he wrote.

> There is nothing that I see for her except a slow building up of private fortunes by agriculture and trade. Our greater mineral deposits and industries have passed into northern hands and the price of labor is fixed here and the dividends will come here and the supplies used there will be brought here and we are left out altogether. Our birthright is sold. Cotton is deposed as King. England is extending its area in India persistently and is also tightening her grip on Egypt with a view to cheaper cotton and food from people she can hold as serfs. We will not be able to set the price of cotton again. It will never rise above 7 cents. So the day of the planter is over. He may exist as a landlord, but not as a planter.
>
> The money powers are now aiding Pennsylvania by drawing all the money from the South to thus cripple our furnaces and force them into northern combinations and control.[13]

The Democratic faith that inflation would break the conspiracy was part of a historical view of political conflict in the United States. Congressman W. H. Denson expressed this orthodox view in a long letter to Robert McKee. Denson saw the conflict over silver as just another phase of "the irrepressible conflict between Monarchy and Democracy, imperialism and free institutions,

[13] George Cruikshank to DuBose, March 28, 1892, DuBose Papers, ADAH.

privileged classes vs the masses, money vs the people, capital vs labor. The doctrines of Hamilton vs the principles of Jefferson." Denson traced the running battle between the money power and the people down through American history. It was a consistent story of large, centralized government, wielded in the interests of the "aristocracy," defeating the democratic forces advocating small government, diffused power, low taxation, and wide distribution of wealth. "The money power has whipped us every crack," concluded Denson, but he called for a fight to the finish on the silver question.[14] While the Populists managed with some justification to locate a few conspiracies in history, Denson portrayed *all* of American history as a conspiracy.[15]

Denson was consistently aligned with the Progressive wing of the Democratic Party. But his identification with the masses and with Jeffersonian principles was shared by politicians of the opposite school. H. C. Tompkins, Chairman of the State Democratic Executive Committee, expressed the standard view when he decried Populism because it would split the Democrats and allow the Republicans to stay in office, "and consequently insures the perpetuation of the power of the latter and the continuance of a system of laws enacted for the benefit of class, that have resulted and could only result in the enrichment of the few at the expense of the many."[16] Mossback papers such as the Mobile *Register* and the Montgomery *Advertiser* vied with each other in anti-monopoly rhetoric. Most Democrats talked as if nothing need be done but to abolish all of the governmental devices fostering

[14] Denson to McKee, July 9, 1893, McKee Papers, ADAH.
[15] See Hofstadter, *Age of Reform*, 71, for his use of this distinction.
[16] Tompkins to McKee, July 9, 1893, McKee Papers, ADAH.

special interests.[17] The nation would then return to a state of Jeffersonian purity, said the gold Democrats.

The fundamental principle of Democracy was negative government. "I believe in that theory of government which minimizes its powers," wrote Tompkins. "I believe government run upon any other theory is bound eventually to become a despotism."[18] Joel D. Murphree, in a widely quoted series of articles in 1896, set forth his understanding of Democratic principles. He not only talked of strict construction of the Constitution and low tariff but also stressed the underlying principles. These were capsulized in a belief in the greatest individual freedom from governmental regulation; government existed merely to maintain law and order.[19] This philosophy, built on a static view of society and buttressed by a complacent faith in the beneficent results of a passive government, was the distinguishing feature of the sound-money wing of the Democratic party throughout the period 1890 to 1910.

There were some Democrats even in the early 1890s who did not accept the ritualistic faith in a minimum of government, but these Progressives did agree with an equally important corollary. They thought the community could best be governed by its natural leaders. This rested on the theory that there was no real conflict of interest within the community. Democratic contempt for the Populist bid for leadership found expression in num-

[17] Mobile *Register*, July 8, 22, 1894. See also the Birmingham *News*, January 5, 1895 for a ringing anti-monopoly editorial, and the Mobile *Register*, July 19, 1894 for an anti-monopoly speech by a railroad president.

[18] Tompkins to McKee, March 13, 1892, McKee Papers, ADAH.

[19] The Troy *Standard*, October 9, 16, 19, 29, 1896. See also the Mobile *Register*, June 24, 1894.

erous attacks by Democrats on the respectability of Populists. One Populist speaker was caricatured in the Democratic press as a "dead cyclops" whose "long, snow white whiskers and hair presented a ghostly appearance," and whose "eyes projected out almost like pot legs." Democrats spoke to audiences with dignity—according to the Democratic press—but the performance of Populist speakers "reminded one of the whoop of a Commanche Indian."[20] Populist officeholders would disgrace the state, argued the Evergreen *Star,*[21] and Gregory L. Smith characterized the Mobile County Populist candidates as very good bricklayers and such, but, after all, not the "proper" men to put in charge of the county.[22] The proper men to run the county or the state were those who had succeeded under the existing system and could therefore conceive of the community as consisting of individuals whose interests were complementary rather than antagonistic.

Democrats knew that Populism was based on an experienced antagonism within the community. The Populist campaign was so socially divisive many Democrats thought that fundamental principles were at issue. "Principles, not men, are at stake," said the Selma *Journal,* which, characteristically, identified those principles as the best interests of the whole community, "the material interests and the prosperity of our state."[23] "The difference between the Democratic and the Populist parties has been told on the stump," reported the Alexander City *Outlook.* "It is this: The Democrats want to support the

[20] Mobile *Register,* August 1, 1894.
[21] Quoted in *ibid.*
[22] *Ibid.,* August 5, 1894. For similar expressions see *ibid.,* May 1, 1894; and Tompkins to McKee, March 13, 1892, McKee Papers, ADAH.
[23] Mobile *Register,* August 5, 1894.

government, while the Populists want the government to support them."[24]

The Democratic conservator of the social order in 1894 was William Calvin Oates. Born on a farm in 1835 in what is now Bullock County, Oates taught school, read law, and served as a colonel in the Confederate army. With the aid of his empty sleeve, acquired during the war, and sharp debating skills, Oates rose rapidly in Democratic ranks. He served one term in the state legislature in 1870 and then in the Constitutional Convention of 1875. In 1880 Oates was elected to the first of seven consecutive terms in the United States House of Representatives.

Oates was one of those self-made men who rigidly defend the system within which they achieve success. In Congress he voted against the Interstate Commerce Commission Act, against the Blair Education bill, against the Hatch Act, against the bill to raise the Agricultural Bureau to the status of a department, and for the repeal of the Sherman Silver Purchase Act. In short, he was a firm advocate of states rights and laissez-faire, and was plainly identified with the right wing of the Democratic Party in Alabama. Oates tried to hedge his support of Cleveland's unpopular sound-money policies by declaring for the coinage of silver at the commercial rate, but this was a meaningless amendment of his sound-money principles. With the aid of Jones and the state Executive Committee, Oates defeated Joe Johnston, a silverite, for the gubernatorial nomination of the Democratic Party by a narrow margin.[25] "We have never said so," admitted

[24] Quoted in Mobile *Register*, July 15, 1894.

[25] *Ibid.*, May 23, 24, 1894. There is no indication that Cleveland used his patronage power to help Oates. Oates to Cleveland, October 26, 1893, Cleveland Papers (microfilm reel 80). Also see the undated list of recommended appointments signed by

the *Choctaw Alliance*, "but it is an undeniable fact, that if Captain Johnston had received the nomination, he would have carried a number of votes that will now go to Captain Kolb."[26]

If the reactionary character of the Democratic nominee provided the voters with a much more real alternative between candidates than would have been indicated by the strikingly similar platforms, the Populist attitude toward labor was an even more glaring contrast. In their platform the Populists made a clear bid for the votes of the miners who were then on the brink of a bloody strike in the mineral district. They wanted the state to remove the convicts from the mines, a new lien law in favor of laborers, and semimonthly paydays rather than monthly. Populists also spoke for the creation of an office of weights and measures, one of whose functions would be to insure that miners who were paid by the ton were not cheated. They called for the popular election of the state mining inspector, along with legislation to prevent children under 13 years of age from working in the mines. These were the most hardheaded proposals in the Populist program. On the other hand, the most ambiguous plank tried to strike a balance between the traditional agricultural demand for a tariff "for revenue only" and the interest of laborers and industrialists in north Alabama in a protective tariff. The Populists called for a

Gaston A. Robbins and James Pugh with an explanatory letter from John T. Morgan to Grover Cleveland, February 5, 1894, Cleveland Papers (reel 82). The choices of the congressional delegation, silverites all (except for Oates and Richard Clarke), were appointed despite the protests of some Oates supporters from Alabama. See M. M. Brannan to Cleveland, May 8, 1893 (reel 75), and Rufus Rhodes to Cleveland, November 27, 1893 (reel 81). Rhodes and Brannan were complaining that all Cleveland's appointments to date had gone to his enemies.

[26] *Choctaw Alliance*, May 30, 1894.

"tariff for revenue" that would also be high enough to protect domestic labor.

The threat to the existing order implied in Populism's espousal of labor's cause was accented by the social unrest throughout the nation. In Tennessee in 1891 and 1892, miners of the Tennessee Coal, Iron, and Railroad Company had gone to war with the company over the question of convict labor. In 1892 the Homestead strike of steelworkers overshadowed the events in Tennessee, but heightened the growing sense of unease in society. Confidence in the status quo was further undermined in 1893 by the collapse of the economy. In 1894 newspapers were full of reports of armies of unemployed men marching on Washington to demand relief, and of thousands of strikes, including the mammoth Pullman strike and the walkout of the United Mine Workers. There was an aura of impending anarchy.

The threats to society were not remote from Alabama. At noon on April 20, 1894 the volatile mineral district was ignited by the 7,000 or more miners who struck in sympathy for the United Mine Workers. On May 7 a mob, evidently made up of striking miners, dynamited and shot up Horse Creek Mines in Walker County. This was the first of a series of violent acts that led Governor Jones on May 25 to order the state militia into Ensley, an industrial suburb of Birmingham. The troops stayed in Birmingham, except for two abortive withdrawals, until August 18th.[27]

The strikers were at a disadvantage. The mine operators had convict labor and were in a region with a surplus

[27] Alabama, *Senate Journal, 1894*, Governor's Message, 40-45, chronicles the strike from the governor's point of view. For a recent account see Robert David Ward and William Warren Rogers, *Labor Revolt in Alabama: The Great Strike of 1894*, University, Ala., 1965.

of unskilled labor. The strikers failed in April and May to get the railway workers to cooperate by not hauling coal mined by nonunion miners. Even so, in early June newspapers reported coal production to be at 60 percent of capacity and that several iron furnaces were banked.[28] But the companies kept operating. Even in July, when the railway strike hit Birmingham, the companies managed to keep the trains running.

In early July Senator John Tyler Morgan made his first speech of the campaign in DeKalb County. With obvious reference to the presence of federal troops in Illinois to cope with the Pullman strike, Morgan said that he was proud that the South was so peaceful, quiet, and law-abiding.[29] While he spoke, three regiments of state militia were policing the labor war that was raging in north Alabama. The strikers numbered between 7,000 and 10,000 men of both races and several nationalities. Five days after Morgan spoke, a ferocious gun battle between the strikers and guards at Pratt Mines left 4 dead and 10 wounded. At the same time, the police found but could not identify a dynamite and a shotgun victim.[30] Ten days later two strikers shot and killed two deputies who were trying to serve warrants on them.[31] Yet in June, while the depression, the strike, and the heated political campaign were roaring through the state, President E. B. Young told a convention of the Alabama Bankers Association that "for the most part our people are happy and contented, with no Coxey armies marching on to Washington."[32]

The Populists were emphatically unhappy, so unhappy

[28] Mobile *Register*, June 2, 1894.
[29] *Ibid.*, July 12, 1894.
[30] *Ibid.*, July 17, 18, 1894.
[31] *Ibid.*, July 25, 1894.
[32] *Ibid.*, June 13, 1894.

they could sympathize with the miners. Based on a common belief in the value of labor and a common sense of exploitation, they constructed a bridge of cooperation between the country and urban labor of which they were proud.[33] It is true that wage-earners and farmers did not have completely compatible interests, but they had common enemies and consequently could expect support from each other on issues that split both the urban and the rural communities.[34] In March, before the strike began, Populists and representatives of the miners met and agreed upon mutual aid. The Populists uniformly condemned Governor Jones for using state troops in a partisan way to break the strike. Peyton G. Bowman, called "blood and bayonets" Bowman by the Democrats, commented that Jones would soon "be trying to run every plough in these mountains with a soldier and a bayonet behind you." The Birmingham *Age-Herald* replied that "no socialist in Chicago and no anarchist in France could have uttered a worse sentiment than that in a public speech, or made a lower appeal to the prejudices and passions of man."[35] The Populists continued to support the outcast miners, and the miners returned the sympathy.

[33] Ozark *Free Press*, February 25, 1897. Writing much later, Joe Manning thought the ills of the city could be cured; *The Fadeout of Populism*, 102-103.

[34] Chester M. Destler, *American Radicalism, 1865-1901*, "Connecticut College Monograph No. 3," New London, 1946, 170. Destler examines the Old Northwest with urban-rural interaction as a major theme. He concludes that Populist-Labor cooperation failed because Populists rejected socialism. Norman Pollack, in Chapter 3 of his book, *The Populists Response to Industrial America: Midwestern Populist Thought*, Cambridge, Mass., 1962, argues that the conservatism of the urban laborers was the cause of the failure.

[35] Mobile *Register*, July 12, 1894; Troy *Jeffersonian*, August 3, 1894.

The mining companies blacklisted most of the white miners who struck, and maintained standing offers to pay their way to coal fields along the Ohio River to get them out of the state. Jones called the strikers and mine operators together in July in a vain effort to settle the strike before the election. The Pinkerton detective Jones hired for undercover work among the miners reported that Populist politicians were busy trying to hold the strike together and keep the strikers in Alabama at least until after the election.[36]

The Democrats won the August election for governor after a bitter campaign with the usual quota of thrown eggs and punched noses. The Populists relied heavily on their appeal for a free vote and a fair count. The Democrats centered on the fact that the Populists not only had the support of the lily-white Republicans within the state, but the financial aid of high-tariff Republicans outside the state.[37] Oates won by a wider margin than Jones had in 1892. Officials counted 192,554 votes, almost 50,000 less than two years before. The most dramatic drops in voter turnout were in the white counties. Oates received 109,160 votes to Kolb's 83,394. The pattern of voting was much the same as in 1892. Before the election Kolb had said that he controlled 37 counties. In the election he carried 34 of the 66 counties, but the margin in each of his counties was quite narrow. The same was not true in the Black Belt. Kolb ran ahead of Oates by 8,000 votes outside the Black Belt, but the tremendous majorities in the same few Black Belt counties carried the state for the Democratic candidate.[38]

[36] See the file marked "Labor Trouble 1894" in the Governor's Office Papers, ADAH.

[37] Mobile *Register*, June 15, 1894. Rogers, "Agrarianism in Alabama," 471-473.

[38] *Ibid.*, 480-481. Montgomery *Advertiser*, August 19, 1894.

The Populists in Alabama faced a very frustrating situation. According to their own view, they had been twice cheated out of control of the Democratic Party and now twice defrauded in the regular elections of 1892 and 1894. The irritations of their position were exacerbated by the fact that Alabama still had no legal provision for contesting elections. The way in which the Populists adapted to this increasing frustration yields another clue to the nature of the movement.

Their growing unwillingness to submit meekly to fraud is best measured by the anticipations of violence that abounded during and after the campaign of 1894. Frustration was beginning to tell. One Populist editor, I. L. Brock, in 1893 advised the Populists to "MEET FRAUD WITH FORCE."[39] This was the counterpart of the Tillmanite battle cry from South Carolina which the Troy *Jeffersonian* echoed a year later, "Ballots or Bullets."[40] Such slogans could be dismissed if they were not accompanied by many other rumors and portents of violence. A Birmingham man warned the *Jeffersonian* that "the Jonesite faction must be kicked out of power, or we may have a sample of the times in bleeding Kansas in 1855."[41] Two months later the *Jeffersonian* observed that the "demagogues in congress do the will of the plutogogues in Wall Street." The paper added ominously that "if relief for the masses does not come through equitable laws it will come through revolution."[42]

Late in June the *Register* reported that the Kolbites in Etowah County were drilling twice a week with shot-

---

Mobile *Register*, August 12, 1894. I have used the *Advertiser*'s figures.

[39] *The Alliance Herald*, May 4, 1893.
[40] Troy *Jeffersonian*, July 27, 1894.
[41] *Ibid.*, March 2, 1894.
[42] *Ibid.*, May 4, 1894.

guns.[43] The Piedmont *Inquirer* was worried about rumors concerning arms shipments from England, military organizations of Populists, and Populists "arming themselves with Winchester rifles and being sworn to do or die in the attempt to have fair elections. Surely fair elections can be secured without resorting to such violent and dangerous methods."[44] But another Democratic paper thought the election would produce violence.[45]

This was evidently not just newspaper sensationalism. In June Horace Hood wrote to McKee that "The devil will be to pay in Alabama after the August elections."[46] McKee chastised Hood for the extravagant language he used to describe the situation. But by July McKee's tone of moderation had changed. In a letter to Senator Morgan, McKee said that federal intervention in the Pullman strike might turn it into a revolution. He severely criticized Governor Jones, "an insane governor de facto, whose authority is the product of multiplied felonies," for doing the same thing in Alabama.[47]

On August 9th, three days after the election, the joint Populist Campaign Committee met and issued an address signed by W. H. Skaggs, A. T. Goodwyn, and John W. Pitts. The address was ambiguous. It called on all true citizens not to submit but to "assert the sovereign power, before which thrones totter, sceptres fall and the outrages of tyrants cease." On the other hand, it did not "advise fighting or lawlessness of any kind. . . ." It called on the people to meet on August 23 at their respective court-

[43] Mobile *Register*, June 28, 1894.

[44] Piedmont *Inquirer*, January 6, 1894.

[45] Brewton *Standard Gauge*, July 19, 1894, quoted in Rogers, "Agrarianism in Alabama," 479.

[46] Horace Hood to Robert McKee, June 13, 22, 26, 1894, McKee Papers, ADAH.

[47] McKee to Morgan, July 8, 1894, copy in McKee Papers, ADAH.

houses to take action that would "be creditable to their revolutionary sires. . . ."[48]

The few protest meetings that were held were poorly attended.[49] The absence of positive leadership may have inhibited them, but it is more likely that the Populists were overcome with post-election depression. A note of disillusionment and bitterness was evident in both the Troy *Jeffersonian* and the *Choctaw Alliance*.[50] As the fall congressional campaign progressed, the *Alliance* regained its sense of outrage; by late October it was expressing regret that the attempted assassination of President Cleveland had failed and prescribing a stiff dosage of hemp for vote-stealers.[51] In September the *Jeffersonian* lapsed into increasingly radical Biblical rhetoric: "And Vengeance will come." "We are on the brink of a revolution. The question is up whether the citizen or the dollar shall rule this country. . . ." And it hinted darkly that "to condone the frauds of 1894 and submit to them . . . would neither be the history of the white race, nor would it be an evidence of 'southern manhood.' "[52]

In October, in the midst of the congressional campaign, the chairman of the two Populist parties called a special state convention of the Jeffersonian and People's Party to meet in Montgomery on November 12 "to consider what action should be taken in regard to the monstrous election frauds that were perpetrated in the last August election and for other purposes."[53] The Tuscaloosa *Journal* hinted that the meeting would provide

[48] Troy *Jeffersonian*, August 17, 1894.
[49] Rogers, "Agrarianism in Alabama," 484.
[50] *Jeffersonian*, August 24, 1894; and *Choctaw Alliance*, August 22, 29, 1894.
[51] *Choctaw Alliance*, October 24, 1894.
[52] September 14, and 21, 1894.
[53] *Choctaw Alliance*, October 26, 1894.

for the organization of a separate state government.[54] Newspapers began to talk of Dorr's Rebellion and remember how in 1872 Democrats and Republicans had organized contesting state legislatures in Montgomery.

Horace Hood had foreseen all of it before the August elections. "There will be two state governments in December each claiming to be the rightful government," he wrote,

> and the sabre will jostle you on the sidewalk and the bayonet will glisten around the state house, while pandemonium reigns within. . . . These are troublous and uncertain times we have entered upon and this is but the beginning of a disastrous end. The end will be liquidation for us all. Men in this community, proud and highminded men, have been forced to beg their friends for fifty cents or a quarter, or anything they could get to buy marketing and something to eat. . . . There are those who do not know, or affect not to know, the condition of the people, and are going like a blind horse toward an awful precipice. There is a gloomy outlook. . . .[55]

The congressional elections held on November 6 cast some light on the psychological condition of Alabama voters. The results showed that a candidate's ideological position mattered much less than his orientation toward the groups contesting for power. Milford W. Howard, the Populist candidate in the 7th District, won a resounding victory over a free-silver Democrat, W. H. Denson. In three other districts Democratic candidates were apparently elected, only to be unseated later by Congress. A. T. Goodwyn, a Populist, successfully contested the

[54] Quoted in the Troy *Jeffersonian*, October 24, 1894.
[55] Hood to McKee, June 13, 1894, McKee Papers, ADAH.

election of James E. Cobb, a free-silver Democrat. Gaston A. Robbins and Oscar W. Underwood, Democrats, had both courted the Alliance and had sought the support of the silver advocates. They were unseated by W. F. and T. H. Aldrich, Republican brothers endorsed by the Populists, who were coal operators and consistent advocates of high protective tariffs and sound money.[56]

Shortly after the election, on November 12, the joint Jeffersonian and People's Party convention met in the Montgomery Theater. Fearing that they would never give up the Capitol once inside, Governor Jones had denied them the usual courtesy of the use of the building. Dr. Grattan B. Crow wanted to seize the Capitol by force and had raised an armed force to help in the venture.[57] The gathering was enthusiastic but took no drastic step. It did vote to finally drop the fictitious dual organization and merge into the People's Party. The delegates also voted not to take any extralegal action until the legislature had had a chance to redress the party's grievances.

In the absence of a contest law, the legislature made short work of the Populist petition which claimed that the Populists had evidence of massive frauds and asked the legislature to disallow the returns from certain counties until the evidence could be heard. On November 17 the General Assembly in joint session ignored the Populist petition and quickly proclaimed Oates the winner of the August election.

Two days later Kolb published a manifesto dated November 17 in his new paper in Birmingham, *The People's Weekly Tribune*—"You, fellow citizens, have twice

[56] Rowell, *A Historical and Legal Digest of All the Contested Election Cases in the House of Representatives of the United States from the First to the Fifty-Sixth Congress, 1789-1901*, 509-510.

[57] Rogers, "Agrarianism in Alabama," 490-491.

elected me governor of this state," and declared ominously, "and this time, by the grace of God and the help of the good people of Alabama, I will be governor. December 1 is the day fixed by the law for the inauguration of the governor. On that date I shall be in Montgomery for the purpose of taking the oath of office and my seat as governor."[58] The headlines of a hostile paper screamed: "KOLB TO BE SEATED IF IT IS TO BE DONE BY SLAUGHTERING THE STATE MILITIA."[59] The newspapers reported that the state militia had been given orders to shoot to kill if necessary.[60] The Anniston *Hot Blast* unleashed its doggerel.

> Reuben! Reuben! I've been thinking,
> And I tell you for your health:
> When you start this bad blood spilling,
> Be sure and spill it from yourself.[61]

December 1, 1894 was a good day for a revolution in Montgomery. The sun shone brightly and the temperature was quite warm at noon when William C. Oates took his place at the spot on the Capitol steps where Jefferson Davis had stood to take the oath as President of the Confederate States of America. Chief Justice Brickell was waiting with the Bible Davis had used in the ceremony 33 years before. These symbols of Southern legitimacy were necessary in view of Oates' cloudy moral claim to the office.

While the inaugural parade passed through the crowded streets on the way to the ceremony during the hour before noon, Reuben F. Kolb took the oath of office

---

[58] Reprinted in the Mobile *Register*, November 20, 1894.
[59] *Ibid.*, November 13, 1894.
[60] *Ibid.*, December 1, 1894.
[61] Quoted in *ibid*.

downtown before a Justice of the Peace. Only a few witnesses and fellow insurgents were present in the drab office on South Court Street. Then the little party of defiant men marched up the hill to the Capitol for Kolb to deliver his address from the traditional spot.

Arriving at the Capitol grounds, they found every entrance blocked by one of the 20 companies of state troops. The troops allegedly were in town for ceremonial purposes and parade duty, but they carried live ammunition. The little group of Populists made its way through the ranks of the troops toward the right side of the big stone steps leading down from the Capitol. A detachment of troops quickly moved between the interlopers and the strategic steps. Governor Jones was on the steps and told Kolb and Warren S. Reese that they could not speak there. Probably at this point a crowd urged Kolb to speak anyway. Kolb turned to the firebrand, Joseph C. Manning, and asked his advice. "Go ahead, Captain," Manning replied, "they may kill you, but you will go down in history as a martyr to the Populist cause."[62]

Kolb refused this invitation to immortality. The small knot of Populists left the Capitol grounds and found an empty wagon nearby on Bainbridge Street. Standing in this wagon and speaking to only two or three hundred people, Kolb made his inaugural address. He insisted he was the lawful governor and demanded that a contest law be passed, but he urged that there be no violence. The crowd dispersed quietly. It was distinctly anticlimactic.

Governor Jones thought his threat of force had kept

[62] Warren S. Reese to Joseph C. Manning, December 2, 1927, in Manning, *Fadeout of Populism*, 142-144. The account of inauguration day has been pieced together from: the Mobile *Register*, December 2, 1894; the *Chicago Tribune*, December 2, 1894; Rogers, "Agrarianism in Alabama," 492-493; and Clark, *Populism in Alabama*, 158-160.

the Populists from trying stronger measures. "They planned to kidnap Oates and myself the day before the inauguration, and to take possession of the Capitol and inaugurate Capt. Kolb," Jones said years later. But the plan failed because "they feared that it would have cost them their lives."[63] The failure was worse than Jones imagined. Few Populists even showed up in Montgomery on inauguration day despite Kolb's plea. Had thousands of angry Populists been in the city on December 1, things might have happened differently, regardless of the troops. But the 83,000 men who voted Populist in August did not feel in December that Populism was worth a revolution or even a show of force.

The Populists backed away from their revolutionary posture soon after the inauguration day fiasco. A few evenings later the Populist legislators met in a quiet caucus and agreed to continue to act within the law until the end of the session. If a contest law were passed, they would abide by its decision. If the legislature did not pass such an act, or if any other oppressive laws were enacted, the Populists would call another convention to decide a course of action.[64] In January, when Kolb sent to the legislature a request for a contest law, he signed it "Governor of Alabama."[65] The General Assembly passed the contest law in February.[66] Because the bill applied only to future elections and not to the election of 1894, three Populists in the House voted against it.[67] Otherwise

[63] Jones to DuBose, September 21, 1911, DuBose Papers, ADAH.

[64] Mobile *Register*, December 8, 1894.

[65] Rogers, "Agrarianism in Alabama," 495.

[66] Alabama, *Acts of the General Assembly, 1894*, 676-679 and 753-763; hereafter cited as *Acts*, plus the year in which the session began.

[67] Alabama, *House Journal, 1894*, 1,004.

they did nothing. When the Populist state Executive Committee met in March it condemned the Democrats for stealing the election, but at the same time it announced that Kolb was abandoning his pretense of being the legitimate governor for the sake of peace, law, and order.[68]

If the Populists were not revolutionaries, neither did they behave like reformers. They repeatedly showed a willingness to vote against reforms to which they were pledged. Populists performed in this bizarre fashion in the biennial legislative session that convened on November 16, 1894. The size of their minority delegation in this legislature was large enough to command consideration from the majority. 35 Populists and 65 Democrats sat in the House of Representatives while 8 Populists and 27 Democrats composed the Senate.[69]

Populists performed variously on minor legislation. They were most consistent in fulfilling their pledges to labor by voting for bills to require the prompt payment of wages and the honest weighing of coal. The same allegiance appeared in their votes against appropriations for the state militia,[70] and against funds to provide a state exhibit at the Cotton States International Exhibition in Atlanta.[71] On a bill to give an enforceable lien to the ginners of cotton, the Populists split. The only votes in the House in favor of yeomen and tenant farmers were Populist votes, but half of the Populists voted with the

[68] Birmingham *News*, March 13, 1895.

[69] Alabama, *House Journal, 1894*, 7-8. *Senate Journal, 1894*, 5. Two Republicans are included in the figure for Populists in the House. For their geographical distribution see Appendix III.

[70] Alabama, *House Journal, 1894*, 757, 758. The Populists also argued that the measure would cost too much money. Mobile *Register*, February 8, 1895.

[71] Alabama, *House Journal, 1894*, 989.

majority for the ginners. This was an important indication of the internal division which in large part gave rise to Populist inability to define objectives for the party. Spot checks of special bills reveal that Populists were inconsistent and divided in their votes on local prohibition and on authorizations for urban bond issues.

The most important issues to face the 1894 legislature concerned taxation, child labor, and the convict lease system. These were issues which remained of fundamental concern to reform-minded Alabamians for the next 15 years or longer; they were the questions that helped to define Alabama Progressivism. When challenged on the grounds of real and immediate need, Populists proved that they were not reformers.

Taxation was always a basic issue. It was on tax policy that Progressives showed their most decisive break with the past and affirmation of the future. The Populists acted differently. In 1894 the state was in debt and running a deficit. One reason was that while the assessed value of property had been climbing since 1876, the legislature had constantly decreased the tax rate from 7 mills in 1876 to 4 mills in the period 1890 to 1894. Early in the 1894-95 session the House passed a bill raising the tax rate to 5½ mills. The Populists voted as a bloc against the tax increase.[72] The constant emphasis on low taxes and inexpensive government in Populist papers leaves little doubt that they were still wedded to the idea of minimum government, despite frequent infidelities of thought. Their fear of debt casts doubt on their grasp of the future needs and direction of society.[73]

[72] *Ibid.*, 371-372. The bill passed by a vote of 53 to 24. Populists voted 24-2 against the bill. Also see Thomas G. Jones to John W. DuBose, January 27, 1914, DuBose Papers, ADAH.

[73] A good example is in the *Alabama Monitor*, December 11, 1896.

The Populist vote could have been a demand for a change in the tax structure, for the tax structure discriminated against the owners of real property devoted to agriculture. But as their performance on the revenue bill showed, Populist motivation lay elsewhere.

Sponsored by Sam Will John, an important Progressive who in 1907 was Comer's floor leader in the House of Representatives, the revenue bill was designed to shift the burden of taxation to the broad shoulders of railroads and other corporations. It provided for an excise tax on bank deposits and intangible assets, and more stringent machinery to make assessments more truthful and less easy to escape.

The John bill faced tough opposition from the friends of railroads and corporations. With the help of the Populists, John staved off attempts to amend or kill the bill. However, when the clerk was reading the bill for the third time just prior to passage, Populist leaders circulated the word among their followers to vote against the bill for "tactical reasons." The House then defeated it 32 to 49. No Populist voted for the bill.[74]

The following day a special committee worked out a compromise, and the House passed it the same day. The compromise omitted the excise tax on corporations and weakened the machinery for assessing property. The legislature passed the compromise bill with the Populists still solidly in opposition.[75]

Populist legislators performed unpredictably on another reform measure sponsored by Sam Will John—one aimed at the convict lease system. The *Register* pointed out that the death rate at Coalburg, operated by the Sloss

[74] Alabama, *House Journal, 1894*, 925-927, 892-894, 942-943. Mobile *Register*, February 9, 10, 11, 12, 13, 14, 15, 1895.
[75] Alabama, *House Journal, 1894*, 943.

Company, was more than twice the mortality rate among convicts in Mississippi and 10 times that of Ohio convicts. Unhealthful conditions and a 66-hour workweek undoubtedly contributed to these figures.[76] There were also nonhumanitarian reasons for abolishing the system. Miners opposed the lease system because convict labor had the effect of setting a ceiling on the wages of free miners and depressed what were already unsafe working conditions. In 1893 Julia Tutwiler, Alabama's great lady reformer, said the system was "one that combines all the evils of slavery without one of its ameliorating features."[77] Governor Jones was proud of the small beginning the legislature had made during his administration toward changing the purpose of the system from profit to self-sufficiency with decent conditions—which was all destroyed under Oates.[78]

Sam Will John felt "that the whole system is a shame to any Christian state, and cannot be too soon blotted out forever."[79] He introduced an amendment which aimed at doing just that. Unfortunately the House tabled his measure by a vote of 34 to 30. In their platform the Populists promised to abolish the convict lease system, yet some of them were distinctly unenthusiastic about fulfilling that pledge; 11 voted against John's reform and 10 voted for it.[80]

The Populists performed with no greater consistency with regard to child labor. Alabama law prohibited employers from compelling women to work more than eight

[76] Mobile *Register*, August 2, 1895.

[77] Moore, *History of Alabama*, 979.

[78] Cory to Jones, November 22, 1892, Jones Papers, ADAH. Jones to DuBose, July 13, 1893, and January 27, 1914, DuBose Papers, ADAH. Alabama, *Acts, 1894*, 856.

[79] Alabama, *House Journal, 1894*, 1,098-1,099.

[80] *Ibid.*, 944.

hours per day, and forbade children under 14 years of age to work more than eight hours per day. Governor Oates recommended that the legislature repeal this restriction in order to lure outside capital into the state. The legislature complied. On December 4 the repeal bill passed, 53 to 7. Perhaps it is significant that of the 7 opposing votes, 6 were Populists, but 17 Populists voted with the majority to repeal the female and child labor law.[81]

The antireform votes of the Populists pose a problem, particularly because their performance in subsequent legislatures and in the Constitutional Convention of 1901 continued to follow the same pattern. The most likely explanation is that the Populists wanted to demonstrate their potential as a balance-of-power voting bloc. Even if this were so, it demonstrates at the least that, unlike the Progressives, the Populists were not primarily issue-oriented. They were, patently, not reformers.

It may be that revolution was not a real possibility in 1894 either, or that there was any danger the Populists would use force or take any extralegal steps. Historians can never be certain. The psychology of rumor, however, indicates that there is danger of violence when rumors begin to assume a specifically threatening form. Before mobs erupt, there is usually a period of unstructured milling about during which the common feelings of members of the mob are frequently mentioned and reinforced by supportive attitudes from other members. This pre-violence condition evidently was closely approximated in Alabama in the fall of 1894 among the Populists. The element possibly missing was the clash between hostile belief systems. Conflicts over ideologies are less easily resolved than conflict over power. When the Alabama

[81] *Ibid.*, 276.

revolution of 1894 did not happen, it was most likely because there was no great ideological division between the opposing forces. The following chapter will explore this possibility.[82]

[82] Neil J. Smelser, *Theory of Collective Behavior*, New York, 1963, 247-248. Berelson and Steiner, *Human Behavior*, 621.

CHAPTER FOUR

The Populist Mentality

What sort of social movement was Populism? Was it reformist or revolutionary? Was it concerned with the here, the now, and the possible, or was it devoted to an outmoded past or perhaps to a chiliastic future? Was the Populist mind rooted in reality or disoriented by anxiety? Much of the evidence needed to answer these questions has been presented above. The missing information has to do with the Populist state-of-mind, an imprecise area of investigation at best, and made more so by the great distances in time and environment between the investigator and the "typical" Populist.

Nevertheless, a good starting point in assessing Populist self-image is a revealing description of the composition of the movement written by an ordinary Populist. This letter to the editor declared that Populism was composed of "that class that makes a country rich, great, powerful, honorable and respectable, the people called the middle class, the people that pay the taxes to support government, produce the country's exports, fight its battles when need be to defend its honor. For you know that neither plutocrats or paupers will expose their lives and their blood in defense of the principles that advance civilization and tend to the uplifting of humanity."[1] Hardworking but poor, Populists had good reason to feel

[1] *The Piedmont Inquirer*, July 14, 1894.

77

angry and defensive. Yet this particular Populist and those he resembled did not think of themselves as members of a persecuted minority, but rather as a victimized majority. Outsiders struggling for entry usually do not question the central norms and values of the class or society to which they aspire; they frequently adopt its standards long before they are actually members, and may zealously overconform to the group's ways after they achieve membership. On the other hand, loyal members who observe the rules and are denied the rewards may begin to wonder what is wrong with the system—the Populists belong in this category. In the 1890s one important rule was that work was morally good and success was supposed to accrue to those having moral worth.[2] It was therefore natural for the hardworking poor to resent those who seemed to work less yet were materially more successful.

Milford W. Howard made a career of expressing the antagonistic feelings of persecuted failures toward "immoral" successes. He himself had played the game of speculator and promoter in the 1880s and lost, so he undoubtedly found the theme congenial.[3] In Congress, where he served for two terms, Howard preached against the concentration of wealth in the United States. "How will you remedy this concentration?" he asked the Congress; "How can you reconcile a nation of paupers to toil in the shadow of splendor and magnificence to support the idle, worthless few?"[4]

And there was to be no mistake about who the idle,

[2] See Irvin G. Wyllie, *The Self-Made Man in America: The Myth of Rags to Riches*, New Brunswick, N.J., 1954, 4, 9, and throughout.

[3] Moore, *History of Alabama*, 529-530. Rogers, "Agrarianism in Alabama," 487, 496-499.

[4] Quoted in *The People's Weekly Tribune*, June 4, 1896.

worthless few were. Howard wrote a book about them: *If Christ Came to Congress*. It was patterned very closely after W. T. Stead's popular exposé, *If Christ Came to Chicago*; Howard even included a map of the red-light district of Washington, as Stead had of Chicago. To leave absolutely no doubt as to where his sympathies lay, he dedicated his book to Grover Cleveland, "President of the United States, and his drunken, licentious cabinet and certain members of Congress."[5]

If Christ Came to Congress, like Edward Bellamy's *Looking Backward*, is a polemical tract thinly disguised as a novel. The main story concerns Jennie Harmon, a pure, sweet, innocent, country girl who comes to Washington to earn a living in a civil service job. She is deceived and ruined and driven to suicide by the corrupt system and the immoral men who run it. But the author is not totally sympathetic with Jennie. After all, she is not compelled to join in the pursuit of success. She "might have gone back and married plain, honest, old-fashioned James Forney, but she rebelled at the thought."[6] The author is also ambivalent in his attitude toward the prostitutes with which the book abounds; they are both sinner and Magdalene. Clearly he does not make up his mind about the power of moral choice to overcome the influences of the environment.

If Christ Came to Congress is lugubriously sentimental, but it does express important attitudes. Its purpose was to impart a sense of the moral depravity of official life in

---

[5] Howard, *If Christ Came to Congress*. For a discussion of William Thomas Stead's prototype, *If Christ Came to Chicago*, Chicago, 1894, see Joseph O. Baylen, "A Victorian's 'Crusade' in Chicago, 1893-1894," *The Journal of American History*, LI, December 1964, 418-434. It should be noted that the maps in Howard's book are out of date.

[6] Howard, *If Christ Came to Congress*, 92.

Washington. The despair of innocent people contrasts sharply with the profligacy and bacchanalian orgies of highly placed people. While sex is the focus of the indictment, gambling, influence peddling, bribery, and drunkenness also get a liberal exposure. "Puritanical ideas of honesty and patriotism" are presented in a good light, while the author condemns modern, urban, loose morality. Howard's heroes are the "middling classes," "the good, honest sturdy yeomen," or the "independent laborers" who are persecuted by the extravagance of Congress and class legislation in the interests of "these gigantic trusts, these rich corporations, these bloated bond-holders and millionaires."

The novel ends with an apocalyptic dream of a revolution in which the mysterious Black Knights create anarchy so the mobs can loot the treasury and distribute all the money to the starving poor. The sequel shows a second stage of the revolution when "peace, plenty and purity" reign because Christ's spirit has been brought to bear on social problems.

Such a striking example as Howard's is a reminder that the South in the 1890s was the sort of society that has frequently spawned millennial movements. Rapid economic changes were threatening the way of life of the small independent farmer and undermining the cohesion and stability of the social structure. In such a situation there may be a paranoiac response among those who feel impotent, exposed, and cast out.[7] The Populists fit this pattern to a considerable extent; certainly their response was aggressive.

Basic to Howard's book, and fundamental to Populism, was the reaction of the people against their traditional

[7] Norman Cohn, *The Pursuit of the Millennium*, London, 1957, 307-314.

leaders. Warren Reese perceived this growing alienation in his important speech at Brundidge, Alabama in August 1891 when he said the people no longer believed that wealth was distributed by society in a just way, "and the people in their sovereign might have determined that there shall be a radical change in our form of government. . . . There never was an instance of the change in the circumstance and temper of a whole nation, so sudden and extraordinary as that which the misconduct of politicians has within the last two years produced in the United States." Reese added that "confidence is a plant of slow growth in one who has been deceived like the laboring classes of this country."[8] Frank Baltzell, before the break with the Democratic party, wrote that "the dirty slush and silly bosh that is given us in answer to our prayers is fast losing [sic] party grip on all honest men, in or out of the farmers' alliance or other orders."[9] Another Populist editor commented that "the politicians have been promising the people relief for the last ten years, but they have never attempted to keep their promises. The people will depend on them no longer."[10] In short, the Populist movement was based on the belief that the people had lost control of their government.

Just as deep imbedded in Populist psychology was the feeling that a conspiracy was afoot to deprive them of what should be rightfully theirs under the existing system with the existing concepts of justice and equity. The right of the laborer to the fruits of his labor, a maxim derived from the Protestant work ethic and not from Marx, was perhaps the most persistently invoked doctrine. "This much talked of labor struggle is not only between em-

[8] *People's Reflector*, November 10, 1892.
[9] *Ozark Banner*, July 7, 1892.
[10] *The Alliance Herald*, July 7, 1893.

ployer and employed, boss and wage worker," said a Populist paper, "but between the doers and the do-nothings, those who give an equivalent for what they receive and those supported by rent, interest and monopoly."[11] "Labor produces all wealth," another Populist paper stated. "Labor should enjoy what it produces."[12]

The bounties of nature were provided by God to be turned into wealth by labor. Therefore idle land was sinful—particularly when there were farmers willing to work who needed land. "See that, Mr. Landlord," the Populists asked in tones familiar to traditional rural classes complaining about land monopoly, "God says the land is His. How come you with more than you can use yourself to the exclusion of others who want and need it?"[13] In all Alliance and Populist platforms there was a demand for the government to reclaim unused land from railroads and alien landholders. These land speculators were good examples of the nonworkers who were trying to subject labor to unjust conditions. "Labor should be king," rang the battle cry, "instead of abject slave."[14]

Populist literature was also saturated with more general conspiracy theories. For instance, the *Alliance Herald* declared that "the Rothschilds are the head and front of the greatest financial conspiracy ever attempted in the history of the world."[15] "The Rothschilds are the kings of the earth, with their faithful allies and watchful co-adjutors in every land," echoed the *Choctaw Alliance*.[16] The Troy *Jeffersonian* confirmed that "the money oligarchy is running the country."[17] Years later Joseph C.

[11] *Choctaw Alliance*, September 12, 1894.
[12] Troy *Jeffersonian*, September 21, 1894.
[13] *Ibid.*, October 12, 1894.
[14] Tuscaloosa *Journal*, October 10, 1894.
[15] May 4, 1893.
[16] September 12, 1894.
[17] May 4, 1894.

Manning still thought that capitalism meant "Invisible Government" and that the people could not trust it.[18] Populists looked out upon the world with hostility and suspicion. They obviously felt oppressed, outcast, and powerless. "Oh wretched people that we are," cried the *Jeffersonian*, "who will deliver us from the oppression of heartless corporations?"[19]

The Populists were in a receptive mood to new doctrines in the early 1890s, as substantiated by their approval of reforms so at odds with traditional Jeffersonian dogma as federally financed rural credit plans, government ownership of railroads, a managed currency, and a protective tariff. But they retained major segments of the old set of values, never breaking completely away. The same platforms and pronouncements that demonstrated Populist willingness to break with the past in search of solutions for their real problems also gave voice to the continued desire for minimum government in the Jeffersonian mold. It is significant that their voting record was more consistent with negative government theory than with a new view of the possibilities of positive action by government.

Populists sometimes ridiculed the dominant overproduction theory of the depression, in favor of an underconsumption theory,[20] and occasionally envisioned a new order of society that would not depend on unbridled competition. Such an order, they thought, would come closer to institutionalizing the brotherhood of man and would provide for the dignity of each individual. Their reforms suggested the use of government to protect weak

[18] Manning, *Fadeout of Populism*, 111.

[19] Troy *Jeffersonian*, August 3, 1894.

[20] Samuel M. Adams in the *Choctaw Alliance*, April 26, 1893; and "Warwick" (I. L. Brock) in the *Alliance Herald*, May 4, 1893.

portions of society against the stronger segments.[21] James M. Whitehead, one of Populism's most able editors, appeared to adopt a forward-looking humanism when he chastised Governor Oates for making derogatory remarks about Whitehead's lack of worldly success. "This thrust on your part," Whitehead countered, "has the appearance of cold blooded cruelty. It convinces me of a thing that I have long suspected, viz. that you have a higher regard for money than for manhood, and you measure men, not by dimensions of the heart, mind and soul, but by the amount of money they may have at their command."[22] The trouble was that Whitehead's humane standards never found an institutional expression; he remained an advocate of Jeffersonian simplicity in government.

The ambivalence of Populists concerning the competitive system indicates that they had not completely liberated themselves from it despite their leanings in that direction. Milford Howard, invoking the image of Christ the Provider, wrote that "if He were here now would He not go among these, His starving children, and feed them, even though He had to convert every stone in the Capitol into a loaf of bread?"[23] But elsewhere in his novel Howard wrote that if Christ came to Congress, "He would, if it were in His power, make it possible for them to earn their bread."[24] This inconsistency was more than an inability to choose between work relief and the dole. When Hilary Herbert, the Alabamian who was Cleveland's secretary of the navy, said that it was the duty of the rich to give liberally to charity in order to allay discontent, the Troy *Jeffersonian* argued in reply that "what the in-

[21] *Choctaw Alliance*, November 23, 1892.
[22] *People's Weekly Tribune*, June 18, 1896.
[23] Howard, *If Christ Came to Congress*, 292.
[24] *Ibid.*, 5.

voluntarily idle want is an equal chance in the struggle for existence."[25] Not a change of rules, but the equitable enforcement of the existing rules was what most Populists desired.

Populism did not offer the exciting new vista of the future that would have motivated an uneducated, insecure, but obviously susceptible electorate.[26] Recent studies of modern revolutions and primitive rebelliousness emphasize the need for ideology.[27] Basic emotions such as hatred or resentment cannot sustain a protest movement for the long term, especially in a political system which continuously accommodates itself to popular pressures. The Populists lacked an ideology that would connect their sad economic plight—which motivated them in the first place—with a train of causation leading back to the political process. All they had were conspiracy theories, and conspiracy theories implied that the situation could be cured by quashing the conspiracy and thereby reestablishing a traditionally just system. Consequently there was little attempt to analyze the system, and solace was gained by heaping a great deal of bad feeling on the supposed corrupters. Populists needed an ideology that would have given cohesion and direction to their unformed yearnings for change.

If anomie is defined as the condition of anxiety resulting from a deterioration in the old belief system when society possesses no common values or morals which

[25] Troy *Jeffersonian*, May 18, 1894.

[26] For interesting comparative cases see Seymour Martin Lipset, *Political Man: The Social Bases of Politics*, 116, 151.

[27] E. J. Hobsbawn, *Primitive Rebels: Studies in Archaic Forms of Social Movement in the 19th and 20th Centuries*, Manchester, England, 1959; and Frantz Fanon, *The Wretched of the Earth*, preface by Jean-Paul Sartre, translated by Constance Farrington, New York, 1965, particularly 111-115.

effectively govern conduct, then clearly the Populists do not qualify.[28] If anomie is the personal bind arising from a discontinuity between culturally induced aspirations and the social structure's limitation on opportunity, then the Populists were definitely eligible.[29] That they perceived the disjunction in their situation is without question, but they did not react by rebelling. The preceding chapter showed that Populists were not willing to launch a physical revolution. The present chapter has emphasized the fact that the Populists were not rebels in the sociological sense of rejecting the existing cultural goals and the institutional ways of attaining them and substituting a new ideology giving legitimacy to fresh values pertaining to ends and means.[30] To be true rebels, Populists needed to transcend the given nature of their society, and they failed to do so.

This is not to say that the Populists did not have occasional glimpses of the problem which had to be solved. "In this country of undeveloped resources, rich in the endowments of nature," they frequently said in various ways, "no man should go idle who wants work. Under a proper distributive system no man who works should be poor."[31] This is a noble sentiment, but it depends on existing values pertaining to the ends and means of society and the substitution of new values.[32] The Populists never

[28] Sebastian deGrazia, *The Political Community, A Study of Anomie*, Chicago, 1948, 73-74, 115-128. DeGrazia uses the late nineteenth century in the United States as an example of anomie.

[29] Robert K. Marton, *Social Theory and Social Structure*, rev. and enlarged edn., Glencoe, Ill., 1957, 162.

[30] An excellent discussion of the concept and literature of anomie is found in Marshall B. Clinard, ed., *Anomie and Deviant Behavior: A Discussion and Critique*, New York, 1964, especially 1-33.

[31] Troy *Jeffersonian*, September 14, 1894.

[32] Merton, *Social Theory and Social Structure*, 140 and note.

went that far, nor did they have a clear conception of how the transition to the ill-defined new order was to take place. Milford Howard, for instance, was not specific as to how the Christian ethic was to be translated into institutions in order to usher in the millennium. He went only so far as to say that the existing situation would be changed by electing pure men. In a similar vein the Populists called "for the masses of the people to stand together in their omnipotence and take control of the law-making power of the government."[33] Power, not a new system, was what the people required.

All social movements contain a mixture of value and power orientations. Even revolutionary movements will cling to cherished values at the cost of losing popular appeal. When power comes to be the dominant consideration in any movement, the group will soften its demands and deemphasize its distinctiveness from the rest of society.[34] This is precisely what happened to the Populists. In their campaign propaganda they did not stress nationalization of transportation and communications, nor the subtreasury scheme, nor the income tax, nor their other advanced proposals. In an effort to appeal to more people they ignored their formal program and resorted to bland slogans. Carrying this tendency to an absurd extreme, the *Choctaw Advocate* in its last issue before the election of 1894 attempted to stir the masses by writing that a vote for Kolb was a vote for "freedom and good government."[35] In their campaigns for state office, the Populists relied heavily on the demand for "a free vote and a fair count." This pointed to a legitimate issue, and

[33] *Ozark Banner*, July 28, 1898.

[34] Ralph H. Turner and Lewis M. Killian, *Collective Behavior*, Englewood Cliffs, N.J., 1957, 373.

[35] Quoted in the Mobile *Register*, August 1, 1894. Also see the *Choctaw Alliance*, August 1, 1894.

it was couched in terms that should have evoked a sympathetic response, but it is significant that it also was concerned with access to office and power. All the indications are that the Populists were a power-oriented protest movement.

Because Populism depended so much on the loss of faith in the old leadership, there remained the question of what would happen if the Democratic Party seemed to respond to the swelling chorus of complaint? The Populists were particularly vulnerable on the silver issue. Illustrating their own lack of internal cohesion and their dependence on issues which were popular common denominators, they had been able to muster agreement on only one measure in the 1892-93 legislature and that was a resolution imploring the federal government to adopt the free coinage of silver.[36] If the Democrats preempted this cause the Populists would be without a symbolic issue, as well as without an ideology. Even more crucial was the question of what would happen if the drive for power on the part of the leaders of Populism resulted in tactics that would shake the faith of an anxious and suspicious people in the authenticity of their own new leaders?

[36] Alabama, *House Journal, 1894*, 625.

Fusion and Confusion

With only a few votes needed to change Populism in Alabama into the majority party, the Populists trimmed their platform to its most modest and broadest essentials and looked hungrily at the estimated 30,000 white Republican votes and untold thousands of black Republican votes that might be had for a price. When the smoke of the resulting battle within Populism had been swept away by the chilly winds of defeat in 1896, the Populists saw their leaders for the first time not as powerful and faithful champions, but as the same frail and fallible politicians who led the two major parties. The resulting disillusion led to disintegration and dispersion.

The Populist State Executive Committee at its meeting in March 1895 not only relaxed the insurrectionary posture of the party but also issued a campaign plan for 1896. Ambitiously calling for the organization of People's Party clubs in every county and every beat, the committee offered to charter any sympathetic organization of "laboring" people in the state. The drift of Populist thinking at the time was also revealed in the constitution of the Reform Press Association which invited the membership of any paper that was "in the fight for fair elections and financial reform."[1] Though there were some

[1] Birmingham *News*, February 2, 1895.

Populists who wished to hold out for the full Omaha platform, the program was being stripped for action.

Shortly after the strategy session of the Populist committee, the first Democratic Free Silver Club in the state was established in Limestone County by Hector D. Lane and Luke Pryor, prominent politicians. The amount of space Democratic newspapers devoted to the silver issue increased markedly as the more resilient members of the Democratic Party began to respond to the popular discontent. Joseph F. Johnston, assuming the leadership of the responsive sector, organized in Birmingham a Free Silver Democratic League, then in September staged an impressive convention in Birmingham. The convention boasted the participation of such well-known figures in the state as Sam Will John, Senator Morgan, Senator Pugh, General Joe Wheeler, Congressmen John H. Bankhead, Gaston Robbins, James E. Cobb, and Jesse Stallings. The mild resolutions of the gathering in favor of free silver and fair elections did not disguise the fact that this was the first open challenge from the non-Populist reform wing of the Democratic Party to the railroad-oriented Democratic machine.[2]

As the silver sympathizers within the Democratic Party began to stir restlessly, the Populists vaguely noted the threat posed to their own party by the silver issue. When a conference of national silver leaders in Washington in March 1895 announced the formation of the American Bimetallic Party and launched national speaking tours of silver orators, Samuel M. Adams responded with an open letter to Alabama Populists. In it he asserted "the new Silver party that is now being formed is but another witness that the People's party is right." He thought the relations between the two parties "should be friendly, and

---

[2] Mobile *Register*, September 10 and 11, 1895.

that no suspicious and unnecessary antagonisms should arise between the two. But at the same time," said Adams, "I want to warn the People's party men of Alabama to be on the alert. We have nothing to gain by following the Silver party. . . ." It was a tricky question, and Adams could not resolve it. "I am in favor of standing by our National platform without compromising a single plank in it," wrote Adams, "and yet at the same time I would like to see the free silver men of this country vote solid for a man for President of the United States who will sign a bill for free coinage of both gold and silver at 16 to 1."[3]

The temptations of success lured the Populists in the direction of the Republicans as well. In 1892 and 1894 Populists had received white Republican endorsement at no particular cost, but R. A. Moseley predicted in February 1895 that the Republicans would run their own ticket in 1896. This served notice that the Republicans would want more in 1896 than the satisfaction of voting against the Democrats.[4]

The discussion of the possibility of fusion between the Populists and the Republicans was brought into the open in June 1895, when Kolb's *People's Weekly Tribune* asked Populist leaders to express their opinions. Kolb, who had favored fusion in 1892 and 1894, now switched sides to oppose it. He was supported by most of the Populist press and by M. W. Howard, Jerry Fountain, Grattan B. Crowe, Samuel M. Adams, J. P. Oliver, J. C. Fonville, A. P. Longshore, A. J. Hearn, Philander Morgan, and S. A. Hobson. The pro-fusion forces were led by Albert T. Goodwyn, P. G. Bowman, W. H. Skaggs, and Frank Baltzell. The lineup was to change frequently over the

[3] Birmingham *News*, April 11, 1895.
[4] Rogers, "Agrarianism in Alabama," 499.

next 18 months, but one fact was constant: there was no correlation between the degree of radicalism of a man's political views and his position on fusion, either local or national.[5]

The fusionists appeared to have control of the party at both the Executive Committee meeting in July 1895 and in a special convention held in November 1895, but their position was precarious. The convention went so far as to establish machinery to work out the details for cooperation among labor, Republican, and Populist forces. But the question was not finally settled until the Populist and Republican state conventions met in Montgomery on April 28, 1896.[6]

In the acrimonious debate over fusion with the Republicans, the lineup of Populist leaders was much the same as it had been since the previous summer, with the exception that Kolb had changed once again and now approved of Populist-Republican fusion within the state. The opponents of fusion advanced and elaborated two main arguments. The first equated fusion with the politics of Reconstruction and sought to trigger the images of corruption, civil disorder, and violations of the racial caste system which were all attached to the myth of Black Reconstruction. The other argument maintained that the Populists would be polluting their reform program by cooperating with the party of high tariffs, the gold standard, and big business. The fusionists answered that Lincoln Republicans were as good as Jackson Democrats in Alabama, and P. G. Bowman pointed out that as a practical business proposition the Populists were getting much

[5] *Ibid.*, 500. Montgomery *Advertiser*, July 25, 1895. Randolph *Toiler*, November 21, 1895.

[6] *Ibid.*, January 30 and March 5, 1896. *The People's Weekly Tribune*, March 19, 1896. Going, "Critical Months in Alabama Politics, 1895-96," 275.

more than they were giving.[7] The appeal of possible votes and power triumphed over the less tangible objections when the fusionists won the crucial roll call in the convention by a vote of 262 to 172.

The situation on the Republican side had changed drastically since 1894. The deep split in the party still existed; in fact, the Republicans were assembled in Montgomery in two separate conventions. The Moseley, or lily-white, wing quickly came to terms with the Populists and meekly endorsed the Populist ticket and platform. This reversal in Moseley's cocky attitude of a year before was occasioned by the fact that he had lost control of the Republican state committee, along with recognition by the National Executive Committee. Supported by Mark Hanna, who was lining up Southern support for William McKinley, William Vaughan had seized the leadership of the black-and-tan faction and captured the party machinery. Vaughan's price for cooperating with the Populists was a bit higher than Moseley's. He wanted, and got, two places on the ticket. The Populists retained their virtue by insisting that the two Republicans named to the Populist state ticket be sincere silver advocates. They were. The Populists went even further and also put J. A. Bingham, another Republican, on the slate. Bingham was a farmer and a former Alliance leader from Talladega County, who had been working for the Populists for several years.[8]

The resulting "cooperation ticket," headed by A. T. Goodwyn, was running on a platform that differed little from the state party's declarations of 1892 and 1894. In the inflated rhetoric of the period, the platform declared: "the toiling masses of the state are linked together in a

[7] Randolph *Toiler*, March 27 and May 8, 1896. *The People's Weekly Tribune*, May 14, 1896. See above, Chapter 1, note 52.

[8] *People's Weekly Tribune*, May 14, 1896.

common destiny and if they will stand together on correct principles for the good of all, who shall say nay?"[9]

The chief nay-sayers were the Democrats. The state convention on April 21 named Joseph F. Johnston as the Democratic candidate for governor over Richard H. Clarke of Mobile, the favorite of the sound-money wing of the party.[10] Johnston had lost the nomination in 1894 to Oates, but with the aid of a quirk in the electoral machinery he had won control of the Executive Committee and prepared the way for a minor revolution in party affairs. In January 1896 Johnston's Executive Committee "let the bars down" by ruling that anyone could participate in the Democratic primaries who pledged that he would vote for the resulting nominee.[11] This was the most direct form of a standing invitation to the Populists to return to the Democratic Party, and was only the first of many such invitations from Johnston. Perhaps because of the Executive Committee's ruling, as well as his long and thorough campaign, Johnston won an overwhelming majority of the convention delegates.

Reflecting the ideological bias of the reform faction, the Democratic platform called for free silver and honest elections, in addition to a more than usual trumpeting of white supremacy.[12] Despite the wide appeal of these sentiments in Alabama, the Jones Democrats were unenthusiastic about the nominee or his principles. William J. Samford, who was to become governor in 1900 as a pacifier of factional strife, perceived the threat of disunity. He noted in his diary that before Johnston's nomi-

[9] *Choctaw Alliance*, May 5, 1896. Randolph *Toiler*, May 8, 1896.
[10] See Thomas G. Jones Papers, ADAH, letters received, November, 1895 through April, 1896.
[11] Going, "Critical Months in Alabama Politics, 1895-96," 274.
[12] *Shelby Sentinel*, July 16, 1896.

nation there was a "great commotion in politics—Clarke and Johnston tearing the party to pieces in the presence of a compact, bold, united enemy—I shall not be surprised (though disappointed) to see the Dem. party defeated in August."[13]

Whether the disaffection of those Democrats of the *Advertiser*'s persuasion would spell defeat for the party in August depended on whether the Populists could stanch the flow of voters back to the refurbished democracy. As the Johnsonites turned their backs on the "gold bugs" to solicit votes from the opposite quarter, the Populists reacted.[14]

Successive chairmen of the Populist Party warned their followers not to be misled by appearances. "You can't get sweet water and bitter from the same spring," wrote Samuel M. Adams in his open letter to the party in the spring of 1895; "neither can you get reform in either of the two old parties."[15] Gilbert B. Deans, in his first statement as chairman on January 23, 1896, advised Populists not to be deceived by Johnston. After all, Johnston was one of the chief instigators of "the midnight conclave of tricksters" who had defrauded Kolb of the Democratic nomination in 1890. Furthermore, the chairman of the Democratic Campaign Committee in 1896 was John B. Knox, a thoroughgoing gold Democrat. Deans told the Populists that the only sure way to reform was for them to stay in the third party.[16]

---

[13] Diary of W. J. Samford, entry for March 11, 1896, in the Southern Historical Collection at the University of North Carolina.

[14] Sam Will John to Robert McKee, February 2, 1897, McKee Papers, ADAH.

[15] Birmingham *News*, April 11, 1895.

[16] Randolph *Toiler*, February 6, 1896.

Risking the possibility that undecided but reform-minded voters in Alabama would not be as sure as they were themselves that the Democratic party was irredeemable,[17] the Populists continued to stress the mild reformism of their call for fair elections and free silver. They repeatedly echoed the theme that Johnston was not a sincere reformer and that the reforms endorsed in the state Democratic campaign would be annulled when the national convention met. So confident were they of this eventuality that at their convention on April 28th they resolved "that our delegates to the national convention are hereby instructed to use all honorable and legitimate means to unite all the financial reformers in one solid phalanx against a polity that has brought want and misery to our once happy and prosperous country."[18] One of the big attractions of a unified reform crusade was that the Populists expected to lead it.[19] Unfortunately for them, the basic premise of their tactics was wrong.

As July 7 and the Democratic national convention approached, it became evident that the silver forces would win control of the national party. Sensing this, and favoring fusion with such a reconstructed Democracy, Chairman H. E. Taubeneck of the Populist National Executive Committee called a meeting in St. Louis of Populist leaders. The St. Louis conference, conforming to Taubeneck's design, issued an "Address to the People" urging Populists to be prepared to give up party for principle. Though Kolb, Manning, and Bowman attended the conference, and though each was on record in favor of fusion

[17] *Ibid.*, May 8, 1896. *The People's Weekly Tribune*, May 14, and May 28, 1896. *Choctaw Alliance*, April 14, 1896. Manning, *The Fadeout of Populism*, 9. The first glimmer of reality broke in the Greenville *Living Truth*, July 2, 1896.

[18] Randolph *Toiler*, May 8, 1896.

[19] *Ibid.*, May 22, 1896.

with the Republicans at the state level, none signed the address.[20] On the other hand, editor Whitehead, who had only reluctantly accepted fusion with Republicans at home, thought the Populists should nominate the Democratic national slate if that party were sensible enough to nominate a free silver advocate.[21] Other Populist papers within the state reacted variously to the prospect of William Jennings Bryan as the Democratic nominee. While some favored endorsing him as the reform candidate most likely to win,[22] others considered fusion with a party so soiled with corruption, gold bugs, and vote fraud as the Democratic Party would be the death of Populism and Populist principles.[23]

Matters were confused even more by the action of the People's Party convention at St. Louis, which began July 22, after the Democrats had nominated Bryan for president and Arthur K. Sewall of Maine for vice president. Unable to obtain simple ratification of the Democratic Party's action, the Populist fusionists agreed to the nomination of Tom Watson for vice president before the convention considered the question of a presidential candidate. This compromise looked like the first step toward an agreement with Democrats to insert Watson in the second spot on the Democratic ticket in return for the nomination of Bryan by the Populists. Consequently, Bryan easily won the Populists' endorsement for president over S. F. Norton of Illinois in a roll call that tested

[20] *People's Weekly Tribune*, June 25, 1896.
[21] The Greenville *Living Truth*, July 2, 1896.
[22] *Choctaw Alliance*, July 14, 1896. Randolph *Toiler*, July 17, 1896.
[23] *The Bessemerite*, July 15, 1896. *Ozark Banner*, July 23, 1896. See *People's Weekly Tribune*, July 23, and July 27, 1896 for quotations on the subject from other Populist papers.

the uncompromising middle-of-the-road sentiment in St. Louis.[24] The Alabama delegation split on this vote. Fifteen voted for Bryan and fusion, while seven went to Norton and a pure Populist ticket.[25] Again there was no correlation between a man's position on the political spectrum and his attitude toward fusion.

The 12 leaders whose attitudes toward both state and national fusion can be reconstructed divided in a confused pattern. Kolb, P. G. Bowman, and Frank Baltzell were in favor of both types of fusion. Grattan B. Crowe, Samuel M. Adams, Milton W. Howard, A. P. Longshore, and Gus Hobson in July all opposed both types of cooperation. Joe Manning and A. T. Goodwyn were willing to work with Republicans but not with national Democrats, while Philander Morgan and J. M. Whitehead took just the reverse position. To make matters worse, Morgan, Baltzell, and Gilbert B. Deans all changed their stand on national fusion between July and November 1896. If fusion brought little else to the Populist Party, it did bring confusion.

In spite of the chaos on the national scene, the Populists faced the state elections on August 3 apparently with determination. The talk in the Populist papers about defending the ballot boxes with force if necessary was not mere bluster.[26] On election day in Chambers County a

[24] Hicks, *The Populist Revolt*, 360-367. Woodward, *Tom Watson, Agrarian Rebel*, 294-301. Robert F. Durden, "The 'Cow-Bird' Grounded: The Populist Nomination of Bryan and Tom Watson in 1896," *Mississippi Valley Historical Review*, L, December 1963, 397-423. Mr. Durden's attack on the Hicks and Woodward reading of the convention battle is also incorporated in his book, *The Climax of Populism: The Election of 1896*, Lexington, Ky., 1965.

[25] *People's Weekly Tribune*, July 23 and July 30, 1896.

[26] *Ibid.*, June 4 and July 23, 1896. Randolph *Toiler*, December 12, 1895. Greenville *Living Truth*, July 9, 1896. Birmingham *Times*, May 27, 1896.

dispute over who was to carry the election box to the county seat turned into a gun battle that resulted in six casualties—three wounded Populists, two wounded Democrats, and one dead Democrat.[27] But this slim Populist victory on the battlefield was not duplicated at the polls. More voters turned out than in 1894, but Johnston's margin was even greater than that of Oates two years before. Though the pattern of the voting was much the same, the Populists carried only 24 counties. Eleven counties outside the Black Belt which showed Populist majorities in 1894 went Democratic in 1896. Even without the heavy Black Belt vote, Johnston would have carried the state.[28] The Democrats were equally successful in the contests for seats in the legislature. Eleven Populists went to the 33-member senate, but the house would be composed of 72 Democrats, 24 Populists, and 4 Republicans. The election proved that the Populists could not compete with an "insider" such as Johnston for the votes of moderate, reform-minded, middle class men.

The political confusion that hampered the Populists before the state election on August 3 was compounded afterward. When the Republicans disentangled themselves from the Populists to run their own slate of electors for McKinley, the Populists were left in a quandary. Should they put their own Bryan-Watson electors in the field in an effort to keep the party together at the risk of hurting Bryan's chances of election, or should they try to negotiate with the Democrats for a fusion slate pledged to vote in the electoral college for whichever combination of Bryan and a vice presidential candidate had the best chance of winning? Actually, the Democrats at the state level had the power to set the terms.

[27] Rogers, "Agrarianism in Alabama," 533.
[28] See the Montgomery *Advertiser*, August 19, 1896 for the returns.

The state Democratic Party was itself severely disturbed by Bryan's capture of the national party. Under the leadership of Thomas G. Jones and aided by the Republican National Committee, a distinguished group of Alabamians decided that party loyalty was not as important as they had previously thought. They joined Charles S. Fairchild and William C. Whitney in forming the National (gold standard) Democratic Party at Indianapolis and in supporting its nominees, John M. Palmer of Illinois for president and Simon B. Buckner of Kentucky for vice president.[29] While reform-minded Democrats professed to be elated that the party was rid of this element, the Populists were glum.[30]

They realized that a Democratic Party responsive to popular pressures and confident of carrying the state, would not only be hard to beat but probably would not be anxious to share its ticket with the Populists. Marion Butler, Chairman of the Populist National Executive Committee, was able to secure divided tickets in 28 states,[31] but the attempt failed in Alabama.[32] On Septem-

[29] Oates to Jones, January 11, 12, 1894. T. G. Bush to Jones, August 18, 1896. Jones to Hector D. Lane, August 14, 1896 and similar letters to other sympathetic politicians in August 1896. Jones to Fairchild, August 14, 1896. Jones to Woodford, September 18, 1896, Thomas G. Jones Papers, ADAH. Early in 1897 Jones was soliciting Woodford and William E. Dodge for funds to back a railroad that Jones and Sol Bloch of Baltimore were organizing. William C. Oates to Charles S. Fairchild, January 6, 1895, Letterbook 66 in Governor's Office Records, ADAH. Fairchild had helped both Jones and Oates float state bonds to refinance the state debt. Montgomery *Advertiser*, August 16, 27, 28, 29, 1896.

[30] Sam Will John to Robert McKee, November 6, 1896, McKee Papers, ADAH.

[31] Paul W. Glad, *McKinley, Bryan, and the People*, New York, 1964, 185.

[32] *People's Weekly Tribune*, September 10, 1896. Rogers, "Agrarianism in Alabama," 542.

ber 3 the Populist state committee met and promulgated a set of electors pledged to Bryan and Watson.[33]

This confronted individual Populists with precisely the same dilemma the party leaders had faced. All Populist voters now had to ask themselves if "the success of [silver] . . . is of more importance to them than the maintenance of the independence and integrity of their party organization."[34] For most Populists, and especially for leaders whose public careers were linked to the Populist cause, surrender to the Democrats was odious.[35] Yet many Populists found the Bryan-Sewall ticket very attractive. A measure of the discomfort caused by the necessity of making such a choice is found in the vacillations of the Randolph *Toiler*. Throughout September it urged that every effort be made to effect fusion with the regular Democrats. But when it became evident in late September that the Democratic state committee was not going to offer to divide its ticket with the Populists, the *Toiler* quickly reverted to the argument that Alabamians could not trust the Democratic Party to bring about reform.

Not everyone was able to accommodate to such inconsistencies, and disgruntled Populist leaders began a general exodus. The first to go was Joe Manning, a fact which at first glance supports the theory that the most thoroughgoing Populists were the most sensitive to Populism's loss of political innocence. As one of the founders of the People's party in the state, and as a member of both the State and the National Executive Committees, Manning was a militant spokesman for Populism. On the other hand, his radicalism extended beyond rhetoric only

[33] *Choctaw Alliance*, September 8, 1896.
[34] *Ibid.*, September 29, 1896.
[35] *Ibid.*, August 4, 1896.

to include electoral reform, and he had been quite willing to cooperate with the Republicans to achieve that. In September Manning announced he was resigning from the Populist Party and would support McKinley for president.[36] He was followed by Guy Sibley, Oscar Hundley, Warren S. Reese, and a few other prominent Populists.[37]

The defectors to Republicanism were not the only Populists having a difficult time deciding on a course of action. Philander Morgan, Senator Morgan's brother who had adamantly opposed fusion with either Republicans or Democrats, began his transit back to the Democratic party by dropping out of politics entirely.[38] Frank Baltzell and Gilbert B. Deans, who had been in favor of some form of fusion with the Democrats on the national level, changed their position and clutched the Bryan-Watson ticket. Some of those Populists who had championed unification of the reform forces behind a single candidate reached a different decision.

Kolb's paper obviously was wrestling with the problem throughout September. On September 24 it carried an article by Jere Dennis, a native radical, who in 1888 had founded the *Labor Advocate*, the organ of the trade union movement in Alabama. Dennis argued that Populists had to remain faithful to Bryan and Watson because only the Populists could battle the trusts and bring them under control.[39] The Populist world was consequently jolted the following week when the *People's Weekly Tribune* changed sides. "What we want," A. B. Brassell wrote by way of explaining the paper's change of policy, "is to elect him [Bryan] and have our humane principles

[36] *People's Weekly Tribune*, September 10, 1896.
[37] *Ibid.*, September 24, 1896.
[38] Philander Morgan to John W. DuBose, November 27, 1895, and July 7, 1896, DuBose Papers, ADAH.
[39] *People's Weekly Tribune*, September 24, 1896.

of equal rights and exact justice to all put in execution!" In view of the fact that a vote for Bryan and Watson was really a vote for McKinley, the *Tribune* and Brassell thought Populists ought to sacrifice their party and vote for the Bryan and Sewall electors.[40]

The Populist Campaign Committee promptly read Kolb and Bowman out of the party and warned "all true Populists no longer to heed them"[41] an action the State Executive Committee endorsed by removing them from the Executive Committee. Frank Baltzell's Alabama *Monitor* now became the official organ of the party.[42] The National Executive Committee, however, dominated by fusionists, refused to discipline Kolb, and some reform papers within the state followed Kolb's example by supporting Democrats in congressional races.[43]

To make matters even worse, the Populists lost their allies in the cities and mining towns of the state. When the Democratic Party accommodated itself to the Populist challenge by moving to the left in 1896, Alabama labor responded by moving to the right—which split the insurgent movement. The leading labor spokesman in the state was J.H.F. Moseley, editor of the *Labor Advocate* and member of the Populist Campaign Committee in 1896. He explained that in view of the fact, "the experience of the past . . . goes to prove that all legislation or good achieved for reform results from compromise, we met the concessions offered in the Chicago platform, accepted the half loaf, and supported the Democratic ticket."[44] The shift in the labor vote was reflected in the decreased Populist share of Jefferson County's vote, from

[40] *Ibid.*, October 1, 1896.
[41] *Choctaw Alliance*, October 20, 1896.
[42] *Ibid.*, October 27, 1896.
[43] Rogers, "Agrarianism in Alabama," 544-546.
[44] *Labor Advocate*, April 22, 1899.

45 percent in August 1896 to 13 percent in the gubernatorial election two years later.

The confused pattern of defection and loyalty was repeated in variations on the theme of fusion in the congressional races. Each district was unique. Republicans in one district endorsed the Populist candidate, but in two others advocated the gold Democrat. Populists endorsed the Republican candidate in two districts, but ran against Republicans in four districts. In the 7th district M. W. Howard defeated a Republican, a regular Democrat, and a gold Democrat. There was ample reason for voter perplexity. One measure of the degree that existed was the number of voters who sat out one of the most exciting presidential elections in American history. There was a decrease of 16.4 percent from the presidential election of 1892, and a drop of 10.6 percent from the gubernatorial election of August 1896.

The Bryan-Sewall ticket got 55.7 percent of the 194,574 votes cast in 1896, while the Republicans won 28.4, the Populists only 12.5, and the gold Democrats 3.3. Together the Populist and Republican allotment of the vote was no bigger than it had been in 1892. Considering the probability that many Republican votes came from disgruntled sound-money Democrats, it is evident that many Populists had drifted back to the Democrats and that the great Populist gains of 1894 had been lost.[45]

Though Jones and company had fared much worse in the election than the Populists, they were not disconsolate. Not only were they largely men of secure social position, but they could expect rewards from both Cleve-

[45] Sam Will John to Robert McKee, November 6, 1896, McKee Papers, ADAH.

land and McKinley should the need arise.[46] They also had the consolation of seeing their main enemy defeated. Shortly after the election Jones wrote to a friend in Kentucky that he was thankful "that the country has been saved . . . and that we are on the march to a higher and better citizenship in the future."[47]

The Populists had no such consolations. They were utterly defeated, and they never recovered. Their immediate reaction to the election was to adopt a brave and confident pose. The *Alabama Monitor* affirmed that "the populists are more needed now and their party commands more [respect] than at [any] time in its existence." It warned that merging with either of the two old parties would mean an end to reform.[48] "Close up your ranks," ordered the *Toiler*, "swear to stand firm for liberty and humanity, and you will live to gain the victory."[49] "Organize. Organize politically. Organize industrially"—was the way to future victory.[50] But the stimulation caused by the stinging defeat was bound to wear off.

As the depressing reality of the situation forced its way into the Populist consciousness, one Populist paper after another gave way to despair. "Many of our people will bid farewell to the Old Year with little regret," the

[46] T. G. Jones' brother was appointed Assistant District Attorney for the Middle District of Alabama by Cleveland before he left office. T. G. Jones himself was appointed Federal Judge of this district by Roosevelt in 1901. Jones was almost desperate for money when he left the governor's office, which is a comment on his personal honesty. He then used his political contacts for business advantage.

[47] Jones to "My Dear Dave," November 6, 1896, Jones Papers, ADAH.

[48] *Alabama Monitor*, November 13, 1896.

[49] Randolph *Toiler*, November 6, 1896.

[50] *Ibid.*, November 13, 1896.

105

Toiler observed on January 1, 1897, "for it has brought little to gladden our hearts and lighten our burdens. While God has been good, man has been wicked and heartless, and oppression and cruelty and wrong have held sway and made countless thousands mourn." "Is there no way to induce the common people to get together and stand by the agencies which promise them relief? The task seems almost hopeless on account of the very indifference of the people. . . ."[51] The cause of this indifference was close at hand: it was fusion.

One Populist paper lamented that "the Angels in Heaven must have wept over the unholy alliance between Populism and Democracy. God's curse is on the Democratic party."[52] C. W. Mathison, the editor of *The Free Press* of Ozark in Dale County, admitted that principle was higher than party; nevertheless, he vowed never again to support "the nominee of a democratic convention for office until that party has squared itself with God. . . ." Mathison was willing for the Populists to enter a completely new party with old Democrats, but he could not trust the cause of reform to the existing Democratic Party, the "monstrous Judas of modern times."[53]

Disenchantment with fusion was a major theme of the Reform Press Association meeting in February 1897. The editors gathered at the Young Men's Hebrew Association building in Memphis and formed a new organization with Frank Burkitt of Mississippi as its president. The meeting called for united action to prove to the country that the People's Party was not dead.[54] But the very need to make such a plea was convincing evidence that the party was thoroughly disrupted.

[51] *Ibid.*, January 1 and 15, 1897.
[52] *Choctaw Alliance*, December 29, 1896.
[53] Ozark *Free Press*, January 6, 1897.
[54] *Ozark Banner*, March 4, 1897.

To individual Populists again politically adrift, Populist leaders who had once appeared as so many Davids seemed in defeat to be similar essentially to the corrupt politicians of the old parties.[55] "Whenever the leaders fall out and fight," observed one Populist paper, "it is then that the masses get a peep on the inside and behold the corruption of the wire-pullers; it is then that the stench becomes unbearable and the plain honest people turn and flee for their lives."[56]

Even more damaging was the stark exposure of the impotence of Populism. Many men had become Populists when they discovered that Democratic leaders either would not or could not manipulate the world so as to bring economic relief and psychic security to the producers. The Populist Party had for a time given them a sense of purpose, a feeling of belonging, an enhanced self-esteem, and a confidence in their ability to gain control over their lives through political power. The debacle of 1896 proved that the Populist Party was also vulnerable, a discovery which came as a crushing blow to those dependent on the party. "All this toil of years," wailed one editor, "together with the fruits of all these sacrifices and privations are today scattered abroad and we are like a flock of sheep without a shepherd."[57]

[55] *Ibid.*, February 5, April 16, and 30, 1897.
[56] *Ibid.*, April 30, 1897.
[57] *Ozark Free Press*, February 11, 1897.

What Happened to the Populists?

"Populism, like Alliancism, is doomed in Alabama,"
said the Mobile *Register* on January 31, 1897. "It
is unable long to survive defeat." Though there was no
doubt that Populism was dying, there was some disagree-
ment as to the cause of the decline. One thing, however,
was certain: Populism did not suffer from an overdose
of prosperity in early 1897.

Despite the wishful predictions of businessmen who
saw an economic upturn in each fluctuation of every index, most Alabamians were still suffering from the depression. "The business outlook is the worst I have seen
since 1874," wrote Sam Will John in early 1897. Colonel
John's pessimism had been reinforced by his attendance
at court in Marion County, where he had not seen one
man "who had on a 'new suit' ", not even the large landowners.[1] Cotton prices did not turn up until late in 1898,[2]
too late to affect the elections of that year. But the Populists were already scattering.

As if by instinct, the Populist press detected the faults
of the campaign of 1896. Perhaps at the time the choice
was not a clear one between principles and party, but in
retrospect it is evident that fusion meant a sacrifice of
principle in the hope of getting the party's candidate

[1] John to McKee, January 31, 1897, McKee Papers, ADAH.
[2] Mobile *Register*, January 31, 1897.

108

elected. "It is folly to convince yourself," warned the *Free Press*, "that the party will die if your candidate is not elected to office."[3]

In the aftermath of defeat, the Populists awoke to the fact that their role could not be to control political power. This realization was accompanied by a burst of latent radicalism. The *Free Press* of Ozark, founded as a "middle-of-the-road" organ after the defection of the Ozark *Banner* to the Democrats during the congressional election campaign of 1896, greeted the new year with a full-dress parade of political theory. The Populists are not Democrats, the *Free Press* said, conceding to the Democrats the strategic position of defender of the Jeffersonian heritage, for the Populists believed in paternalism. Theirs was not the Hamiltonian brand espoused by the Republicans, said the paper, but a much broader and more democratic sort of paternalism that was not enslaved to special interests.[4] The first practical application of this policy—government ownership of railroads and telegraph companies—was an original Populist demand which previously had been collecting dust in Alabama.

The new Populist belligerency was still tempered by a discreet respect for capitalistic values. As the *Alabama Alliance News* put it, Populists merely feared that "capitalist production of farm crops will compete out of existence the small farmer." The paper wanted the government to protect the status of the small farmer with various devices, including an "anti-bucket-shop" law (to prevent speculating in crop futures). Such a law was justified by the notion that society had the right to limit the property rights of an individual if the individual inflicted evil on society. Similarly the *Alabama Alliance*

[3] *Ibid.*, June 24, 1897.
[4] *Ibid.*, January 21, 1897.

News thought the government should one day have a duty to provide employment at a living wage to all who might apply.[5]

These expressions represent Populism's commitment to governmental intervention as a mechanism for solving the problems created by material progress and social change, but that commitment remained ambiguous. Just before his *Alabama Monitor* folded, for instance, Baltzell denounced the forces driving for a new constitution in Alabama because he feared that their ambitious goal of modernization would force the state into ruinous debt.[6] Unable to break with the fear of debt, and the ethos of self-help of which it was part, the Populists turned instead to another American tradition—the belief in equality.

Sometime during the era of the American Revolution, and specifically in the Declaration of Independence, Americans had dedicated themselves to the ideal of equality. It had never been realized, and never would be, but the devotion to the ideal remained in the form of a fundamental assumption that republican institutions were unworkable in a land with a wide disparity in the distribution of wealth.

Though the Progressives later spoke circumspectly of promoting economic growth for all, the Populists after 1896 talked openly of redistributing the wealth. "The real issue is not whether we shall have hard times or good times, prosperity or panic in the abstract," reasoned the Randolph *Toiler*, "but it is whether that prosperity now monopolized by the few shall become the inheritance of all."[7] It was axiomatic to Populists that the "more evenly

---

[5] *Ibid.*, January 16, 1900.
[6] *Alabama Monitor*, December 11, 1896.
[7] Randolph *Toiler*, July 30, 1897.

property or wealth is distributed among the people the more prosperous, contented, and happy that the people will be."[8] The trouble was that under the existing "forced and unnatural" system of distribution, wealth was the monopoly of the few. The *People's Banner* gloomily predicted no hope for a change to a more equitable system of distribution in 1898. In fact, the paper casually blamed the great concentration of wealth on the contraction of money.[9] The Populist solution was still to take the control of money away from the monied classes and give it to government, and then put government back in the hands of the producing classes.[10]

The champions of the producing classes had four basic options in 1897 and after. They could join the Democrats, join the Republicans, withdraw from politics altogether, or remain with the Populists. Historians have speculated about the typical experience of Populists after 1896. If Alabama is representative, all of the alternative paths were followed by various proportions of the People's Party.

Withdrawal was the most popular option. One way for a man to defend himself psychologically when defeat threatens to damage his image of himself is to quit trying —in the case of the Populists, to cease political activity. Joe Manning understood the dynamics of losing when he remarked that it was impossible to keep voters interested in the Populist Party as long as they were certain the Democrats would win, by fair means or foul.[11] Repeated defeats and the consequent defeatism, in addition to the

---

[8] *Ibid.*, February 25, 1898.

[9] Quoted in *ibid.*, January 28, 1898. Also see *ibid.*, February 25, 1898.

[10] *Ozark Banner*, July 28, 1898. Ozark *Free Press*, July 29, 1897.

[11] Manning, *Fadeout of Populism*, 41.

disillusioning effect of the campaign of 1896, sapped the strength of the Populist Party nearly to the vanishing point.

Defeatism was reflected most directly in the fact that the growing political apathy among Alabamians affected Populists more than Democrats. The Populists never came as close to winning the governorship as they had in 1892, when voter participation was at its peak. The gap between them and the Democrats generally grew wider thereafter as participation declined; this was true in spite of the fact that the major portion of the lost voters was composed of Negroes whose votes in one way or another had gone to the Democrats. The great bulk of the 26-percent drop in voter turnout between the gubernatorial elections of 1896 and 1898 occurred in the Black Belt, and represented the growing Negro acceptance of de facto disfranchisement and perhaps a growing reluctance on the part of white politicians to count uncast Negro votes now that they were no longer so crucial. Voter withdrawal was much less outside the Black Belt, but there obviously were many more missing voters than can be accounted for simply by Negro disfranchisement and apathy. The differential impact of voting truancy is dramatically in evidence when one considers the 14 counties in which the Populists were in the process of losing their majority position. There the decline in the number of voters was an abnormally high 19 percent, approximately double the county average outside the Black Belt. Many more white Populists than white Democrats were giving up on politics.

Of those Populist voters who did not adopt the ego-protecting device of taking a holiday from politics, most became Republican voters. This is strongly suggested by the high positive correlations, shown in Appendix II, between Republican voting strength in the election of 1902 and Populist performance in the elections of 1892, 1894, and 1896, whereas there was no significant relationship between Republican strength in 1888 and Populism. To prove that *most* voting ex-Populists voted Republican is impossible, but a sound inference can be drawn from the voting returns and a series of assumptions. In 1888, when Negroes were still voting though perhaps not with complete freedom, and when they still comprised the bulk of Republican support, the Republicans polled 57,177 votes in the presidential election.[12] This represented a little over 32 percent of the total vote. In 1902, with virtually no Negroes voting and the total electorate reduced by one-half since 1888 and by almost two-thirds since 1892, the Republicans received 24,423 votes in the gubernatorial election, or approximately 27 percent of all votes.[13] Unless white Republicans were fantastically immune to the epidemic of nonparticipation, the relatively steady Republican share of the vote would have been possible only with the substantial accretion of new voters. Assuming that white Republicans suffered the same rate of attrition as white voters in general, and assuming that the figure of 30,000 white Republicans, which was accepted at the time, was not an underestimation, as it most surely was not, then there should have been no more than 10,000 old-line, white Republicans voting in 1902. This means that at least 14,000 white voters were recruited elsewhere to vote Republican in 1902. Even if allowance is made for new voters, and assuming that no more than 65,000 of the 115,000 Populist votes in 1892 belonged to white ex-Democrats, it is clear that most ex-Populists who were still voting in 1902 must have voted Republican. A somewhat simpler indication of this tendency for ex-

[12] Burnham, *Presidential Ballots*, 261.
[13] Montgomery *Advertiser*, November 16, 1902.

Democratic Populists to shift to the Republican party is revealed in Table 3. In the 7 counties that had a Republican vote of less than 10 percent in 1888, which are therefore the counties that are most free of the distorting effects of a well-established white Republicanism or of Negro disfranchisement, the electorate's involvement in Populism in the 1890s left a heavy residue of Republicanism.

TABLE 3

Populism Leads to Republicanism, Voting Performance in 7 Previously Democratic Counties (in percent)

County	Negro 1900	GOP 1888	Pop 1896	GOP 1902
Coffee	23	0	58	22
Covington	30	5	55	17
Crenshaw	31	10	54	14
Dale	25	1	57	40
Geneva	18	0	62	45
Henry	44	0	50	9
Pickens	49	1	45	17
averages	28.5	2.4	54	23.4
state averages	43	33	41	27

Typically, leaders preceded the masses into the Republican Party. Even before the election in November 1896, several had made the conversion. Joseph C. Manning, the fervent "apostle" who founded the People's Party; Warren S. Reese, one of the most radical of the Populist spokesmen; and Guy Sibley, the moderate son of a prominent family, were immediate converts. Oliver Day Street, A. P. Longshore, John C. Fonville, and Gilbert B. Deans, all of them ambitious politicians, were to follow at later intervals.

Some leaders plotted other courses. Milford W. Howard, congressman, moralist, sentimentalist, and rhetorical revolutionary, remained with the Populists until 1904 and then dropped from political sight. Grattan B. Crowe, the professional healer but advocate of righteous violence, followed an identical course. W. H. Skaggs emigrated. In 1898 he declined to help O. D. Street's campaign for Congress in the 7th district, writing to Street, "the Populist party is dead" because the people had lost faith in their leaders.[14] Unable to believe that the Republican Party in the South was sufficiently free of corruption to serve as a vehicle for reform, and unable to return to the discredited Democratic Party, Skaggs moved to Chicago and continued his activities in behalf of the "pure people" in concert with the socialists and assorted reformers of that city. There was one Populist newspaper in the state which similarly continued for a time as a socialist sheet, but socialist efforts to recruit leaders from among the Populists in Alabama produced no tangible results.[15]

Some Populist leaders found the transition back to the Democracy quite congenial. Reuben F. Kolb was received with open arms by the Democrats during the fall campaign of 1896. He had a long career ahead of him as a Democratic candidate, a candidate noted neither for

[14] Skaggs to O. D. Street, September 21, 1898, Street Papers, University of Alabama.

[15] Skaggs to DuBose, January 2, 1905, DuBose Papers, ADAH. Skaggs' liberalism extended to race relations, but he returned from Chicago in 1901 to vote for disfranchisement. *The People's Protest* was published in Cullman, but the only issues extant run from September 8 to November 24, 1899. For a revealing attempt at recruiting by a socialist see Thomas N. Freeman to Oliver D. Street [n.d.], 1903, Street Papers, University of Alabama. Populism did carry over into socialism in some states: Grady McWhiney, "Louisiana Socialists in the Early Twentieth Century: A Study of Rustic Radicalism," *Journal of Southern History*, XX (August 1954), 315-336.

his radicalism nor his success. After several subsequent defeats, "Run Forever" Kolb was finally elected in 1910 to a 4-year term as Commissioner of Agriculture. He was back where he started in 1886, but this time he would not anger the Democratic potentates. An even more striking case of conversion was Tyler Goodwyn, editor of the out-spoken Wetumpka *Reform Advocate* and the son of the Populist candidate for governor in 1896. Tyler Goodwyn returned to the Democratic Party, where he enjoyed prominence as an able legislator and chairman of the State Democratic Executive Committee. Interestingly enough, he became one of the most respected spokesmen for railroad and corporation interests in the state. In 1907 he led the legislative opposition to Comer's Progressive program.

Only two leaders provided continuity between Popu-lism and reformism after the turn of the century. One was Zell Gaston who in 1904 resigned from his post as Pro-bate Judge of Butler County and moved to Birmingham to go into partnership with Jesse Stallings, a labor lawyer and reform-minded congressman. Peyton G. Bowman, the fiery stump speaker from Birmingham, was the other. He remained active in municipal politics and in 1908 served on the State Democratic Executive Com-mittee. He and his law partner, Charles P. Beddow, acted as Progressive spokesmen for urban labor. But these links through urban labor between Populism and Progressivism were few. Other ex-Populist leaders did not retain their fervor for reform.

The depth and extent of the curdling process which affected some old Populists is a difficult question, but there were a few extreme cases. Tom Watson of Georgia is the classic example of a Populist who took off after racial and religious scapegoats in his later years.[16] But as tragically ironic as Watson's reaction was, it was no more warped than the perversion of equalitarian reformism eventually adopted by one Alabama Populist. Milford W. Howard became an apologist for fascism! His ecstatic report on Mussolini's Italy was published in 1928 as *Fascism: A Challenge to Democracy*. Howard admitted that he had been an advocate of direct democracy and of the collective ownership of the means of production. But "as the quality of our leadership at times seems to decline, the theory of the equality of all men no longer thrills many thoughtful minds. Many question whether the voice of the people is after all the voice of God." Howard was completely captivated by the mysticism, racial eugenics, and elitism of Italian fascism, even though these things were repudiations of his Populist heritage of equality, tolerance, and materialistic reform.

The element of Populism that made fascism so appealing to Howard was that which developed from a longing for *Gemeinschaft*, the traditional community. Howard was evidently affected by the feeling of spiritual renaissance, the apparent selfless dedication, and the sense of belonging in Italian fascism. He concluded that the pastoral, simple, agricultural society with a strong leader was the best society possible in this world.[17]

Howard's case is a striking example of what happens to frustrated urges to create a more just society, but it should not be read as the typical Populist reaction to defeat. At the time Howard discovered fascism, Joseph Manning, in his book, *The Fadeout of Populism*, was reasserting the old Populist class antagonisms, condemning persecution of Negroes, and calling for an increase of

[16] Woodward, *Tom Watson, Agrarian Rebel*.
[17] Howard, *Fascism: A Challenge to Democracy*, New York, 1928.

Christian love and democracy as a cure for social ills. In 1924 W. H. Skaggs published *The Southern Oligarchy*, a long indictment of the reactionary political practices and social policy of the alliance of large planters and industrialists which had defeated Populism. Skaggs also reasserted his faith in democracy and bitterly condemned racism, the Ku Klux Klan, peonage, political corruption, "Bourbonism," child labor, and the convict lease system.[18] Commoner than the disillusionment of Howard or the persistently protesting voices of Manning and Skaggs was the return of Kolb and Goodwyn to the right wing of the Democratic Party. Samuel M. Adams, I. L. Brock, and Philander Morgan all followed this trail; they were willing to forget reform.

One of the reasons for the prevalence of this route was that the Populists were actively pursued. One Democrat wrote to young Oliver Day Street: "your father [T. A. Street] and yourself could be of great service in leading this [silver] wing of the democracy in this section of the country. . . . Why can't you both come in and help?"[19] Governor Joseph F. Johnston saw his opportunity clearly. "The Populists are in a hopeless tangle," he wrote in 1897. "They are torn to pieces and never was there such opportunity to rally all who want good government, honest and wise laws bearing equally on all and allowing all to live and prosper."[20] He became the chief suitor of the defecting Populists.

Johnston solicited the aid of Philander Morgan, Sen-

[18] Skaggs, *The Southern Oligarchy: An Appeal in Behalf of the Silent Masses of Our Country Against the Despotic Rule of the Few*, New York, 1924.

[19] J. E. Brown to O. D. Street, December 14, 1896, Street Papers, University of Alabama.

[20] Johnston to DuBose, August 19, 1897, DuBose Papers, ADAH.

ator John Tyler Morgan's cantankerous younger brother, as soon as he heard that Phil Morgan had refused to support Goodwyn in the summer of 1896. Morgan could not bring himself to support Johnston then, so he remained silent. But he ended the year in ill health, in debt, and in possession of Kolb's old *People's Weekly Tribune*.[21] After suspending publication for a few months he appointed John DuBose to be editor of the *Tribune*. Morgan professed to see the major threat to Johnston coming from a union of Republicans, gold Democrats, and fusion Populists. He wanted his paper to unite the middle-of-the-road Populists with the Johnston wing of the party.[22] Perhaps Morgan was feverish when he had this hallucination, but it may also have been brought on simply by the need for money. He applied to Johnston for financial aid—and got it.[23]

Johnston expertly used his power of patronage to secure the loyalties of wavering Populists. He appointed I. L. Brock, editor of the *Cherokee Sentinel*, to the probate judgeship of that county, for instance, and received valuable support and guidance in return. "By-the-way," wrote one of Johnston's friends on the University's Board of Regents, "I had a long talk with J[unious] P. Oliver (Populist member of the Board) and I am satisfied Governor Johnston made a shrewd 'political stroke' in his appointment. He appeared indifferent to accepting at first, he said, but now 'hopes for some great leader (like Bryan)

[21] Sam Will John to Robert McKee, September 3, 1897. John W. DuBose to McKee, September 4 and 5, 1897, McKee Papers, ADAH. DuBose to Chappell Cory, March 29, 1897, Cory Papers, ADAH.

[22] Philander Morgan to Johnston, January 29, 1897, Governor's Office Records, ADAH.

[23] Johnston to John W. DuBose, August 19, September 1, 1897, DuBose Papers, ADAH.

to fully unite the silver forces.' We put him on the Executive Committee and he seemed well pleased." No one's political virtue was safe with a man like Johnston on the make. Money for ailing newspapers, offices for needy politicians, prestige for status-hungry leaders—his courtship was thorough.

Nor did Johnston spare the rhetoric. He and DuBose exchanged ideas about what the editorial lines of the *Tribune* should be and found that they were in full agreement. "There can be no general prosperity under existing laws, and there is none," the Governor wrote to the editor, continuing: "Laboring men are barely subsisting: they have had slice after slice taken from their wages until bone is beginning to appear. . . . I am fighting all organized plunderers and neither asking nor giving quarter. I shall continue it without regard to personal results. If I should go down I know that justice will be done in the end. The trouble is that we lack cohesion."[24]

It was the lack of cohesion that all of Johnston's considerable political skills were aimed at remedying. He always maintained a respectful fear of the coterie of politicians from which he had wrested control of the party and state.[25] Therefore he tried to keep politics in Alabama sharply polarized in the public mind. His enemies were the machine, lackies of Wall Street, and gold bugs. He recruited Populists in an effort to reinforce his forces for the expected counterattack. In the fall of 1897 Johnston wrote to his secretary that "the Pops are coming back bodaciously into the party. . . ."[26]

Johnston was elated at the apparent success of his policy of an opening to the left. But his achievements

[24] *Ibid.*, August 19, 1897.
[25] *Ibid.*, September 1, 1897.
[26] Johnston to Cory [n.d., but probably November 1897], Cory Papers, ADAH.

were deceptive. Not only did more of the prominent Populists who remained active in Alabama politics become Republicans than Democrats, but the ex-Populist Democrats he recruited later became so doubtful of the personal rewards of reform politics that they transferred loyalty to the right wing of the Democratic Party when it returned to power in 1900. They never returned to the left wing, even when it was rejuvenated by B. B. Comer in 1902.

But in 1897 it seemed there was something to gain by bidding for support of the Populist constituency. The returning ex-Populists might add considerable strength to the reform segment of the Democratic Party, which Johnston had finally led to victory in 1896. That segment had offered Alabama voters and lawmakers a Progressive alternative since 1890, and its efforts were just beginning.

CHAPTER SEVEN

The Progressive Alternative

During the 1890s Progressivism and Populism were contemporary rather than sequential. Progressivism, the alternative to Populism, was a substantially different reaction by a separate set of men to the same enemy Populism faced—the dominant industrial wing of the Democratic Party. What Progressivism lacked before 1902 was a viable combination of issues to forge a winning coalition among the electorate. The chief concerns and top-echelon leadership that characterized the unmistakably Progressive Comer administration after 1906 had been growing since before 1890 and were evident in Governor Johnston's administration. The victories of Johnston in 1896 and 1898 as the leader of the silver faction of the Democratic Party showed that genteel reform could command a following. These victories were shallow and indecisive, however, and produced little legislation. Though the issue of race had proven ineffective in preventing the defection of the alienated to the Populist Party, it did inhibit the solidification of the groups interested in various types of moderate reforms. Though they lacked consolidation, the ingredients for a solid Progressive movement were present in Alabama during both the vigorous and the declining years of Populism.

One example of potential for a Progressive movement in the 1890's was the existence of Democrats in Alabama who were unhappy about the political corruption and lack of responsiveness of the Democratic Party, but who could not vote Populist because of the social disintegration such a vote allegedly invited. Horace Hood, editor of the Montgomery *Journal*, was one of these. Hood sided consistently with the progressive wing of the Democratic Party. From 1897 to 1901 his paper was the semi-official organ of the Johnston administration, and in 1907 Governor B. B. Comer rewarded Hood's services to Progressivism by appointing him Sheriff of Montgomery County. "It only demonstrates what you said ten years ago," Hood wrote to fellow journalist Robert McKee in disgust after the convention of 1890 had denied the nomination to Kolb, "that when the party began to steal votes from the opposition it would soon begin to steal votes within its ranks, and then comes trouble. This was a fight between the politicians and the people, and the politicians— bold, unscrupulous politicians like Joe Johnston—won. The people—the honest masses—submit this time. But the future is dark."[1]

Similarly, many proto-Progressives experienced a moral revulsion at the election of 1892. Robert McKee wrote afterward that "there can be no re-uniting but upon the basis of reorganization and a total abandonment of the 'party-law' of the Jones Convention."[2] Chappell Cory not only shared McKee's disdain for the corrupt methods used to secure Jones's election, he shared McKee's dislike of the Populist leaders: "It is not in men without conscience themselves, like Kolb and Baltzell to check the tide toward moral bankruptcy."[3] As these men of the

[1] Hood to McKee, June 1, 1890, McKee Papers, ADAH.

[2] McKee to Willis Brewer, August 7, 1892, and McKee to James E. Cobb, March 26, 1893, McKee Papers, ADAH.

[3] Chappell Cory to McKee, June 18, 1893, McKee Papers, ADAH.

19th century themselves might have described their dilemma, they were between the Scylla of corrupt Democrats and the Charybdis of unworthy Populists.

Rufus Rhodes, editor of the Birmingham *News* and constant supporter of Comer Progressivism, began his 18-year battle against "moral bankruptcy" in 1892 by criticizing Jones as the machine candidate. Jones, sensitive as ever, replied that if he (Jones) was the machine's candidate for Governor, then Rhodes was the machine's delegate to the National Democratic Convention. "It would be perfectly idle to discuss how I came to be a delegate to the National Convention," Rhodes responded. "I was elected by the 'machine' in the sense that I was elected by the Convention that nominated you, and in no other sense whatever, for the 'bosses' that is, the railroad commission and the railroad gang of attorneys who are and have been running the party—had it in for me and tried to defeat me. Governor, if Democracy is to continue in power in Alabama these men will have to be shelved from place and power." Rhodes also denounced the *Advertiser* and the "Cleveland straightouts" who were wrecking the party with their intransigence. "I shall do all in my power to destroy them, and mark my words, their days are numbered."[4]

Daniel S. Troy was one of those who wanted to number the days of the Democratic machine. Born in 1832 the son of a North Carolina Whig legislator, he moved to Alabama when quite young, read law with his brother-in-law, and was admitted to the bar at the age of 19. After the Civil War, in which he served as a Confederate officer, he entered a law partnership with his father-in-law, Governor Thomas H. Watts, also an ex-Whig. He was very successful in law. His partners included Henry C.

[4] Rhodes to Jones, August 31, 1892, Jones Papers, ADAH.

Tompkins, long the Chairman of the State Democratic Executive Committee, and Alex T. London, who became a prominent Progressive gadfly after 1900. Troy was also director of the Elyton Land Company, which developed Birmingham, and was the president of the Alabama Fertilizer Company. His position was solidly respectable.

With Sam Will John, Horace Hood, Rufus Rhodes, and other middle-class professional men, Troy suffered from a tender conscience because of the fraudulent machine rule in the state and all its unethical ramifications. A second factor motivating him toward Progressivism was the fact that he was a small manufacturer and booster of industrial progress who resented the economic restrictions imposed by railroad freight rates.

Troy was among the first in the state to discover the railroad "issue." He was preaching against the dangers of railroad exploitation as early as 1876,[5] and in 1880-81 played a key role in establishing the state railroad commission.[6] He was supported in these early bouts with the railroads by Robert McKee, who was then editor of the Selma *Southern Argus* and who was until the turn of the century the most renowned commentator on public questions in Alabama.

McKee was an unreconstructed Jeffersonian. In 1876 he campaigned against railroad influence and in favor of a low tax rate and repudiation of the Reconstruction debt.[7] McKee never changed his bias. He opposed the Constitutional Convention of 1901 out of fear that it would raise the tax rate and destroy the constitutional limit on the rate of taxation. In the 1890s he cast a pro-

[5] Going, *Bourbon Democracy in Alabama, 1874-1890*, University, Alabama, 1951, 134. Moore, *History of Alabama*, 596.
[6] Going, "Establishment of the Alabama Railroad Commission," 366-385.
[7] Moore, *History of Alabama*, 589.

test vote or two for the Populists, but was never fully sympathetic with their socially divisive rhetoric nor with their moves toward an increased utilization of the state. More fundamentally, he never trusted the character of their leadership. Few of them were of the natural planter aristocracy which McKee thought should rule. Despite the fact that McKee rejected both modern industrialism and the theory of active government which was endorsed by the Progressive movement, it was the accession to Progressivism after 1901 of the large class of "planters" in Alabama who shared McKee's outlook that made possible the success of that movement.

It was at just such men as the comfortable but principled "planters" for whom McKee spoke that Troy aimed his major antimachine strategy in 1895. After the 1894 election Troy had condemned the Populists for their threats of violence.[8] In 1895, after the legislature and Jones had refused to offer any sort of redress, Troy changed his position. He became convinced the only way to obtain free elections in Alabama was to organize and apply enough physical force to get the ballots cast and counted fairly. He wanted a convention of silver forces to meet and perhaps form the basis of cooperation between Populists and reform-minded Democrats. Troy got various Populist leaders to join him in issuing a call for a convention to meet in Birmingham on November 13, 1895.

The Progressive-Populist coalition that Troy contemplated never materialized, for several reasons. Troy envisioned an independent ticket endorsed by the Populists but headed by Robert A. McClellan and Sam Will John.[9] McClellan had been making independent-sounding state-

[8] Troy *Jeffersonian*, August 24, 1894.
[9] Troy to John W. DuBose, July 27, 1895, DuBose Papers, ADAH.

ments in public, but declined to have his name connected with the Populists in any way.[10] Populism was not respectable. Horace Hood and John W. DuBose supported Troy's move while it lasted, but with Troy's death in October it became obvious nothing would come of the effort. The conference for free silver and fair elections was held anyway, but in November. It turned out to be a purely Populist affair, whose main concern was the issue of fusion with the Republicans. It did serve to commit the Populists further to a moderate program of electoral and financial reform, but the conference did not recommend the independent candidates which Troy had hoped would serve as a rallying point for political reunification.[11]

That one of the independent candidates Troy was counting on—Sam Will John—chose another method of fighting the machine, indicates perhaps an even more powerful explanation for the failure of his plan. John joined the forces of Joe Johnston in a Democratic free silver campaign which was launched with a convention in Birmingham on September 10, 1895. This conference also boasted the participation of Senators Morgan and Pugh, General Joe Wheeler, Congressmen John H. Bankhead, Gaston Robbins, James E. Cobb, and Jesse Stallings. Johnston's announced purpose was not only to further the cause of silver but to reform the Democratic Party.[12] The movement resulted in Johnston's capture of the state Democratic Party and victory in the governor's race of 1896.

One of the men most elated with Johnston's victory

[10] McClellan to DuBose, August 4, 1895, DuBose Papers, ADAH.
[11] Rogers, "Agrarianism in Alabama," 506-509.
[12] Mobile *Register*, September 10, 11, 1895.

was Braxton Bragg Comer. At that early date, Comer was the foremost exponent of the movement seeking to obtain effective regulation of railroad rates, a movement that had originated among merchants and small manufacturers of the major urban centers. In 1890, while the political campaign was still raging, the Montgomery Commercial and Industrial Association passed a resolution condemning the Railroad Commission and calling for a thorough investigation of its activities—or rather its lack of activity.[13] Earlier the same year the firm of Comer and Trapp of Anniston had also complained to the Commission about the local rates, which put an effective tariff wall on their trade to the east. Comer withdrew this initial complaint in November 1890,[14] but did not give up his fight for lower freight rates in Alabama; he kept at it with varying degrees of success for the next 25 years.

Braxton Comer, like Kolb, was from Barbour County, and like Kolb was a member of a prominent Alabama family. There the resemblance ends. Comer, born in 1848, was just young enough to miss the Civil War, being a cadet at the University of Alabama in 1865 when it was burned by raiding Yankee troops. Unlike many other Southern boys at the time, Comer was able to pursue his education after the war at Emory and Henry College in Virginia, from which he was graduated in 1869. Then he returned to Barbour County to manage the inevitable plantation at the same time Kolb was farming and looking for the way to repair his depleted family fortunes.

The biggest difference between Comer and Kolb, how-

[13] Birmingham *Age-Herald*, July 10, 1890.
[14] Doster, *Railroads in Alabama Politics*, 87-88.

ever, was that Comer soon made the economic transition to agricultural capitalism, while Kolb was trying to find a way to make the family farm pay. Comer first became an absentee merchant-landlord, as so many other large landholders were doing. But he did not stop there. Although he never quit operating his family's land, he moved in 1885 to Anniston where he founded a wholesale grain and commission business with Sydenham B. Trapp.[15]

It was in the bustling new town of Anniston that Comer discovered Georgia's local railroad rates were so much lower than Alabama's that he could not compete with Georgia merchants. The reason was clear to him. In 1879 Georgia had created a railroad commission with mandatory powers to fix rates. The solution, Comer thought, was simply that Alabama should have one, too.

While the Alabama Railroad Commission was telling him in 1890 why it could not act on his complaint, Comer moved to Birmingham. There, because Birmingham was a competitive basing point for railroads, he found the cheap rates and commercial opportunity he sought. He first operated a grain mill whose products bore the trademark "Jim Dandy," and was in banking for a time. That he was immediately successful is suggested by the fact that he was able to lend money during the dismal days of 1893 to the Tennessee Coal, Iron and Railroad Company, the largest corporation in the state and later Comer's archenemy.[16]

Comer's greatest success came in cotton manufacturing. He started Avondale Mills in 1898 and built it into an enormously profitable enterprise. The impulse to

[15] Allen Johnston Going, "The Governorship of B. B. Comer," unpub. master's thesis, University of Alabama, 1940, 1-2.
[16] Ethel Armes, *The Story of Coal and Iron in Alabama*, Birmingham, 1910, 426.

found a big cotton mill in Birmingham came from Comer's participation in the Birmingham Commercial Club with its New South, booster spirit. Indeed, he and his constant newspaper supporter, Rufus Rhodes of the Birmingham *News*, helped to organize the club in 1893. Success was typical of B. B. Comer. But his success with the cotton mill was particularly characteristic because the personal profit which it brought was inextricably linked to the genuine public spirit with which it was undertaken.

Success did not spoil Comer. With unwavering devotion, he pursued the goal he thought would bring greater profits to the merchants, cheaper goods to the farmers and consumers, and greater opportunity for local manufacturers through cheaper raw materials. He had been in Birmingham only a short time when the rate-reform movement appeared there. In October 1890 Comer and other Birmingham wholesale merchants received invitations from George F. Gaither, President of the Alliance Exchange, to confer on the problem of railroad rates.

This conference, which took place on October 22, 1890 at the offices of the Alliance Exchange in Birmingham, posed the crucial problem of whether or not city merchants and discontented farmers could cooperate in a campaign against a common enemy. The participants in the meeting not only expostulated vigorously about the unjust Alabama freight rates, but took specific steps to remedy the evil. J.R.P. Durham, serving as chairman of the meeting, appointed three merchants to serve on a committee to draft a bill to present to the legislature; Comer was one of them. To represent the consumers and farmers Gaither appointed Reverend Samuel M. Adams, Newton N. Clements, and R. W. Beck. The meeting resolved "that the Georgia law be recommended to the committee for adoption," and the cooperation between merchants and farmers was off to a good start.[17]

Prospects for pushing the legislation through the General Assembly were excellent. The legislature elected in the summer of 1890 was known as the "Alliance Legislature" because 11 of the 33 senators and 69 of the 100 representatives were affiliated with the Farmers' Alliance.[18] Newton N. Clements, who helped draft the railroad bill, became Speaker of the Alabama House of Representatives soon after the legislature convened on November 11, 1890. Samuel Adams was the floor leader of the Alliance forces, and R. W. Beck, the state Alliance lecturer, was also a member of the House.

On November 26 Adams introduced the bill to give the Railroad Commission mandatory powers to fix rates. It created considerable interest, to say the least. The committee on commerce and common carriers held extensive hearings on the bill in December and January. William J. Wood, the new 3rd vice president of the L & N, led the fight against the bill. Wood received considerable help from the press, particularly the *Advertiser* and Mobile *Register*.[19] On February 7, 1891 the committee reported out the bill adversely. No one made a serious effort from the floor to put the bill on the calendar despite the overwhelming strength of the Alliance in the legislature; it was dead.[20]

In view of such favorable prospects for passage, the precipitous defeat of the bill requires some explanation. One historian has argued strongly and simply that the

[17] Birmingham *Age-Herald*, October 23, 1890.
[18] Clark, *Populism in Alabama*, 114.
[19] For a succinct statement of the railroad case see the Mobile *Register*, January 21, 1891.
[20] Alabama, *House Journal, 1890*, 688. Mobile *Register*, January 31, 1891.

Alliance and the Populists in Alabama were not anti-railroad.[21] Their performance over a number of years confirms that they never mounted a concerted attack on their professed enemy. But this hardly explains why Alliance and future Populist leaders were so anxious in the fall of 1890 to cooperate in regulating railroads if they were not really anti-railroad, why railroad interests always tried so hard to defeat Populists, why Alabama Populists should be so different from Populists the country over, or why Alabama Populists used anti-railroad rhetoric and included anti-railroad planks in their platforms if they were not hostile to railroad interests.

One (simple) explanation was bribery. During the campaign of 1892 Governor Jones charged that Kolb had taken Adams to Nashville during the Christmas recess of the 1890-91 legislature to confer with Wood and other L & N officials, and that Adams had then changed his position on the railroad regulation bill. This was a correct statement of fact. But Jones' former and future employers were greatly perturbed by the implication of bribery. With some skillful tightrope-walking, Jones was able to placate the L & N without withdrawing his charge in public.[22] Even so, it would have taken literally an incredible amount of bribery to kill the bill as thoroughly as it was killed in 1891. The explanation must lie elsewhere.

If the analyses of the first four chapters of this book are correct, then the political situation had changed between the fall of 1890 and February 1891, so that Adams

[21] James F. Doster, "Were Populists Against Railroad Corporations? The Case of Alabama," *The Journal of Southern History*, XX (August 1954), 395-399.

[22] Russell Houston to Jones, January 9, 1892; William J. Wood to Jones, January 10, 1892; Jones to Houston, January 11, 1892; Houston to Jones, January 14, 1892; Jones Papers, ADAH.

and the third-party-oriented Alliance leaders could no longer afford to give the impression that reform was possible short of a revolutionary change in the nature of political leadership and in the location of political power. The Populists were always more interested in *who* should rule than in reform, but they were hardly friends of the railroads.

Despite the failure of railroad reform when its cause was deserted by the agrarians in 1891, Comer and the city merchants refused to drop the idea. As the nineties wore on, more and more men were making the same commitment that Rufus Rhodes had made when he broke with Jones in 1892—"that these men will have to be shelved from place and power." Everyone knew that railroad interests were closely intertwined with courthouse rings across the state, with iron and coal companies, with foreign corporations, and with the Jones faction of the Democratic party. Because the various facets of the enemy were so well unified, it seemed natural to bring together the three main streams of Progressive reform: the men seeking to regulate railroad rates and practices, those working for humanitarian measures, and those desiring to cleanse politics. Such a Progressive force offered to that portion of the electorate which balked at Populism an alternative method of combating plutocratic corporations without rending the fabric of society.

The Birmingham Commercial Club served Comer as the Power base for his attack on the railroads. In 1895 the club was seeking out new industry for Birmingham, helping Comer launch his idea for a $100,000 cotton mill, petitioning the legislature through Sam Will John to grant Birmingham power to levy a two-mill education tax, and defeating a bill in the legislature which would have allowed the Southern Railway to seize the independently controlled Alabama Great Southern, and thus prevent the Seaboard Airline from entering Birmingham with a competitive east-west route.[23]

In the midst of this fight between competing railroads, Comer launched another tirade against railroads-in-politics. "The incontinent greed of the politicians and the railroad has taken the place of the vile swindle of the black Republicans," ran a typical Comer sentence, "and as in radical days lobbyists infest the capitol and the clink of money is heard."[24] Comer praised Jones for sending troops to Birmingham to control the striking miners, an act Comer was later to duplicate, but he accused Jones of putting the Railroad Commission into the hands of railroad servants. It was time for the Democrats to reform, Comer insisted.

The Commercial Club agreed. At its meeting on May 3, 1895 Gen. R. D. Johnston declared: "the greatest difficulty that now confronts this club in securing the location of industries in this city is the railroads. . . . The truth is, that the great railroad systems centering in this city have combined together so that no road can give Birmingham a fair rate without war on it from all lines. They have parcelled out the state among them like sovereign lords, and no competing line can enter their territory without a bitter war. I desire the club to make a square and open fight for justice to this city. . . ."[25]

[23] This fascinating episode can best be followed in the Birmingham *News* from January through March 1895. For the status of railroads in the South in 1900 see John F. Stover, *The Railroads of the South, 1865-1900: A Study in Finance and Control*, Chapel Hill, 1955, 280-81.

[24] Birmingham *News*, February 7, 1895. Thomas G. Jones replied with characteristic lack of restraint in the Birmingham *Age-Herald*, February 13, 1895.

[25] Birmingham *News*, May 4, 1895. The railroads had done exactly as he claimed. Milton Smith and Samuel Spencer met at

The Birmingham *News* and the *Age-Herald* began editorial campaigns the next day. Throughout 1896 the Birmingham merchants kept up their pressure on the Railroad Commission for lower rates.[26] But their great opportunity came when Joseph Johnston became governor. Johnston depended to a considerable degree on support from the movement for railroad regulation, the political purists, and the humanitarian reformers. He revealed this dependence when he appointed Chappell Cory as his private secretary. Cory was not only in sympathy with the various reformers, he had been secretary of the Birmingham Commercial Club and was on intimate terms with its members. Comer wrote to him in December urging him to "forget not the old club in this hour of need. Please look after our bill close and wire me if you think I can do any good."[27]

The bill to which Comer referred was the Railway Commission bill. It provided for an elective rather than appointive commission with power to set rates, instead of merely reviewing and approving the rates set by the railroads. Under the proposed legislation the shipper would not have to sue for redress. The commission could direct railroads to reimburse shippers injured by a de-

---

Kenesaw, Georgia on October 28, 1894 and agreed to divide the South between them. See the "Louisville and Nashville Railroad Company, Hearings before the Interstate Commerce Commission. . . ." U.S. Congress, Senate Documents, 64th Cong., 1st Sess., 1915, Vol. XXX, No. 461, pp. 369, 379-386, and throughout. Smith testified that they were never successful in carrying out their agreement and that from 1902 on, the roads were not on good terms. *Ibid.*, 377-378. Historians are just beginning to appreciate the inability of railroads to make their conspiracies work. Gabriel Kolko, *Railroads and Regulation, 1877-1916*, Princeton, 1965.

[26] Doster, *Railroads in Alabama Politics*, 95-96.

[27] Comer to Cory, undated [January 1897], Governor's Office Records, ADAH.

parture from commission regulations and the railroads were liable to criminal penalties if they did not comply. Based on the Georgia law, the bill was drawn by W. J. Boykin and introduced in the House by Reid Barnes, a Comer associate from Opelika in Lee County. William W. Brandon, a Tuscaloosa politician and future governor of the state, dropped the bill into the Senate hopper to start it on its stormy career.

The Barnes-Boykin bill sailed through the Senate with little opposition and was passed on February 2 by a vote of 18 to 7. It met stiffer opposition in the House where the railroads had a strong lobby working and many friendly Representatives. Ariosto A. Wiley, attorney for the Atlantic Coast Line and political friend of Thomas G. Jones, led the fight against the bill. The governor used his patronage in support of the measure, while outside the legislature the war of words in the press was heated.

Newspaper accounts of the debates in the House of Representatives conjure up scenes of the wildest disorder. Representatives were shouting in confusion while lobbyists buttonholed legislators in the aisles and corridors. On the final vote, the railroad reform bill was defeated 53-36. The Populists split 11-8 against the bill after its Democratic supporters ignored A. P. Longshore's hint that Populist support might be bought by giving them one place on the new commission. The Republicans cast five votes against the bill. A change of only nine votes would have brought passage.[28]

Despite their near success, Comer and his committee from the Commercial Club were discouraged. In his bi-

[28] Boykin to Johnston, December 29, 1896, Governor's Office Records, ADAH. Alabama, *House Journal, 1896,* 534, 783, 814, 857, 884. Mobile *Register,* January 30, February 3-5, 1897. Doster, *Railroads in Alabama Politics,* 43-45, 97-101.

ennial message to the legislature in 1898 Governor Johnston again recommended an elective railroad commission, but even though several railroad reform bills were again introduced no such bill was introduced and no other reform measure was reported out of committee.[29] The efforts of the railroad reform movement shifted direction. For the five years after their defeat in 1896-97, the movement's leaders engaged in fruitless attempts to get their way by direct negotiation with the railroads and the Railroad Commission. When they returned to the political arena after 1900, they were well aware of the difficulties of having their way with a legislature filled with railroad retainers and men elected on issues other than railroad reform.

There were arrows other than railroad reform in the political quiver carried by Joseph F. Johnston. These as yet lacked the power and direction required to carry them to the target, but they were undoubtedly there. Johnston had written McKee in 1894 that the state was "in a bad fix. . . . My mission is to build up not destroy, to unite not separate; to bind together, to bring peace, and to unite our party once more for the principles that all of us love. I have arranged to do without the Ringsters!" Johnston's emphasis on constructive unity was characteristic of Progressive thought. He also captured the peculiar way in which Progressives used the democratic myth. Populists often equated the government with the people and championed rule by the people. But Progressives tended to think of popular rule differently. For them, the people needed leaders to direct and perhaps control their inherent strengths. "The people are more powerful than any machine," wrote Johnston, "and only

[29] Alabama, *House Journal, 1898*, 17.

need an honest and [illegible—'bold leader'?] to direct their power."[30]

Of course, Johnston saw himself as the required hero. Entering upon his task of leadership with great gusto and some success, he revealed the tone and direction of that leadership in his first inaugural address, delivered on December 1, 1896.[31] He communicated the details to the legislature separately.[32] The address struck the keynote of orderly development under equitable and humanitarian government. This was the Progressive message; in reflecting the Progressive emphasis on social unity, it received praise from all elements of the community.[33] These terms—order, equity, development, humanitarianism—do not denote separate categories of Progressive concern so much as they designate interrelated facets of a single, economically self-interested, ethically shaped, middle-class attitude toward life.

Johnston's frank invitation to Northern capital to come into the state to develop the under-utilized natural resources was particularly significant. His desire to encourage manufacturing took the form of a tax exemption bill which he signed into law during his first administration. Further doubt about Johnston's desire for reform is stimulated by the fact that he had come from the ranks of capitalists and industrialists and that his Populistic stance was more than a little artificial. When the rigidity of old

[30] Johnston to McKee, January 19, 1894, McKee Papers, ADAH.

[31] Alabama, *House Journal, 1896*, 365ff.

[32] *Ibid.*, 368-387.

[33] W.P.G. Harding to Johnston, December 1896, Governor's Office Records, ADAH. Harding was then second vice president of the First National Bank of Birmingham and was later the governor of the Federal Reserve Board. John W. DuBose to Chappell Cory, March 29, 1897, Cory Papers, ADAH. *Choctaw Alliance*, December 8, 1896.

age set in, Johnston froze in place considerably to the right of center. But the picture of him as a reformer should not be obliterated. In his initial speech as governor, while praising the good that corporations did, Johnston thought "a wise supervision is absolutely essential to prevent abuse of the powers conferred upon them."[34] When the tax exemption for manufacturers was passed in a more generous form in his second term as governor, Johnston vetoed it as an inequitable measure, and some portions of his program aimed at taxing and curbing the very concentrations of wealth that he invited into the state. In his first address he also emphasized the fact that Alabama's raw materials had to be fabricated at home if the population was to benefit, an argument Comer later emphasized. It was never clear from Johnston on whose terms and at whose expense progress was to be obtained, the population or the capitalists? An ambiguous commitment to progress and equity at the same time was not unique. To be of two minds about many things was inherent in the social position of the middle class.[35] The same ambiguous attitude toward outside economic interests later showed up with telling force in the administration of Governor Comer.

The program Johnston proposed to the legislature contained measures aimed at development, equity, and humanitarianism, but the taxing and spending activities of government provided a crucial test of Progressivism. The tax structure of Alabama was weighted in favor of large property owners. In addition, assessors were frequently accused of allowing the rich to escape without listing all of their property. Johnston pointed out that the total assessed value of real and personal property in 1890

[34] Alabama, *House Journal, 1896*, 379.
[35] Hofstadter, *Age of Reform*, 134.

was about one-third the figure computed by the federal census for the same year. More important was the fact that similar land varied in assessment from county to county. Apparently mules could lose value just by crossing a county line. To correct these evils and to increase state revenue, Johnston wanted changes similar to those Sam Will John had proposed in 1894.

To meet the problems of nonassessment, under-assessment, and unequal assessment which arose from having an elected tax assessor in each county and no central authority, Johnston proposed a new tax commission appointed by the governor, with assistants in each county and the power to oversee and correct the work of the county assessors. J. J. Mitchell of Lauderdale County hailed the measure as a way of taxing the rich men who owned two-thirds of the property in the state that went untaxed. Despite opposition from the railroads, their friends in the press, and the Populists, the tax commission bill became law.[36]

A companion measure designed to help shift the burden of taxation was included in the revenue bill Johnston supported. Its most controversial provision was a tax on the fair market value of the capital stock of corporations, as well as the real and personal property of corporations. This was the franchise tax, which became the hallmark of progressive tax legislation. The *Register* and the *Advertiser* attacked it vigorously as double taxation that would drive capital away from the state. E. L. Russell, president of the Mobile and Ohio Railroad and Governor Johnston's friend, went to Montgomery to testify against the provision before the Judiciary Committee on

[36] Alabama, *Acts, 1896*, 521. Alabama, *House Journal, 1896*, 389, 603, 673, 814, 819, 834, 857. The bill was enrolled on February 3, 1817. Mobile *Register*, January 27, 29, February 2, 1897.

February 8. When the revenue bill passed the House two days later by a vote of 47 to 20, the "double tax" on corporations was no longer included.[37]

The same fate befell Johnston's financial program in the 1898-99 session. The governor wanted to increase the levies for licenses and fees, but the myriad businesses the increase would affect so emasculated the schedule in the biennial revenue act that very few changes were actually made. In the 1898 session the House passed a measure that would have placed a tax for the first time on the gross income of corporations, but it was defeated in the Senate. As with the other major thrust for equity—railroad reform—the Progressive spirit was willing, but the legislature was still weak.

Progressive concern for giving everyone a fair and equal chance, as they interpreted the phrase, was shown in Johnston's early interest in business regulation other than railroad reform. A law enacted at the 1896 session of the legislature limited the interest rate of building and loan associations to 10 percent.[38] An effort in the 1898 session to lower the general legal interest rate to 6 percent failed in the Senate after passing the House. Another effort to protect the public from the economic power of sometimes predatory but always necessary aggregations of capital was the beginning of efforts to regulate the insurance companies which did business in the state. The 1896 legislature made the Alabama Secretary of State ex officio Insurance Commissioner, with the power to suspend the license of any company that did not meet certain financial and operating requirements. The act also pro-

[37] Alabama, *Acts, 1896*, 1,489. Alabama, *House Journal, 1896*, 694, 994, 1,000, 1,023, 1,277, 1,295, 1,300, 1,305, 1,318. Mobile *Register*, February 4, 6, 9-11, 1897.
[38] Alabama, *Acts, 1896*, 854.

vided him with a deputy insurance commissioner whose sole duty it was to enforce the code. In addition to the usual license fee, insurance companies were henceforth required to pay an additional tax of one percent of the premiums they collected within the state.[39] These steps comprised an important beginning in the regulation of largely out-of-state sources of capital which had come to be deeply resented by Alabamians and Southerners in general.

Another aspect of the desire for the establishing of equitable standards was the wish of many men for laws to insure fair election practices. One act of the 1896 session met the demands to liberalize the Sayre election law, which had been designed to limit the potential Populist electorate. Governor Johnston advised the legislature in his inaugural address of 1896 that there was no longer any threat from that quarter so that it was possible to institute fair procedures. The new law eased registration requirements. It provided that a person living outside a town of 5,000 population did not have to register unless he moved out of his precinct. The new requirements aided town and city voters, against whom the old law had militated, by a provision which opened up registration books at the polls on election day.[40] The 1898 session added to the electoral safeguards by following the governor's recommendation for a new primary law. Johnston's suggestion in 1896 for breaking up local political cliques and rings fell short of the demand for mandatory statewide primaries that had been growing since 1891.[41] The resulting law bound voluntarily held county primaries with the protection of all the criminal penalties

[39] *Ibid.*, 1,377. Mobile *Register*, February 16, 1897.
[40] Alabama, *Acts, 1896*, 1,186.
[41] Jones, "A History of the Direct Primary in Alabama," 148, 197.

that applied to regular elections.[42] But Johnston's success ended here. In 1899 the legislature defeated his proposal for the election of solicitors rather than their appointment by the legislature, where free wheeling political deals were the normal mode of decision, instead of merit. The governor's effort to get lobbying banned from the capitol went unheeded for the moment.

The significant thing about the Progressives' desire for social and economic development was that they wanted to use governmental action to stimulate such progress. Like Comer after him, Johnston thought the state was justified in spending beyond its current revenues for measures which would eventually pay for themselves in economic progress. For instance, progress required that better roads be built, but the counties were not fulfilling their obligation in this regard. In both 1896 and 1898 Johnston recommended that the legislature initiate a system of central planning for the state road system and look for a more adequate means of underwriting the cost of a modern system. This was not done. Johnston also wanted to increase the state's efforts to attract worthy (white) immigrants who would create additional wealth for the state by their industry. The dream of an immigrant influx was an old one in the South, and despite the interest of governors of all political persuasions and the activities of the state immigration commissioner, it continued to be just that—a fond dream.

Education was not only a sure way to material progress, it had the added feature of creating moral progress and better citizenship as well. Johnston devoted more space to education in his 1896 message than to any other single subject. The legislature moved toward implementation of Johnston's pledge "to develop our public schools

[42] *Ibid.*, 162. Alabama, *Acts, 1898*, 126.

to the limit of fair taxation . . ." when in the 1898 session it raised the general appropriation for education from $350,000 to $450,000 and provided an additional one mill tax for school maintenance.[43] Another act improved the administrative machinery of the educational system.[44] The legislature also established in 1898 the Boys Industrial School, the companion institution of the Girls Industrial School authorized by the previous Johnston legislature. Both of these measures had been championed by the Alabama State Federation of Women's clubs, an organization just beginning to make itself heard in legislative halls. The two industrial schools were designed to reform and care for wayward and orphaned youth.[45] Their goal went beyond the normal ones of a public education system to stimulate material progress, to aid in moral improvement, and to make the competitive system more equitable by equalizing the advantages of birth; it extended to humanitarianism.

The most controversial humanitarian legislation that Johnston sponsored, and which attacked the position of the interstate economic interests and their allied local politicians, was the bill to abolish the noxious convict leasing system. Dr. Russell M. Cunningham, physician for the Tennessee Coal, Iron, Railroad Company, was intimately acquainted with the high death rate and degrading conditions among convicts leased by the state and the counties to private mining companies. He stimulated the legislature to appoint a joint committee which investigated the situation during the recess in January 1897. The report of the committee did much to expose the public to the realities of the convict lease system.

The Cunningham Committee found that mine opera-

[43] Alabama, *Acts, 1898*, 69, 217.
[44] *Ibid.*, 217.
[45] *Ibid.*, 70, 75, 158.

tors were quite happy with the system, especially as a check against strikes.[46] It also found that the death rate for convict miners was four times the rate for free Negro miners in the same county and 10 times that for free white miners.[47] The committee recommended abolition of convict leasing and the institution of a system that would pay for itself and yet would aim at the reformation rather than the punishment of convicts. Cunningham's bill would have done just that.

Cunningham skillfully managed his bill through the Senate, only to be thwarted in the House. Ariosto A. Wiley, the man who had arranged the defeat of the Progressive revenue bill, got the House to pass his own bill on convict leasing with only 12 negative votes. He saved the mining companies from the economic hardship of having to pay wages to their labor and at the same time indirectly benefited his own railroad employers who depended on the bulk freight traffic generated by the coal mines. His bill provided for some health safeguards but left the lease system intact. The conference committee appointed to reconcile the two bills accepted the Wiley version on the day before adjournment. Consequently, the legislature passed no bill at all. The convict leasing system proved to be an extremely tenacious parasite.[48]

Governor Johnston, as did all other governors, deplored lynching. He not only called on all good people to aid in its suppression, but suggested concrete ways of discouraging the practice. Among his suggestions were the use of special sessions of court, rapid trials, and the full use of the state militia. It is a commentary on the powerlessness of the Negro community, as well as the

[46] Alabama, *House Journal, 1896*, 640.
[47] *Ibid.*, 629-630.
[48] *Ibid.*, 622-656, 1,311-1,314.

145

foreshortened limits of white humanitarian endeavor, that the two Johnston legislatures never even discussed the anti-lynching suggestions.

But the Progressives' urge to put "fair play" into the law did not extend to Negro grievances. Indeed, when it came to insuring ethical conduct in elections, Progressives and other white Alabamians eliminated the theft of Negro votes by eliminating Negro voting.

The Movement for Disfranchisement

The two decades 1890 to 1910 was the era of disfranchisement not only in Alabama but throughout the South. Mississippi led the way in 1890 with the Second Mississippi Plan, which provided for a poll tax, a literacy test with a property qualification as an alternative, and an "understanding clause" as a loophole for poor whites. South Carolina (1895), Louisiana (1898), Alabama (1901), and Virginia (1902) also turned new constitutions to the purpose of barring Negroes from politics. North Carolina (1900), Georgia (1908), and Oklahoma (1910) accomplished the same thing with constitutional amendments, while Tennessee (1890), Texas (1902), Florida (1889), and Arkansas (1891) legislated the poll tax as a prerequisite for suffrage.

Of the states passing major disfranchising measures only in Mississippi did the move come before the outbreak of the Populist revolt. There the movement seems to have been pressed originally by white counties and then taken up and controlled at the convention by Black-county forces, with the result that the restrictions served to bar many whites as well. In South Carolina the Tillman wing of the Democratic Party sponsored the cleansing of the electoral process, while in Virginia and Georgia it seems to have been spearheaded by progressive, antimachine political groups. The variation in the intrastate and intra-race political conflicts that conditioned the disfranchising process in each state led V. O. Key to the conclusion that "the groups on top at the moment, whatever their political orientation, feared that their opponents might recruit Negro support."[1]

But this begs the question of why disfranchisement occurred at a particular time, and it does not do justice to the complexity of motivations that influenced Alabama's route to disfranchisement. It was not simply a matter of racial prejudice; there was much more than a simple straight-line course to the disfranchising convention of 1901 from the time in 1890 when Governor Thomas Seay became the first prominent Alabamian to propose a convention.[2]

The first complicating factor was that Negroes were not the sole target of disfranchisement. Governor Johnston urged disfranchisement initially as a way of ridding the electorate of a class of voters that was "a constant menace to its [the state's] growth and to the security of life and property. . . ."[3] Johnston did not identify the menacing voters, but they were evidently not all of one color because he thought a substantial poll tax was the

---

[1] Woodward, *Origins of the New South*, 321, 335. Dudley O. McGovney, *The American Suffrage Medley; The Need for a National Uniform Suffrage*, Chicago, 1949, 60, 72, 110, 123-124. V. O. Key, Jr., *Southern Politics in State and Nation*, New York, 1949, 550. Albert D. Kirwan, *Revolt of the Rednecks: Mississippi Politics, 1876-1925*, Lexington, Ky., 1951, 63. George B. Tindall, *South Carolina Negroes, 1877-1900*. Columbia, S.C., 1952, 74. Charles E. Wynes, *Race Relations in Virginia, 1870-1902*, Charlottesville, Va., 1961, 56. Vernon Lane Wharton, *The Negro in Mississippi, 1865-1890*, Vol. XXVIII of "The James Sprunt Studies in History and Political Science," Chapel Hill, 1947, 209.

[2] Alabama, *House Journal, 1890*, 33.

[3] Alabama, *House Journal, 1896*, 386.

best method of purging them. In the late stages of the struggle William C. Oates argued forcefully that any voting test adopted should apply to all alike, and Thomas G. Jones justified disfranchisement as the best guarantee against a new threat to property in the form of a Populist revival.[4] Jones always insisted, sometimes angrily, that the large majority of Negroes had legitimately voted for him; thus his rationale points to white Populists as the unwanted voters.

The fear of the Populist vote was not just a matter of hindsight. The first serious attempt at disfranchisement in 1892 had as its target the Populists. The initial proposal for disfranchisement was discussed at the Democratic convention in the summer of 1892, but the convention postponed a decision. Soon after the legislature convened on November 16, 1892 the matter came up again, now in the form of a bill to provide a literacy and property test for the ballot, sponsored by the speaker of the House of Representatives, Francis L. Pettus of Dallas County, in the heart of the Black Belt.

Though the judicial committee reported the Pettus Bill favorably, it was killed in February 1893 when Populists joined right-wing Democrats to defeat 22 advocates of disfranchisement. Both sides of this curious coalition feared the same thing: the loss of votes—white votes in the case of the Populists, black votes for the Democrats. Disfranchisement had to await political tranquility.

The growing sense of outrage at the blatant corruption involved in state elections, combined with the decisive defeat of the Populists in the election of 1896, made that year seem propitious. By the time the biennial session of the legislature met in November 1896, every business

---

[4] Mobile *Register*, January 19, 1901. Montgomery *Advertiser*, January 31, April 11, 16, 1901.

149

and commercial organization and all but five of the Demcratic newspapers in the state had endorsed a call for a constitutional convention. In October 1896 the Alabama Commercial and Industrial Association appointed an impressive committee headed by H. L. McKee of Selma, to petition the legislature and lobby for a convention. The Alabama Education Association also had a committee working for a new state constitution.[5]

There were, of course, reasons other than disfranchisement for wanting to call a constitutional convention; these reasons complicated the picture considerably. Most of them hinged on the facts of change and the problems of growth which created needs unmet by the Constitution of 1875. The authority to levy special local taxes for education, an expansion of the borrowing capacity of municipalities, the power to use state funds for internal improvements, a stronger state railroad commission, abolition of the convict lease system, provisions for statewide primaries, reorganization of the overworked state judicial system, changes in the tenure and method of choosing various public officials—all had champions in powerful sectors of society and all required constitutional revision.

There were also opponents of constitutional revision. The Mobile *Register* reported that railroads and other corporations, fearing stricter regulation and discriminatory taxation, were using their influence against the convention bill.[6] They were not the only interests that looked on the 1875 constitution as a bulwark against destruction.

[5] Alabama, *House Journal, 1896*, 397. Malcolm C. McMillan, *Constitutional Development in Alabama, 1798-1901: A Study in Politics, the Negro, and Sectionalism*, Vol. XXXVII of "The James Sprunt Studies in History and Political Science," Chapel Hill, 1955, 238-239.

[6] February 2, 1897.

Real estate owners feared higher rates of taxation; the Black Belt feared that the basis of apportionment might be changed from total population to the number of actual voters or some other basis, and destroy their base of power in the large Negro population; Negroes and poor whites feared disfranchisement; and officeholders feared a change in the political system they had learned to manipulate so advantageously.[7] The task of placating enough of these hostile interests to secure a majority for the convention bill was a formidable one.

Late in the legislative session the constitutional convention bill (H. 631) picked up a powerful supporter when Governor Johnston added his endorsement.[8] With the scales seemingly balanced by the addition of this final counterweight, the House of Representatives took up the bill on February 11 with the galleries overflowing and the lobbies active. The debate was heated but disingenuous. With the exception of a few Populist speakers who spoke frankly about the effects of disfranchisement, the discussion generally did not touch on the exposed nerves of real interests. The House passed the bill by the narrow vote of 49 to 44, with the Populists in solid opposition.[9]

Strange things happened to the bill in the Senate. Oscar Hundley of Huntsville offered an amendment providing for inspectors from at least two parties at each polling place during the referendum and election of delegates. If the Populists were granted this safeguard, perhaps they would support the bill. An attempt to table Hundley's amendment failed 13-16; then without warning, Willis

[7] Alabama, *Acts, 1896*, 1,186.
[8] Mobile *Register*, February 10, 1897.
[9] *Ibid.*, February 12, 1897. Alabama, *House Journal, 1896*, 1,044.

151

Brewer moved to table both the amendment and the bill! His motion carried 18-11 with Populist support.[10]

Just why the sudden reversal of fortunes is a difficult question. Black Belt senators were split down the middle. Half were opposed to the convention and favored the Hundley amendment, apparently so that the bill would become unacceptable to Democrats everywhere, while the other senators from the Black Belt took the opposite stance. Eight Populists, five Black Belt Democrats, and four Democrats from districts with a hardy Populist vote combined to defeat the bill. In the House only 5 of 31 representatives from the Black Belt voted against the bill, and those weathervanes of railroad sentiment, A. A. Wiley and A. M. Tunstall, voted for it.

Nevertheless, the most logical explanation for the defeat of the convention bill is that certain railroad and corporate interests were opposed. "I understand," Kolb wrote to Johnston while the bill was pending, "that every influence is being brought to bear upon members of the legislature . . . in opposition to the bill and that said influence is being led by some if not all the Rail Road Corporations. You understand the power of such influence and if some counter influence is not inaugurated I fear the result. . . ."[11] Kolb's fears were well founded.

The voting patterns on the other major measures during the session show that the issue of disfranchisement cut across ideological lines. Most of the support for the constitutional convention, which meant different things to different people, came from representatives who had opposed one or both of the railroad and tax commission reform measures. But 40 percent of the "yes" votes for

[10] Alabama, *Senate Journal, 1896*, 1,044. Mobile *Register*, February 17, 1897.
[11] Kolb to Johnston, n.d. [December 1896], Governor's Office Records, ADAH.

the convention came from supporters of both the railroad reform bill and the tax commission bill. That Progressive-oriented legislators were in the forefront of the convention movement at this point in time is indicated by the fact that very few of the men who voted progressively on the reform bills failed to support the constitutional convention bill.

William W. Brandon was one of the few who voted for reform but opposed the convention. He had promised the Populists in the campaign that he would oppose disfranchisement if they would support him. He kept his word. Similar men from north and southeast Alabama probably shared with Brandon and the Populist leaders the need to conciliate a fearful poor-white constituency. These "no" voters were not numerous. Twice as many of the no votes came from opponents of one or both major reform measures. Though they killed the convention bill, they could not kill the issue, and the issue played an important part in the election of 1898.

Populism was barely functioning in 1898. The convention in early May named Gilbert B. Deans to lead the Populists into battle once again, but the old zeal was gone. Deans, along with numerous editorials, called attention to the problem of low morale among the faithful by exhorting them not to be disheartened and by rehearsing the old cliché about the darkest hour coming just before day.[12] The convention tried to respond to this urging in the platform. Starting with government ownership of utilities, and ranging through a long compendium of reform measures to a call for better schools and roads, the platform sounded a defiant note. Somewhat in conflict with this brave new front, however, was the platform's demand that counties cut expenditures to a bare minimum

[12] Randolph *Toiler*, April 18, May 6, July 15, 1898.

and that the state legislature repeal the Johnston administration's new tax laws. Populists evidently still refused to make the philosophical adjustments called for by their desire for new governmental services. The one thing clear above all else was that the Populists opposed a constitutional convention.[13]

On April 20, while President McKinley was signing the ultimatum to Spain and the joint Congressional resolution recognizing the independence of Cuba, the Democratic convention met in Montgomery to reply to the Populists. No one was surprised when the convention renominated Johnston and endorsed his administration and its efforts to make all classes of people bear the burdens of taxation. True to form, the platform embraced the newly discovered but "eternally true" principles of the Chicago platform. Because the document made no mention of disfranchisement, which became the chief campaign issue anyway, the *Cherokee Sentinel* concluded later that "the Democrats were hypocrites."[14]

The campaign was uncommonly placid for Alabama. There were two occasions on which speakers were mistreated, but on only one of these was physical harm involved,[15] and though a few Populists threatened armed resistance if they were counted out, their threats did not have the old tone of determination.[16] One distraction from the campaign was the war with Spain, which was in progress between convention time and election day on August 1. The approach of the war was met with the same range of opinion in the Populist papers as in the Democratic. If anything, the Populists were less con-

---

[13] *The Cherokee Sentinel*, May 12, 1898.
[14] *Ibid.*, April 28, May 19, 1898. Mobile *Register*, April 21, 22, 1898. Randolph *Toiler*, June 3, 1898.
[15] *Ibid.*, August 5, 1898.
[16] Mobile *Register*, July 16, 1898.

cerned than the Democrats about the situation in Cuba. But it had the effect of forcing news of Alabama politics to the inside pages of newspapers.

It might be argued that the events in Alabama were more important to the nation and would one day have a greater impact on world opinion than the episodes at Manila Bay and San Juan Hill. While one Alabamian, Richmond Pearson Hobson, with his heroic but irrelevant deed in the bay of Santiago de Cuba, was helping to extend liberty abroad, other Alabamians were preparing to limit it at home.

The Populists—or those who were still active—did what they could to preserve democracy. Gilbert Deans took special pains to emphasize the plank in the platform opposing the calling of "a State Constitutional Convention for the purpose of disfranchising the poor and illiterate."[17] He denied again that Populists or Negroes were calling for social equality, but he noted that the same men who stole the Negro's vote and kept him in ignorance and poverty preyed equally on the poor white.[18]

The August election was even more disastrous than usual for the Populists. Johnston had no difficulty in carrying the state, by a vote of 110,551 to 50,052, while losing only 10 counties.[19] Though there was some evidence that Negro Republicans were not enthusiastic about supporting Populists,[20] the Republican Party again advised its members to support the Populist nominees, and fusion between Republicans and Populists at the county level was widespread despite the experience of 1896.[21] There were even some attempts by Populists and

[17] Randolph *Toiler*, May 13, 1898.
[18] *Ibid.*, July 15, 1898.
[19] Alabama, *House Journal, 1898*, 84-85.
[20] Mobile *Register*, August 2, 1898.
[21] F. H. Lathrop to J. H. Bingham, October 18, 1900; and

Democrats to merge through joint primaries, but these usually broke down under the weight of mutual suspicion.[22]

One Populist politician explained the defeat by observing that "there is an apathy among plebeians in all the parties, because they are tired of so much politics when they are getting nothing out of it. . . ."[23] Others agreed.[24] The problem was that the Populists depended more on the plebeians than did the other parties. In Cherokee, where Deans had a small majority in a county that was normally overwhelmingly Populist, the *Sentinel* said apathy explained it all. "There has been no increase in the Democratic vote in this county, but there has been a falling off in the Populist vote."[25]

Whatever explains the Populist defeat, almost everyone agreed at the time on the meaning of the Democratic victory.[26] The headlines of the Mobile *Register* crowed, "The Election Means a New Constitution."[27] The situation suddenly changed during the fall, however, when Johnston began to reassess his own support for the new constitution. His ambition was to occupy John Tyler Morgan's seat in the United States Senate. The only prob-

---

T. W. Powell to O. D. Street, August 22, 1898; Street Papers, University of Alabama.

[22] *The Alabama Alliance News*, February 8, 20, 1898.

[23] Alfred G. Lee to O. D. Street, August 20, 1898, Street Papers, University of Alabama.

[24] George F. Gaither to Street, August 20, 1898, Street Papers, University of Alabama.

[25] August 4, 1898. See the voting analysis of apathy in the preceding chapter. For evidence of the fact that lower class withdrawal is not only normal but personally functional, see Arthur J. Vidich and Joseph Bensman, *Small Town in Mass Society; Class, Power, and Religion in a Rural Community*, Princeton, 1958, 69-70, 290-291.

[26] *Cherokee Sentinel*, August 11, November 10, 1898.

[27] Mobile *Register*, August 2, 1898.

lem with this noble ambition was that John Tyler Morgan was still sitting in his Senate seat and gave no indication of seeking a softer perch despite his advanced age. Johnston cast about for the most likely source of an anti-Morgan majority. To his discomfort, the most likely source of new votes was the Populist Party, and it was adamantly opposed to the constitution. As the *Alabama Alliance News* put it, "We doubt the honesty of purpose which is crying for a new constitution."[28]

Knowing that the Populists were not essentially interested in protecting Negro suffrage, Johnston temporized and looked for a means of disfranchising Negroes while placating white Populists. On November 18, 1898, in his biennial address to the new legislature, Johnston suggested that perhaps disfranchisement could be accomplished more cheaply and less divisively by a constitutional amendment rather than through a convention and a new constitution. Disfranchisement by amendment would give the Populists a better check on the untrustworthy Democrats, so Populists hailed the governor's message as a victory. "But really," commented the *Toiler*, "it begins to look like we have got a very good POPULIST GOVERNOR. When he ordered the bars let down we regarded it as a trick to beguile the unwary, but now the Governor has slipped around the gap and hopped in himself!"[29] But Johnston was actually still sitting on the fence. Which pasture he would find greener remained to be seen.

One factor beginning to affect Johnston's outlook was that the issue of disfranchisement, as well as the legislature itself, had been adopted by his enemies. Reflecting this shift in complexion, the lawmakers chose Russell M.

[28] *Ibid.*, August 30, 1898.
[29] Randolph *Toiler*, December 2, 1898.

Cunningham as President of the Senate and Charles Waller as Speaker of the House. Cunningham, who later ran for governor against B. B. Comer, championed certain humanitarian reforms, but was connected politically with the old Jones wing of the party. Waller had been a Johnston supporter, but in 1898 he was feuding with the governor over the Back Tax Law which was unpopular among property owners. A more serious sign of the drift of opinion was the election of Massie Wilson, a gold Democrat, as clerk of the House of Representatives over John F. Burns, a silver Democrat. In addition to these indications, the first Democratic caucus of the legislature voted to exclude anyone who had not voted the Democratic ticket in the election in August 1898. The caucus received one ex-Populist but turned away four others who applied for admittance, which put a serious crimp in Johnston's plans to bring all of the Populists into the party on his side. The Mobile *Register*, a barometer of standpat business opinion, revealed the nature of the legislature of 1898-99 when at the end of the session it praised it as a legislature of character and ability which with only one exception had passed no bill that was not for the general good.[30]

The issue dominating the legislature was the battle over the bill calling for a referendum on the question of a constitutional convention. A few days before the legislature convened on November 16, 1898, the Managing Committee of the Alabama Commercial and Industrial Association for the New Constitutional Convention met in the Exchange Hotel in Montgomery.[31] Because Negro disfranchisement was the issue on which it could get the broadest consensus, the committee decided its best tactic

[30] Mobile *Register*, February 21, 1899.
[31] *Ibid.*, November 13, 1898.

158

was to stress the need for suffrage reform. In addition, its task was to convince those who looked on the Constitution of 1875 as their protection that there was nothing to fear from a new constitution. The committee felt the most damaging apprehension was fear of higher taxes. Therefore it decided that the public should be assured that the existing constitutional limit on the rate of taxation would not be changed in the new constitution. This began the move to secure approval of a constitutional convention by guaranteeing the continuation of the special privileges of influential groups and by using Negro disfranchisement as an omnibus to transport progressive business purposes.

The friends of the new constitution wasted no time. On December 5, as the campaign in the newspapers was building, Democratic members of the legislature held a joint caucus and decided to take some action on the question despite the fact that some of the members had made campaign promises to oppose any move for a new constitution. The caucus appointed a committee of 10, five from each house, to draft the legislation and referred to it a number of resolutions designed to enlist the support of important interest groups. These resolutions proposed that the legislature bind the Constitutional Convention in three basic ways: not to disturb the vote of war veterans (a reassurance to poor whites), not to change the basis of representation (a bid for Black Belt support), and not to alter the existing limits on the amount or agencies of taxation (a guarantee evidently desired by most groups other than Progressives).[32]

While the committee was drafting the proposed legislation, another discussion was going on in Washington which was not without its ironic connection. On Decem-

[32] *Ibid.*, December 3, 6, 1898.

ber 6 President McKinley sent to Congress the report of the Commission on Hawaiian Government. The relevance was not only in the fact that one of the two senators on the Commission was Alabama's John Tyler Morgan—the Commission's report was itself significant. The Commission proposed to safeguard the government of Hawaii with property qualifications for holding office and with property and literacy qualifications for voting. The Southern way was becoming the American way,[33] or was it the other way around?

No matter where the innovation originated, this was but another of many indications that the South no longer need fear the interference of the federal government in racial matters. In *Williams v. Mississippi* the Supreme Court in 1898 upheld Mississippi's disfranchising provisions. This completed the work the Court had started in the Civil Rights Cases of 1883 and the *Plessy v. Ferguson* decision of 1896 (approval of separate but equal facilities for the two races on railroads). The president reinforced the growing confidence of Southern whites that their will could be made law in racial matters when in his 1898 State of the Union address he refrained from mentioning the matter of Republican concern for the status of the Negro in the South.[34]

There is no doubt that Southerners perceived the changed attitude of the North. Emmett O'Neal told the Alabama Constitutional Convention in 1901 that "the acquisition of the Sandwich Islands, the Philippines, Porto Rico and the control of Cuba has forced the race problem to the attention of the whole country and in the

[33] Woodward, *Origins of the New South*, Chapter 12. Francis Butler Simkins, *A History of the South*, 2nd rev. edn., New York, 1953, 356-357.
[34] Mobile *Register*, January 8, 1899, December 15, 1898.

wise solution of this question we have the sympathy instead of the hostility of the North." Edgar Gardner Murphy was even more explicit in explaining the situation to Booker T. Washington. "The North has decided to allow the XVth Amendment to stand," he wrote, "which decision guarantees to the South a full representation in Congress for every Negro of voting age. And the North has also decided not to interfere in the internal affairs of the Southern States, so that each Southern State can count the Negro out in the election, and count him in for representation. This is the view of the 'practical' men at the South. They are entirely satisfied. . . ."[35]

On December 8, 1898 the Mobile *Register*, for instance, noted with complete satisfaction both the Hawaiian commission's recommendations and the report of the caucus committee of the Alabama Democratic Party which aimed at much the same thing. The committee of 10 decided that the bill providing for the referendum and the convention should also include the reservations embodied in the resolutions of the party caucus of December 5. It also decided that the referendum should be held in July and the convention in August. By this time, 57 representatives and 16 senators had pledged to support the bill.[36]

Supporters of the bill rushed frantically to get it through before the Christmas recess in order to take advantage of the disorganized state of the opposition. The bill passed

[35] *Official Proceedings of the Constitutional Convention of the State of Alabama, May 21st 1901 to September 3rd 1901*, Wetumpka, Ala., 1941, III, 2,783. Other delegates made the same observation: I, 8; III, 3,003; III, 3,087. This four-volume reprint of the stenographic record will be cited hereafter as *Proceedings of the Convention*. Edgar Gardner Murphy to Booker T. Washington, March 28, 1900, B. T. Washington Papers, Library of Congress.

[36] *Ibid.*, December 9, 1898.

the Senate handily with only slight changes on December 10, by a vote of 17 to 11.

The going was tougher in the House. Because the procedures preliminary to passage required a minimum of three days, the bill had to be introduced no later than December 10 to come to a vote before adjournment. Consequently the bill's opponents merely had to delay its introduction. In a wild session on December 10, with a combination of strongarm tactics and shrewd parliamentary maneuver, supporters managed to introduce the bill.[37] The author of the successful strategy, which included locking the chamber doors to prevent losing a quorum, was A. M. Tunstall, the son of the same operator who had masterminded the deal that put Jones in the governor's chair and who had obtained passage of the pro-Black Belt reapportionment bill in 1891.

As the constitutional convention bill awaited the governor's signature, there occurred an interval in which Alabama, the South, and the nation seemed to pause as if to acknowledge the importance of the event. It was one of those rare times when people are momentarily conscious of the passing of one era and the beginning of another. By fortuitous but not unrelated circumstance, a Republican president was on a rare and friendly visit to the Deep South, and on December 15 Alabama legislators traveled to Atlanta to mark the occasion. Heading from Atlanta to Montgomery the following day, with the Alabama legislators aboard as the honor guard, the presidential train stopped in Tuskegee, Alabama, the home of the author of the Atlanta Compromise for racial harmony. There Booker T. Washington spoke to the gathering about the role his institution was playing in the search for a solution to "one of the greatest problems

[37] *Ibid.*, December 11, 13, 1898.

162

ever given to man to solve." His purpose, said Washington, was to teach his people to put "brains and dignity into the common occupations of life. . . ." In reply President McKinley praised Tuskegee Institute for its efforts "to cultivate and promote an amicable relationship between the two races." McKinley also sang the praises of the idea of self-help that the Institute was furthering through its emphasis on practical industry. "An evidence of the soundness of the purpose of this institution," said McKinley, "is that those in charge of its management evidently do not believe in attempting the unattainable. . . ."[38]

Leaving Mr. Washington behind in Tuskegee, the president continued on with the Alabama legislators to the state capitol, where the largest crowd ever seen in Montgomery had gathered to welcome the Yankee leader. Banner headlines and a three-column picture in the newspaper announced his expected arrival for what proved to be a prolonged celebration of sectional reconciliation. The main ceremony of the day was held in the hall of the House of Representatives where the Confederate States of America had been born and where William McKinley now joined in singing both "Yankee Doodle" and "Dixie." His short speech, echoed by all of the other speakers of the day, emphasized the obliteration of sectional antagonism. The crowd responded with tremendous cheers and applause. The *Advertiser* commented that "it was a scene calculated to live forever in the minds of those who understood its significance."[39]

Its *significance* was put in bold relief when, after the president had left Montgomery to return to Washington, the government of Alabama returned to its task of un-

[38] Montgomery *Advertiser*, December 17, 1898.
[39] *Ibid.*

doing what the national government had spent so much blood in doing some three decades earlier. Governor Johnston signed the Constitutional Convention Act the following day—December 17, 1898.

The bill contained six major restrictions on the power of the convention: (1) the convention was not to remove the capitol from Montgomery; (2) it was not to change the tax limits; (3) it was not to grant the power of taxation to private persons or corporations; (4) it was to insure that no county or town could levy taxes to exceed one-half of one percent except in certain cases and in order to service the debt contracted before 1875; (5) it was to insure that all property would be taxed at the same rate; and (6) it was to provide that the entire population would continue to be the basis for apportionment in the state. These pledges took care of the fears of the Big Mules and the Black Belt, but certain promises were notably absent. There was no pledge not to disfranchise white men or veterans, nor was there a promise to submit the new constitution to the people for ratification.[40]

Focusing on this last inadequacy of the act, Bibb Graves, who was later a Comer partisan in his campaign for railroad regulation and still later a progressive governor of the state in the 1920s, introduced a bill requiring the convention to submit the new constitution to the people for ratification, but it got nowhere.[41] Other opposition to the convention developed from the same quarter. John W. A. Sanford wrote to Robert McKee urging him to help form an organization to fight the calling of the constitutional convention. Colonel Sanford, a venerable, old-line Democrat, noted that Sam Will John, W. H. Denson, and Horace Hood were all

[40] Mobile *Register*, December 21, 1898.
[41] *Ibid.*, January 25, 1899.

active in opposition to the convention.[42] These men represented the humanitarian side of Progressivism, a point of view to which Johnston wished to appeal. In fact, they were all friends of Johnston.

When the state convention of the Democratic Party met on March 29, it seemed Johnston's enemies were in the ascendancy. Not only were such notables as R. H. Clarke and W. C. Oates prominent among the delegates, but the convention named as its permanent chairman William Dorsey Jelks. Jelks was the editor of the Eufaula *Times*, a state senator, a future governor of the state, and a gold Democrat.[43] The convention endorsed the constitutional convention and pledged the party to two restrictions in addition to the ones embodied in the act itself. It promised that no white man would be disfranchised, no matter how illiterate, and it guaranteed that the new document would be submitted to the people for ratification. These concessions to poor whites completed the neutralization of the opposition. The Big Mules and the Black Belt already had their reassurances.[44]

Johnston did not accept the judgment of the legislature and his party's convention. After canvassing the views of the members of the legislature, on April 20 he called a special session of the General Assembly to meet on May 2, 1899 for the purpose of repealing the Constitutional Convention Act.[45] This decision to oppose the convention was not an act of idealistic bravery, it was cold calculation. Johnston's secretary noted that he was not only ambitious and energetic, but unflinchingly realistic. "What I like about the man as an official," Cory

[42] John W. A. Sanford to Robert McKee, March 20, 1899, McKee Papers, ADAH.

[43] W. D. Jelks to Jones, March 16, 1896, Jones Papers, ADAH.

[44] Mobile *Register*, April 1, 1899.

[45] *Ibid.*, April 11, 1899.

wrote, "is, that he is not a saint whom the rascals can fool."[46] There were many other men in the state who noted the same characteristic in Johnston but did not count it as an endearing quality.[47] In any case, as the politicians chose sides in the days between the call for the special session and its meeting, the political facts on which Johnston had based his calculations became more apparent.

Even though men who were interested in Progressive reforms, and consequently sympathetic to Johnston, had played a prominent part in the early stages of the movement for a constitutional convention, the simple fact was that they were no longer in control of the movement in 1899.[48] Such men as G. L. Comer, W. D. Jelks, John B. Knox, Sydney J. Bowie, and George Harrison were the leaders of the convention advocates. They were all gold Democrats, linked to the interests of railroads and industrial corporations. One ex-Populist wrote that his "sympathies were with the Governor on the repeal of the Convention Bill. Not, however, because I was so strongly opposed to the convention, but because of the opposition I felt towards the crowd that would have dominated it. The old Palmer and Buckner fellows were able to get control of the party machinery, and I regard them as the common enemy."[49] The *Labor Advocate* also complained that special interest groups controlled the

---

[46] Chappell Cory to Robert McKee, January 5, 1897, McKee Papers, ADAH.

[47] For the judgments of two bitter enemies of Johnston see R. W. Cobb to McKee, July 20, 1898, and Frank O'Brien to McKee, May 17, 1899, McKee Papers, ADAH.

[48] That Johnston was aware of this fact was revealed in his debate with Senator Morgan on November 18, 1899. Mobile *Register*, November 19, 1899.

[49] I. L. Brock to John G. Winston, June 11, 1899, in the file marked "Applications—Judge of Probate—Cherokee County," Governor's Office Records, ADAH.

State Democratic Convention.[50] Frank O'Brien, whose testimony should be sound on this point because he was a bitter enemy of Johnston, wrote that "a very large majority of the people of the state were opposed to the holding of a constitutional convention, for the reason that they were afraid of the corporate influence."[51] Johnston himself later explained his position on the convention by saying that he "found the attorneys and employes of corporations had been able to control the nominations" for the constitutional convention and that if he had allowed it to be held, "the convention would have been in the hands of the representatives of the corporations, the gold-standard men, and the Palmer and Buckner bolters."[52]

That it had alienated some of Johnston's friends and supporters made the decision a tough one. Jim Nunnellee, editor of the Selma *Times* and a state senator, Charles Waller, and Charles M. Shelley were important figures who decided disfranchisement was more important than the threatened change in factional control. Conspicuously absent from Johnston's camp were also those hard-headed businessmen such as B. B. Comer who wanted the state to regulate railroad rates and perform other services for small business. Robert J. Lowe, Frank S. White (later Comer's campaign manager), and Hugh S. D. Mallory (heir to the leadership of the Comer faction in 1910) all made valuable contributions at various times to the cause of "business progressivism."[53] But in 1898 they opposed Johnston.

[50] Birmingham *Labor Advocate*, April 22, 1899.
[51] O'Brien to McKee, March 20, 1899, McKee Papers, ADAH.
[52] Mobile *Register*, November 19, 1899.
[53] George B. Tindall has used this term to describe the elements of the business community in the 1920s that wanted the state to improve its services to the public. "Business Progressivism: Southern Politics in the Twenties," *South Atlantic Quarterly*, LXII, Winter 1963, 92-106.

The convention question in fact split the leadership of the embryonic Progressive movement. The humanistic Progressives followed Johnston in hopes of shaping victory with the help of a dwindling Populist electorate. The business Progressives, in a characteristic gesture, co-operated with the enemy in a common attempt to rid society of what they considered to be a threat to order. At the same time, they were acting against the long-term interests of their political faction in an attempt to achieve immediate institutional reforms at the constitutional convention.

The opposition to Johnston seemed overwhelming. On April 21, after he had issued the call for the special session, the State Democratic Executive Committee met in Montgomery and by a vote of 18 to 7 passed a resolution providing for a vigorous campaign for the convention and against repeal. The spirits of the group were lifted by a strong endorsement received by telegram from Senators John T. Morgan and Edmund W. Pettus and Representative John H. Bankhead.[54] The *Register* gleefully found Johnston's newspaper support almost non-existent; only 15 papers it saw were in favor of repeal. Three were Republican, two were Populist, and three were out-of-state; only seven were Democratic papers within the state. On the other hand, 83 Democratic papers in the state had come out for the Constitutional Convention.[55]

The governor probably was not greatly distressed by the weight of this opposition. Newspapers had no votes in the legislature, and Johnston had been busy among legislators neutralizing his enemies and reinforcing his friends with patronage.[56] He knew he had the votes for

[54] Mobile *Register*, April 22, 1899.
[55] *Ibid.*, April 21, 1899.
[56] R. T. Ervin to Morgan, April 10, 1899, Morgan Papers,

repeal.[57] The count would be close, however, so it was essential to Johnston that the Populists not desert him.

The governor had cause for concern on that score. At the January meeting of the State Democratic Executive Committee, Judge Zell Gaston appeared as a spokesman for the Populists. He suggested that if the Democrats gave some recognition to the Populists in the campaign for the convention, the Populist Party would advocate voting for the Constitutional Convention in the referendum.[58] The Committee did nothing about the offer at that time because victory seemed assured without Populist help.

Things looked different in May. During the evening of May 4 Robert J. Lowe and A. M. Tunstall went before a caucus of Populist and Republican legislators to offer essentially the same deal Gaston had asked for in January. Tunstall said that if the Populists would vote against repeal, the friends of the convention would amend the act by increasing the number of delegates from 133 to 166. They would then place on the Democratic state ticket for the at-large delegates any 30 Populists named by the Populist State Committee. It was an attractive offer. Nevertheless, even though the chairman of the Populist State Committee wanted to accept, the caucus voted to decline Tunstall's offer and vote against the convention.[59] This was one Tunstall deal that did not work.

Library of Congress. Johnston was notoriously adept in the use of patronage. At least two legislators who had voted for the convention in the regular session abstained from voting in the special session after having received appointments from Johnston.

[57] Johnston told Sam Will John that he had 65 representatives, including 15 Populists, lined up on his side. John to John Tyler Morgan, April 20, 1899, Morgan Papers, Library of Congress.

[58] Mobile *Register*, January 27, 1899.

[59] *The Southern Argus*, May 5, 1899.

On May 4 the House passed the repeal bill by a vote of 57 to 35.[60] The Senate followed suit four days later in a roll call that showed 17 in favor of repeal and 14 for the convention.[61] By changing a few votes in each house the governor had achieved his victory; but he could not keep the issue down. It emerged again as the central concern of the campaign of 1900. The main engagement of that campaign was the battle between John T. Morgan and Johnston for a seat in the U.S. Senate. The legislators who were to choose between the two men were in reality selected at the county conventions and primaries of the Democratic Party, held between November 1899 and April 1900. These same primaries and conventions, and 54 of the 66 counties held primaries, selected delegates to the state convention which in turn chose the party's nominee for governor. The primaries were therefore doubly important.

The order of battle was much the same as for the skirmish in the spring of 1899. In spite of the fact that he was an advocate of the free coinage of silver, Morgan enjoyed the support of the gold faction, whose members knew a lamb even when he was dressed in a wolf's clothing.[62] Reflecting the fact that gubernatorial and senatorial clashes would be decided at the same election, the Morgan camp joined forces with William J. Samford who was running for governor. Possessing appealing attributes, not the least of which was his traditional attitude toward the role of government leading inevitably to policies of low taxation and retrenchment, Samford was a

[60] Mobile *Register*, May 5, 1899.

[61] Alabama, *Senate Journal, Special Session, 1899*, 37.

[62] Sam Will John to John Tyler Morgan, April 20, 1899, Morgan Papers, Library of Congress.

farmer from Lee County who was not firmly identified in the public mind with either faction.[63]

Opposing Samford for governor were three candidates, all from the Johnston wing of the party: Charles M. Shelley, Charles Waller, and Jesse Stallings.[64] They hoped to deny Samford a majority in the state convention by winning enough delegates from the areas and segments of the population where they had special personal or ideological appeal. Then, in a repetition of the strategy that had defeated Kolb in 1890, they would combine behind one of their number and capture the nomination.

The struggle for the gubernatorial nomination in 1900 amounted to little more than a diversionary action, for the main forces were engaged in the assault on the Senate seat. Beginning with a debate in Limestone County on November 18, 1899, the campaign between the senior senator from Alabama and his former political protégé revolved acrimoniously around the central issue of the constitutional convention. Recalling his boyhood in a slaveless but anti-Negro family, Morgan spoke in favor of the convention without reservation. Johnston, while claiming to be just as good a white supremist as Morgan, opposed the convention in the name of economy and on behalf of that 16 percent of the white population who were illiterate. The contestants modulated this dominant tone with a number of secondary issues. Johnston tried to identify Morgan with plutocratic and monopolistic corporations, and condemned Morgan's frank championing of imperialism. Johnston's supporters suggested

[63] Mobile *Register*, November 11, 1899, January 11, 1900.
[64] Samford to Morgan, May 3, 1900; Jefferson County Campaign Committee to Morgan, February 3, 1900; C. W. Hooper to Morgan, April 3, 9, 1900; Morgan Papers, Library of Congress. Mobile *Register*, March 30, 1900.

Morgan might desire the same sort of government for Alabama that he favored for Hawaii.[65] Morgan's forces countered by pointing out Johnston's part in a questionable sale of University of Alabama lands to a private corporation. The two men also argued about which one had brought more capital into the state and which adhered most strictly to business principles. But the real conflict lay elsewhere. Johnston appealed to the fear of rule by a powerful oligarchy and Morgan sought to exploit racial fears.[66]

That racial fears were stronger was immediately apparent in April after the last primaries had been held. Morgan won, in all 54 counties that held primaries, a stunning victory which the Democratic legislative caucus merely confirmed when it voted 115-0 on November 15 to send Morgan back to Washington.[67] The congratulatory messages that poured in on Morgan in April interpreted the victory as an endorsement of clean politics and good government, as those slogans were understood by right-wing Democrats. Sydney J. Bowie, an ex-Congressman and railroad lawyer, enthused: "political morality and public decency have been signally vindicated."[68] Samford wrote that the people had returned Morgan in order to rebuke Johnston's machine tactics.

Samford also had a victory to celebrate. On April 26 the delegates chosen in the primaries met in the State Democratic Convention and nominated Samford over his

[65] Mobile *Register*, November 11, 1899.
[66] *Ibid.*, January 5, 14, 17, 20, 1900. See the 16-page pamphlet of Johnston-Morgan correspondence in the 1899 folder of the John Tyler Morgan Papers, Library of Congress. Mobile *Register*, March 30, 1900.
[67] Mobile *Register*, November 16, 1900.
[68] Bowie to Morgan, April 17, 1900, Morgan Papers, Library of Congress.

three opponents on the third ballot. His winning total of 246 votes was gathered from every section of the state, while Stallings, Waller, and Shelley had each run strongest in their home counties and those adjacent, though Stallings' connections as a labor lawyer won him a few delegates far from home.[69] The reform faction of the Democratic Party was now in full retreat.

The one certainty coming out of the election was that there would be a constitutional convention. Frank S. White, Morgan's campaign manager, announced after the primaries that "Morgan's victory is a triumph for better politics in Alabama. It means a constitutional convention. The state can no longer do without it. Alabama can not exist with a foundation under it of corruption at the polls. The constitutional convention and the elimination of fraudulent elections are bound to be the results."[70]

White was right, or at least his prediction was accurate. The state House of Representatives passed the convention bill promptly on December 1, 1900 by a vote of 65 to 17,[71] and the Senate approved it on December 7 after a 22 to 8 roll call.[72] Acting Governor W. D. Jelks signed it four days later.[73] The act provided for the same restrictions as that of 1898. The two essential reservations were that the new constitution was to include all of the existing limits on the state's power to tax, and was to provide for the same basis of apportionment as then prevailed. This time the act also required the governor to submit the new constitution for ratification. Governor Samford reinforced this provision later in the face of

[69] Montgomery *Advertiser*, April 27, 1900.
[70] *Ibid.*, April 17, 1900.
[71] Alabama, *House Journal, 1900*, 351.
[72] Alabama, *Senate Journal, 1900*, 318-320.
[73] Alabama, *Acts, 1900*, 224.

mounting skepticism by issuing his own personal pledge to submit the new constitution to the people.[74]

Before these reservations could be put to the test, the convention needed to be approved by the referendum set for April 23, 1901. If the elections of the previous August were any guide, this would be no problem. The total turnout had been only 162,000 and the Populists and Republicans had made a miserable showing. The Populist Party was in such disarray that A. T. Goodwyn at the beginning of the campaign of 1900 recommended that it disband and support Johnston and Stallings,[75] but the stubborn counsel of Frank Baltzell prevailed.[76] The Populists called a state convention for May 2, but with only six counties represented, nothing was done. A second attempt on May 30 produced a state ticket headed by Grattan B. Crowe, but he polled only 17,543 votes in the August election against Samford. The Republican candidate, John A. Steele, gathered another 28,291 votes, mostly outside the Black Belt. The *Living Truth*, then in the throes of transition to the Democratic Party, noted that the Populist primary had drawn only half of the number of voters who had participated in 1898.[77] Apathy was continuing to make inroads into the old Populist electorate.

Consequently the referendum on the question of the constitutional convention was an anticlimax. It would have taken something dramatic to block the convention at the referendum, and nothing dramatic happened. The Democratic State Committee met January 15, 1901 and declared the convention to be a party issue. The party

[74] Montgomery *Advertiser*, April 11, 1901.
[75] Mobile *Register*, November 17, 1899.
[76] Greenville *Living Truth*, December 14, 1899.
[77] *Ibid.*, June 1, 1900.

convention later issued a platform which reaffirmed the party's commitment to all of the limitations on the convention embodied in the act and which declared in unmistakable language that the time had come to remove the Negro from politics.[78] Significantly the chairman of the convention was Jones G. Moore who, along with T. G. Bush, was the state's leading ideologue among the defenders of the railroads. The State Committee put the campaign in the hands of John V. Smith, who in 1904 was to be Comer's opponent in the race for the presidency of the Railroad Commission. Smith had been the campaign manager for Samford in 1900 and was rewarded with an appointment to the commission by Acting Governor W. D. Jelks. Jelks also appointed Wiley Tunstall to his old post on the commission, from which he had been barred by Populist and Johnstonian opposition in 1895. A. M. Tunstall, his son, was the chief legislative architect of the convention bill. Thus there could be no mistake about who controlled the movement for disfranchisement.

The canvass was a veritable crusade for white supremacy and honest elections, two concepts that became interchangeable. The campaign committee of the Democratic Party flooded the state with literature and distinguished speakers. Frank S. White, soon to be the organizing genius of Alabama Progressivism, stated the purpose of the convention campaign when he told the convention of the Jefferson County Democratic Party that "time has demonstrated that the negro has no capacity to rule, but a great capacity to ruin. The negro . . . was disfranchised years ago by fraud and the purpose now was to do it by constitutional enactment."[79]

[78] Montgomery *Advertiser*, January 16, March 20, 1901.
[79] *Ibid.*, March 15, 1901.

Senator Morgan gave disfranchisement a boost with an endorsement in which he advised that the less talk there was about disfranchisement, the better it would be.[80] If he did not feel guilty, at least he felt uncomfortable about the fact that there were men who would find disfranchisement immoral. Not all of these fault-finders were outsiders. One Populist reader found Morgan's position ludicrous. "Our sympathies are with the 'oppressed of all nations,' " J. Culpepper wrote in reply to the senator. "Our sense of justice to distant people is keen, I reckon our 'conscience is void of offense' while we calmly plan to do our neighbors and fellow citizens injustice."[81]

Even though most active Populists, as well as the black-and-tan Republicans, opposed disfranchisement, there were others who agreed with Senator Morgan. Such diverse ex-Populists as Reuben Kolb, Joseph Manning, and William Skaggs approved of disfranchisement. The *Choctaw Alliance* deserted the ranks of Populist opponents of the bill to urge its readers to vote "yes" in the referendum. Charles P. Lane, a leading white Republican from Huntsville, came out in favor of disfranchisement, as did many other white Republicans who thought only the Negro stood in the way of their respectability.

The longing of Southerners for self-respect had something to do with the desire for disfranchisement. Southerners, after all, were Americans, and as long as electoral fraud was such a blatant part of the state's political life the strain on the consciences of the white people would be great. Yet they feared the results of an uncontrolled Negro electorate. To think of disfranchisement as a reform, then, as a cleansing of the electoral process, was a rationale that allowed whites to do what they wanted

[80] Montgomery *Advertiser*, March 22, 1901.
[81] *Ibid.*, March 31, 1901.

176

to do and feel good about it. True, it was a bit like sweeping dirt under the rug in order to present a clean house, but at least it honored the ideal of cleanliness. A resident of the Black Belt expressed this feeling in 1891 in explaining why the Belt was tired of the burden of controlling the Negro vote. "They don't love to soil their clothes," he said, "they want the black cloud lifted somehow, anyway, but surely and finally."[82]

The system was not only burdensome, it was precarious. The eruption of Populism had delayed the relief the Black Belt wanted and had stirred up a latent fear of real Negro power. Charles H. Greer of Perry County assured the constitutional convention in 1901 that "we people of the Black Belt do fear such [Negro] domination. . . ." Greer described the system of organized electoral fraud aptly as a " 'magnificent system' that can not be inherited or perpetuated. . . . It is Christianity, but not orthodox. . . . It is wrong but right. It is justice but injustice. It is life instead of death. That this subordination will continue, we do not believe."[83]

It was akin to closing banks to prevent bank robberies, but many Southern whites sincerely thought of disfranchisement as a reform. In spite of the fact that many true reformers endorsed it, the legitimacy of its reform credentials should be questioned. One need do no more than identify the men who were in control of the movement. They were hardly reformers. In fact, they represented the institutions that were the unwilling objects of reform. Further, the legislature that passed the Constitutional Convention bill and that had been elected after the campaign of 1900, in which disfranchisement was the issue, was thoroughly committed to the status quo.

[82] Birmingham *Age-Herald*, February 2, 1891.
[83] *Proceedings of the Convention*, III, 3,079-3,080.

While the newspapers and public speakers were amplifying the message that a "yes" vote in the referendum would mean reform and white supremacy, the legislature turned down attempts to enact a child labor bill, an anti-trust bill, a compulsory school attendance bill, a uniform text book bill, and an attempt to appropriate more money for schools. Another clue to the nature of this legislature was that it chose Alfred M. Tunstall as its acting speaker of the House, after the onset of the fatal illness of Speaker Francis Pettus, the author of the original disfranchising bill in 1892-93.

It is no surprise, then, that the chief threat to the disfranchisement movement was the widespread distrust of its leadership.[84] The friends of the measure compensated for this by emphasizing their notion that the convention would be dominated by the "best men in the state" and that no one had anything to fear from the best men. "Best men" meant those whose worth was emblemized by success in business or the professions.[85] Indeed, these were the men in Alabama who reversed the trend of one hundred years of democracy and faith in the common man by transmuting the right of universal suffrage into a privilege for a select few.

The April 23 referendum approved the Constitutional Convention 70,305 to 45,505.[86] Despite the importance of the issue and the fervor of the campaign, participation was at an all-time low. What opposition there was, as Appendix IV shows, predictably came from the "wiregrass" section of southeast Alabama, the hill counties, the mining towns, and the old Populist beats in general.

[84] *Ibid.*, March 17, 1901.
[85] *Ibid.*, January 16, April 20, 1901. Mobile *Register*, January 19, March 9, 1901.
[86] Montgomery *Advertiser*, April 25, 1901.

Of the 24 counties that voted against the convention, 17 had returned Populist majorities in 1896 and 4 of the remaining 7 showed Populist voting strength in 1896 above the state average. True to their pledge, patriotic poll managers neutralized any Negro opposition brave enough to present itself.[87] The large majorities for the convention in the Black Belt made it seem as if Negroes were voting for their own disfranchisement, but nothing could be further from the truth. There was, however, an air of tragic resignation. "It is good bye with poor white folks and niggers now," wrote one Negro editor, "for the train of disfranchisement is on the rail and will come thundering upon us like an avalanche, there is no use crying, we have got to shute the shute."[88]

[87] McMillan, *Constitutional Development in Alabama*, 260-261 and 261n.

[88] Huntsville *Journal*, April 20, 1900.

The Negro and Disfranchisement

E mancipation Day was celebrated on January 1, 1901 in Negro communities throughout Alabama just as it had been for many years. Numerous Negro speakers enumerated and detailed the progress of Negroes since the Civil War: progress made in literacy, land ownership, business, the professions, and the aggregate of personal achievements that reflected material progress. Measured against the lowly status of Negroes 35 years before, these advances seemed spectacular. But measured against the promise of American life, they were not great enough to dissuade whites from their belief in the doctrine of Negro inferiority. Some people felt Negroes had failed their test as Americans and deserved to be proscribed. Others, such as those for whom Tom Heflin spoke, feared that Negros were succeeding too well. For whatever reason, most white men in Alabama agreed on the necessity of disfranchisement. It was the biggest and most important downward readjustment in the long and bitter process of redefining the Negro's place in Southern life.

The trend in race relations had been evident in the South ever since Florida enacted the first Jim Crow law in 1887.[1] The tendency was to replace informal, fluctua-

[1] C. Vann Woodward, *The Strange Career of Jim Crow*, new and rev. edn., New York, 1957, 90-91, and "The Case of the

ting, and nonuniform patterns with legal, static, and uniform methods of treating Negroes. For example, Negroes could vote and participate in politics in various ways in some places during the 1890s. In other places countless stratagems of dubious morality were employed to neutralize or utilize their votes. The Constitutional Convention, said James Weatherly, was called to replace "this revolutionary method by legal machinery. . . ."[2]

The revolutionary methods had grown out of the vague feeling among many whites that there was something impermanent and not right about existing relations between the races. As a friend wrote to John W. DuBose, probably in 1902, "The Civil War . . . did not settle the problem. It is still unsettled and must remain so until settled right." But with no model of "right," there was no agreement on the spheres of life from which even the deferential Negro should be excluded.[3]

Consequently the pattern of race relations was highly fluid in Alabama in the period 1890 to 1910. Inconsistency was the primary characteristic.[4] The law in its various guises brought increasing order to the situation, and in doing so abolished both the freedom and the in-

---

Louisiana Traveler," in John A. Garraty, ed., *Quarrels That Have Shaped the Constitution*, New York, 1964, 145-158. Guion Griffis Johnson, "Southern Paternalism Toward Negroes After Emancipation," in Charles E. Wynes, ed., *The Negro in the South Since 1865; Selected Essays in American Negro History*, University, Ala., 1965, 103-134.

[2] Mobile *Register*, April 23, 1901.

[3] E. Y. Morris to John W. DuBose, n.d. [November 1902], DuBose Papers, ADAH.

[4] Newspapers sometimes used courtesy titles in referring to Negroes. See Birmingham *News*, February 21, 1895 and Birmingham *Age-Herald*, March 12, 1890. Negroes were evidently included on the venires of circuit courts in the early 1890s but not at the turn of the century. See the Huntsville *Gazette*, June 27, 1891 and Huntsville *Journal*, May 30, 1901.

security that went with inconsistency. The workings of the law could be seen in various fields. The city council of Montgomery passed an ordinance segregating the seating on streetcars in 1900. A Negro boycott that year failed to reverse the decision.[5] Jim Crow did not come to the railroad stations until January 6, 1902, when the Alabama Railroad Commission issued an order to the railroads operating in the state to maintain comfortable waiting rooms for their passengers. The order also required railroads to furnish separate waiting rooms for the two races.[6] The last company of Negro state militia, the Capitol City Guards, was not disbanded until 1905.[7] Meanwhile Birmingham's mayor announced that the new Birmingham jail, famed in folk song and pamphlets of protest, would be segregated at last.[8]

While recognizing the law's creative role in the structure of segregation, the growing separation of the races did exist independent of the law. This separation was even extended to the domain of death. A Negro newspaper noticed in 1900 that the Mississippi legislature had ordered the removal of the remains of the Honorable James Lynch from the white cemetery where they had rested since his death.[9] Two years later a Birmingham paper reported that "Will Mathis has requested Judge Lowry to have his hanging at a different hour from the time that the negro, Orlando Lester, will be hanged, and also that he be hanged from a different set of gallows."[10]

[5] Anniston *Union-Leader*, August 23, 1900 and Anniston *Baptist Leader*, September 13, 1900. Typically white papers had little to say about Negro news.
[6] Birmingham *Age-Herald*, January 7, 1902.
[7] Greenville *Living-Truth*, November 17, 1905.
[8] Birmingham *Age-Herald*, March 30, 1902.
[9] Mobile *Southern Watchman*, April 14, 1900.
[10] Birmingham *Age-Herald*, January 16, 1902.

Labor was a particularly sensitive area of race relations. The vice president of the Alabama Federation of Labor in 1902 was J. H. Beanes, a Negro, who was host for the organization's annual convention in Selma in that year. Community pressure was strong for the meeting to be segregated, but there was resistance. A delegate from Typographical Union Local 104 in Birmingham stated that "rather than see one accredited delegate, black or white, thrown out of this convention I would go to the woods and hold this meeting."[11] Union locals were thoroughly segregated, but conventions and governing bodies admitted Negroes in order to protect unionism from an increasingly hostile Negro labor force.

Perhaps nothing better captures the flux of patterns of segregation in the South at the turn of the century than the case of a Southerner with an impeccable pedigree, Mary Custis Lee, the daughter of Robert E. Lee. In 1902 she was arrested on the Washington, Alexandria & Mt. Vernon Railroad for refusing to move from the Negro section of the car where she had taken her seat. She was not a freedom rider; she simply was not aware that there was a law segregating the races on that railroad, and evidently was not used to such a practice being dictated by custom.[12]

Pathological evidence of the disturbed state of race relations was available in the statistics on lynching. The 10-year period 1889 to 1899 witnessed the most dramatic rise and decline of lynch law. The peak years were 1891 and 1892; in each year 24 people were dispatched by mobs in Alabama. The low point of a mere four lynchings was reached in 1900. But in 1901, a year of prosperity and rising cotton prices, contrary to the notion

[11] *Ibid.*, April 3, 22, 24, 1902.
[12] *Ibid.*, June 14, 19, 1902.

183

that the frequency of lynchings fluctuated in response to deviations from the long-term trend in cotton prices, there were 16 mob murders. It was no accident that disfranchisement was the single most important public issue that year.[13] This raises the question of the cause of the ebb and flow in this form of physical aggression. It is certainly true that "respectable" groups in society carried on campaigns to discourage people from resorting to rope and faggot. Thomas G. Jones went so far as to argue that the Thirteenth and Fourteenth Amendments gave federal courts jurisdiction in lynching cases against mob members who deprived Negro victims of equal protection and due process of law. Governor William Dorsey Jelks (1901-1906) was sincerely devoted to the prevention of lynching, for which he suffered some criticism. He was deeply disturbed by the fact that "human life is about as cheap in Alabama as it is anywhere. . . ." Yet he was unable to get lynchers convicted even when the evidence appeared overwhelming. In view of the continued immunity of lynchers it would seem that some factor other than social disapproval was responsible for the decline of lynching.[14]

[13] Arthur F. Raper, *The Tragedy of Lynching*, Chapel Hill, 1933, 30-31. National Association for the Advancement of Colored People, *Thirty Years of Lynching in the United States, 1889-1919*, New York, 1919, Appendix II. Also see the foldout map of lynchings in the Southern Commission on the Study of Lynchings, *Lynchings and What They Mean*, Atlanta, 1931.

[14] Henry S. Lynn, Jr., "Thomas Goode Jones and His Public Philosophy," unpub. senior thesis, Princeton University, 1966, 108-110. Alabama, *Acts, 1903*, Governor's Message. Paul Speake to Lieutenant Governor Russell M. Cunningham, October 5, 1904, Governor's Office Records, ADAH. Between 1900 and 1930, 132 people were lynched in Alabama. Though convictions were obtained in only three of the cases, this was a higher ratio of convictions to cases than the national average. James H. Chadbourn, *Lynching and the Law*, Chapel Hill, 1933, 13. Three

It is likely that the high rate of extralegal sanctions against Negroes in the 1890s was related to the fluidity and uncertainty in patterns of race relations. The potential for conflict was greater as long as patterns of permissible conduct were poorly defined and changing. At the end of the decade and after, as legal devices were used increasingly to define and make uniform the prescribed boundaries of the permissible in race relations, anxious whites felt less need to assert their superiority. The Negro leader and president of Alabama A. and M. College at Normal, W. H. Councill, sensed this when he told an Emancipation Day audience in 1901 "that the salvation of the negro in this country depends upon drawing the social lines tighter, tighter all the while, North and South. The moment they become slack the white man becomes brutal—the negro goes down forever."[15]

Councill's statement also reflected the deepening disillusionment of Negroes in the face of their increasing proscription. This despair was expressed in the half-dozen extant Negro newspapers in Alabama. As the 1890s wore on, Negroes postponed their quest for full citizenship through political self-assertion and turned to the more traditional paths favored by Booker T. Washington and W. H. Councill.[16] Accommodation, material

convictions were obtained after an Elmore County lynching in 1900. Governor Jelks pardoned all but the main instigator after they had served one year of a 10-year sentence. Birmingham *Age-Herald*, June 9, 1902.

[15] Mobile *Register*, January 2, 1901.

[16] August Meier, *Negro Thought in America, 1880-1915: Racial Ideologies in the Age of Booker T. Washington*, Ann Arbor, Mich., 1963, traces the gradual shift in Negro thought in response to worsening conditions from an ideology emphasizing "integration" and political rights to one stressing the themes of self-help, racial solidarity, and emigration.

self-improvement, and dependence on upper class whites seemed to be the only choice short of emigration for Negroes. H. C. Binford, schoolteacher, city alderman, and newspaper editor, in 1899 told his readers: "there is nothing in politics for us, it makes no difference which side wins none of them want the Negro." A year later he glumly admitted that "we have gotten use to being slighted and have ceased to kick. What's the use?"[17] Negro newspapers of all shades of opinion put increased emphasis on the need to acquire education and property.[18]

Prospects were so gloomy that Washington thought that "before we [Negroes] can make much progress we must decide whether or not the Negro is to be a permanent part of the South."[19] Not only was there a Negro emigration movement of unknown strength, and white propagandists of colonization like John Temple Graves, Thomas Pearce Bailey, and John Tyler Morgan, but newspapers were full of plans to replace the Negro labor force and population of the South with white immigrants. The atmosphere was so tense that W. H. Councill surrendered to pessimism. In a controversial article in *The Forum* in 1899 he arrived at the conclusion that everything the Negro had was at the sufferance of the whites and that there was no future for the Negro in America.[20]

Councill's despair led to two patterns of thought. On the one hand there was the policy of accommodation—and Councill was an expert accommodator. In 1901, as always, he needed funds from the state government, and

[17] Huntsville *Journal*, November 10, 1899, February 1, 1901.
[18] *The Christian Hope*, March 22, 1901. *The Journal*, December 8, 1899. *The Truth*, August 26, 1905. Tuscaloosa *Chronicle*, December 17, 1898. *Southern Watchman*, December 23, 1899.
[19] Huntsville *Journal*, October 13, 1899.
[20] William H. Councill, "The Future of the Negro," *The Forum*, XXVII (July 1899), 570-577.

applied to Governor Samford hat-in-hand. His letter argued that the state was getting a good deal because "all of this vast property is deeded to the State of Alabama. The State has donated money only for a normal school which is putting into rural districts as well as the towns teachers who are not only competent to teach, but who are in harmony with the institutions and customs of the South." To complete this example of the policy of accommodation, Councill's request was endorsed by General William C. Oates who played the role of upper-class paternalist. Oates wrote that he thought "Councill a good man and fine manager of this school and politically all right."[21]

The other fork of Councill's two-pronged pessimism was the assertion of a perennial American Negro myth, "repatriation." The redemption of Africa from barbarism by American Negroes was a satisfying dream for Negroes who were alienated from American life and suffering from a poor self-image.[22]

The progressive alienation of Negroes sprang from several sources. One prime cause was the dwindling sphere of economic opportunity. Negro newspapers in Alabama were aware, as was Councill, of the Negro's weakening position in the job market. But while the Negro is anxious to work," commented the *Southern Watchman*, "there are those who are using every effort to deprive him of the wherewithal to earn his daily bread."[23]

[21] W. H. Councill to Governor W. J. Samford, January 4, 1901, with an endorsement by W. C. Oates, January 18, 1901, in the folder marked "Bids for Bonds 1905," Governor's Office Records, ADAH.

[22] Councill, "Future of the Negro," 577.

[23] September 2, 1899. That Negroes were faring progressively worse in the job market was common knowledge at the time.

But it was the total impact of adverse change that Negroes experienced. One Negro newspaper reacted with bitterness, indignation, despair, bewilderment, and resignation:

> The 'Jim Crow' car law, which forces the respectable and the disrespectable Negro to travel in the same car is infamous enough, an insult is being added to injury continually. Have those in power forgotten that there is a God, and do they not know that every seed of unjust discrimination sown will in some due time come up. . . . The Negro is as docile as he can be . . . and day after day he is reminded through the daily papers . . . that some additional project is on foot, or is about to be promulgated to stand as a menace to his development, or a curb to his ambitious manhood . . . and we wonder what the harvest will be.[24]

Leaders of the white community were as aware as Negroes were of the deterioration in race relations, for the future of the Negro was a popular topic of public discussion. One evidence of this concern and interest was The Southern Society for the Promotion of the Study of Race Conditions and Problems in the South. Edgar Gardner Murphy conceived the idea and quickly enlisted Hilary Herbert and a blue-ribbon membership. The result was a widely publicized meeting in May 1900 in Montgomery. The conference aired a broad range of opinion, from John Temple Graves' call for colonization of Negroes in Africa to William A. MacCorkle's insistence that Negroes be treated as citizens.[25] A Negro observer re-

---

See Carl Kelsey, "The Evolution of Negro Labor," *The Annals,* XXI (January-June 1903), 55-76.

[24] Mobile *Southern Watchman,* May 12, 1900.

[25] *Race Problems of the South: Report of the Proceedings of the First Annual Conference Held Under the Auspices of the*

ported that there was no support for Graves' proposal nor for the argument of a North Carolina man that Southern states ought not to educate Negroes. Other speakers evidently met significant opposition when they expressed their belief in the inherent inferiority of Negroes, when they maintained that Negro criminality was getting worse, and when they thought that Negro religious life should be guided and controlled by whites. Everyone was opposed to lynch law.[26] According to Murphy, even the Northerners agreed that enfranchising Negroes was a mistake.[27]

This is an important indication of the state of informed opinion at the time of the Alabama Constitutional Convention. Booker T. Washington himself was yielding before it. In November 1899 he had tried unsuccessfully to rally Negro opposition to a disfranchising measure pending before the Georgia Assembly.[28] At the same time, however, he was talking of backing an educational qualification for suffrage as a means of insuring that Negroes would be judged on the same basis as whites. G. W.

Southern Society for the Promotion of the Study of Race Conditions and Problems in the South at Montgomery, Alabama, May 8, 9, 10, 1900. Hilary Herbert served as president, Edgar Gardner Murphy as secretary, and J.L.M. Curry as one of the vice presidents. Jeff Falkner and James Weatherly, leading railroad lawyers, were among the prominent Alabamians involved. Herbert continued in his role as spokesman of the white South on race relations. See James Ford Rhodes to Herbert, November 12, 1904; Herbert to Theodore Roosevelt, November 12, 1904; Theodore Roosevelt to Herbert, November 12, 1904; Hilary Herbert Papers, University of North Carolina.

[26] Mobile *Southern Watchman*, May 19, 1900.

[27] Edgar Gardner Murphy to Booker T. Washington, March 28, 1900, B. T. Washington Papers, Library of Congress.

[28] Booker T. Washington to T. Thomas Fortune, November 7, and 10, 1899, B. T. Washington Papers, Library of Congress. Woodward, *Origins of the New South*, 323, 337-338.

Atkinson of West Virginia questioned the wisdom of such a deal with white leaders. Atkinson advised Washington that he thought the Democratic leaders of the South were using Washington and that any voting law would be administered so as to discriminate against Negroes.[29]

As later events proved, it was naïve of Washington to think registrars would apply suffrage tests fairly to both races. Atkinson grasped the essential evil of the Southern system when he understood this. But Washington understood that he had very little choice; he was simply trying to use his contacts among white leaders to make the best deal possible under the circumstances.[30]

The problem was, those bent on disfranchisement were no longer restrained by the federal government or by opposition from within the state. The small force of 14 Populists and Republicans in the 155-member convention could do little, though they stood fast against limiting suffrage. The sizable opposition to disfranchisement registered in the referendum, more interested in white votes than black, was not nearly sufficient to block the powerful coalition whose divergent interests happened to focus on disfranchisement. There was so little resistance of any kind that there was little need to camouflage the purpose and intent of the convention.

"And what is it that we want to do?" asked John B.

[29] G. W. Atkinson to Booker T. Washington, October 20, 1899, B. T. Washington Papers, Library of Congress.

[30] Meier, *Negro Thought in America, 1880-1915*, 100-118. A convenient introduction to the interpretations of and literature about Washington is Hugh Hawkins, ed., *Booker T. Washington and His Critics: The Problem of Negro Leadership*, "Problems in American Civilization," Boston, 1962. Many of the controversies about Washington will be solved with the appearance of the forthcoming biography by Louis Harlan.

Knox in his presidential address to the Constitutional Convention of Alabama as it opened its deliberations on May 22, 1901. "Why it is within the limits imposed by the Federal Constitution, to establish white supremacy in this State."[31] The subordinate position of the Negro race was about to be written into the fundamental law. "Our purpose is plain," delegate Thomas Watts asserted some days later. "It is not denied by any man upon the floor of this Convention or in this State."[32]

There was such a consensus on disfranchising Negroes that the main question facing the convention was not whether to do it but how to do it without violating the federal constitution on the one hand and the pledge not to disfranchise any white men on the other hand.

The committee of the convention in charge of the delicate task of drafting the suffrage article was the Committee on Suffrage and Elections, composed of 21 lawyers and including 9 members from the Black Belt. The chairman of the committee was Thomas W. Coleman from Eutaw in Greene County. Coleman was a graduate of Princeton and the University of Alabama Law School, a former Associate Justice of the Alabama Supreme Court, an officer in the Confederate army, a member of the Constitutional Convention of 1875, and the president of the Merchants and Farmers Bank of Eutaw. Of such stuff was the convention made.[33]

While the rest of the convention settled down for an uncomfortably hot and contentious summer of parliamentary maneuvering involving the important side issues of the convention, which will be discussed in the following chapter, the Suffrage Committee met for the first time

[31] *Proceedings of the Convention*, 1941, I, 8.
[32] *Ibid.*, II, 2,389.
[33] McMillan, *Constitutional Development in Alabama*, 263, 266-267.

191

on May 29 and began its long and arduous task of shaping a suffrage article. It drew on the suffrage provisions of other Southern states, as well as many ordinances submitted by delegates, sent by constituents, and published by newspapers.[34] Through the month of June the committee debated in private the sundry suggestions of how best to disfranchise the Negro. Even without diabolical registrars, the constitution could eliminate Negroes by applying tests that took advantage of differing social conditions. Property tests, literacy tests, residence requirements, the poll tax, and disqualification for conviction of certain crimes all fell into this category.

The central problem was how, or whether, to provide for the whites who would be disfranchised by the anti-Negro provisions unless some special loophole were created for them. There is no doubt that many people in the state envisaged the disfranchisement of poor whites as well as poor Negroes.[35]

In his opening address President Knox provided a rationale for those wishing to disfranchise whites while not violating the pledge of the party. On the one hand there were 236,476 white males of voting age of whom 31,681 were illiterate but who were not to be disfranchised. On the other hand there were 181,345 Negro males of voting age of whom 107,946 were literate and who were to be disfranchised. "We are pledged," said Knox, " 'not to deprive any white man of the right to vote,' but this does not extend unless this Convention

[34] A good analysis of the various proposals is in *ibid.*, 274-279.
[35] *Ibid.*, 279-280, 285-288, 292-295. The *Advertiser*, the *Register*, and the Alabama Press Association (by a vote of 19 to 11) favored ignoring the pledge not to disfranchise whites. The other two major dailies, the Birmingham *News*, and the *Age-Herald*, also opposed the grandfather clause.

chooses to extend it beyond the right of voters now living."[36]

The Committee on Suffrage and Elections accepted Knox's rationalization. When it finally made its recommendations on June 30, the majority report was a grotesquely complicated document that eventually became Article VIII of the new constitution with very few alternations.

Article VIII, as finally passed, contained two distinct "plans." The permanent plan contained the disfranchising provisions, the qualifications that were to be a permanent part of the organic law. The temporary plan consisted of the devices designed to permit those of the favored race (or party) who would not be able to qualify under the permanent rules to register under special provisions. The temporary plan expired on January 1, 1903.

The permanent plan set up a most elaborate maze through which one had to grope to claim the privilege of becoming an elector. The basic conditions for registration were that a person must be a male citizen, or alien who had declared his intention of becoming a citizen, 21 years of age who had resided in the state for two years, the county for one year, and the precinct for three months. The second requirement was the ability to read and write any article of the United States Constitution, unless physical disability caused the deficiency. Except for the physically disabled, the prospective elector also must have been engaged in some lawful employment for the greater part of the preceding 12 months. If this requirement could not be met there was the alternative property qualification of 40 acres of land on which the prospective elector lived, or the ownership of real or personal property assessed for taxes at a value of $300 and on which

---

[36] *Proceedings of the Convention*, I, 8.

the taxes had been paid. There was, in addition, a long list of disqualifying crimes, including vagrancy. Having become an elector, the last cul-de-sac in the labyrinth was the cumulative poll tax of $1.50 per year that had to be paid on or before the first day of February preceding the election in which the elector offered to vote.

Those who could meet all but the literacy and property qualifications were provided with loopholes that were to be open for only a few months. For this purpose Louisiana's famous "Grandfather Clause" was adapted by Alabama, indeed the only novelty of the suffrage article, so that it became the "Fighting Grandfather Clause." This device allowed those to register who had served honorably in the land or naval forces of the United States or Confederate States in any war from 1812 on, or who were descendants of such veterans. If this were not enough, there was the further provision to register "all persons who are of good character and who understand the duties and obligations of citizenship under a republican form of government."

From July 23 to August 3 the convention gave itself over to a remarkably frank debate on the suffrage article. The most significant attack on the article came from an important group of men who questioned the "Fighting Grandfather" clause. In their minority report, they pointed out that the clause set up an arbitrary standard which discriminated against citizens of the United States on the basis of race and was therefore a violation of the federal Constitution. They also asserted that it was undemocratic, that it insulted white men by requiring less of them than of Negroes, that it was open to manipulation, fraud, and perjury.[37] These men wanted suffrage requirements that applied to all alike.

[37] *Ibid.*, I, 1,264-1,266. The United States Supreme Court in a 5-3 decision handed down on April 27, 1903 refused to rule

William C. Oates, the chief spokesman of the minority of the Committee on Suffrage and Elections, received support on the floor from Thomas G. Jones who spoke in the tradition of patrician paternalism. George P. Harrison and Stanley H. Dent, prominent men who had been colleagues of Jones in the gold Democratic Party in 1896, also signed the minority report. Senators Morgan and Edmund W. Pettus made their opposition known in letters to the convention.[38] The instructive thing about this opposition to the grandfather clause was that it was not all of one coloration.

The fourth signer of the minority report was Frank S. White of Birmingham who doubled at the convention as the leader of Comer's crew of railroad regulators. J.L.M. Curry was also opposed to providing loopholes for ignorant white men,[39] and Robert J. Lowe of Birmingham, Chairman of the State Democratic Executive Committee and a man with some Progressive leanings, thought the grandfather clause was "the very repudiation of fairness."[40]

Evidently, the Big Mules and the Progressives shared a pessimism about human nature as well as a passion for social order. Much of the discussion of the grandfather clause and white suffrage was based on a belief in the existence of a large, powerful, and dangerous portion of the population that was "ignorant and vicious."[41] The convention was dedicated to limiting the suffrage to the

---

against Alabama's grandfather clause. Justice Harlan dissented magnificently, but Justice Holmes for the majority noted that the court could not grant relief to the plaintiff unless it was prepared to supervise voting within the state. *Giles v. Harris*, 189 U.S. 475 (October term, 1902).

[38] *Proceedings of the Convention*, III, 2,863 and 2,797.
[39] Mobile *Register*, May 22, 1901.
[40] *Proceedings of the Convention*, III, 2,826.
[41] *Ibid.*, III, 3,569; IV, 4,708; and II, 2,691.

"intelligent and virtuous." Samuel Blackwell, a Progressive from Morgan County, expressed his desire to put the suffrage only in the hands of competent men so as to insure good government. He affirmed his belief that "nature has marked the weak and incompetent to be protected by Government, rather than to be the directors of the Government."[42]

This outlook received support from Alabama's most famous reformer, Edgar Gardner Murphy. The crusading rector of St. John's Episcopal church in Montgomery wrote an "open letter" to the Constitutional Convention, in which he voiced his opposition to the grandfather clause. Then in the midst of a campaign to free the state of the evil of child labor, Murphy expressed doubts about the natural goodness of man. His social reforms were essentially aimed at putting institutional limits on human capacity for evil. But he also believed in secular progress, in industrialization, and in improving the material and moral condition of man. He wanted to release the creative energies of men who were cramped and rendered inefficient by human institutions. An aristocracy of the educated would achieve that progress,[43] so limiting suffrage to the "intelligent and virtuous" was a step in the right direction.

It is quite likely that some of the opposition to the grandfather clause was influenced by personal obligations

[42] *Ibid.*, III, 3,024.

[43] Daniel Levine, "Edgar Gardner Murphy: Conservative Reformer," *The Alabama Review*, XV, April 1962, 100-116; and *Varieties of Reform Thought*, Madison, Wis., 1964, 78-94. Edgar Gardner Murphy, *Problems of the Present South: A Discussion of Certain of the Educational, Industrial and Political Issues in the Southern States*, New York, 1905; *The Basis of Ascendancy: A Discussion of Certain Principles of Public Policy Involved in the Development of the Southern States*, New York, 1909.

to Booker T. Washington who was actively soliciting the aid of white businessmen for a letter-writing campaign.[44] Murphy and Oates, in particular, were on easy terms with him, and Thomas G. Jones was appointed to a federal district judgeship in October 1901 by his grace. Washington's most open move was a petition to the convention signed by 15 prominent Negroes which humbly asked that Negroes be allowed to share in the choice of their rulers.[45]

This "humble and unnecessary" petition was not well received in some quarters of the Negro community. The *Southern Watchman* stigmatized Washington as "the white man's ideal Negro" and entered an eloquent plea for racial justice. "Do not show us how to be men and then blame us for being men," wrote the *Watchman*, which claimed to be speaking for "every intelligent Negro in America" when it asserted "that they are not satisfied with the present condition of things in the South."[46]

Neither protesting Negroes, with whatever tone of voice, nor sympathetic whites could budge the majority. Defending the suffrage article from attacks on the left as well as the right, the convention tabled the minority report by a vote of 109 to 23. The "no" votes were cast by the opponents of the grandfather clause, joined by Populists and Republicans who were against the whole idea of suffrage restriction in spite of the inducements offered by the temporary plan.

---

[44] Belton Gilreath to Booker T. Washington, July 9, 1901, B. T. Washington Papers. For the role of Washington in Jones' appointment see Bond, *Negro Education in Alabama*, 209-210. Washington's role was public knowledge at the time, and Southern whites were further annoyed in the fall of 1901 by his luncheon with Theodore Roosevelt at the White House.

[45] *Proceedings of the Convention*, I, 191.

[46] Mobile *Southern Watchman*, June 1, 8, 1901.

To Knox and Coleman and other prominent champions of the clause, the most beautiful thing about the temporary plan was that it was temporary. Delegates who represented poor-white voters, whose support for the new constitution the compromise was designed to secure, made several attempts to widen and lengthen the loophole. A minor irony is the fact that the principal doctrinal support for belief in the common (white) man, or in the "democratic myth," was white supremacy—the doctrine that "the white man was always qualified to vote. He inherits his qualities. . . . The meanest white man in the State is within the saving clause. . . ."[47] The adherents of such a philosophy failed in their attempt to make the grandfather clause permanent,[48] and the convention also defeated other attempts to postpone the terminal date of the temporary plan.[49]

In order to move the convention in the other direction representatives from the Black Belt tried to raise the age at which a man became exempt from the poll tax from 45 to 60. This was in reality a fight over white disfranchisement. After a series of close votes that indicated the restrictionists had a slight majority, the issue was compromised by setting the age of exemption at 45, but providing that the legislature could raise it to 60.[50] Similarly, for fear of creating opposition to the new constitution in the ratifying referendum, the convention gave north Alabama its way by defeating the Black Belt's attempt to raise the property requirements for suffrage.[51]

[47] *Proceedings of the Convention*, III, 3,052-3,053; the speaker is Mike Sollie.
[48] *Ibid.*, III, 3,450.
[49] *Ibid.*, III, 3,052, 3,116-3,117, 3,125, 3,141. The two votes were 64-53 and 63-49.
[50] *Ibid.*, III, 3,402, 3,405, 3,409, 3,411. McMillan, *Constitutional Development in Alabama*, 301-302.
[51] *Proceedings of the Convention*, III, 4,877.

The only victory won by those who wanted to expand the electorate beyond the limits set by the majority of the Committee on Suffrage and Elections came in regard to aliens. The majority report had reversed existing practice by not providing for the registration of aliens who had declared their intention of becoming citizens. On the motion and initiative of C. P. Beddow, a spokesman for Birmingham labor, the convention changed the majority report so that "first paper" aliens could register and vote. Beddow won another victory by getting the wording of the article changed so that strikers would not be proscribed by the ban against persons who were not regularly employed.[52]

The meager results of attempts to change the suffrage article might give the impression that the debates were dull. Nothing could be further from the truth.[53]

Among other things, the debates disclosed the gnawing sense of guilt that permeated the convention. They bore witness to the recent suggestion of Professor C. Vann Woodward that the peculiarities of the Southern identity owe much to the un-American experiences of defeat, poverty, and guilt. Every time electoral fraud was mentioned, every time a delegate argued that the suffrage article did not violate the Fifteenth Amendment, every time the pledge not to disfranchise any white man was explained away, the uneasy conscience was briefly exposed. Dr. Russell M. Cunningham remarked in a revealing jest that he had often in his life wanted to be a lawyer. "This is one time," he said, "I am glad that I am not. If I were a lawyer I would not only be expected to have a conscience, but I would also be expected

[52] *Ibid.*, III, 3,188, 3,224, 3,238.
[53] *Ibid.*, II, 2,704 through III, 3,099. The suffrage article was approved for engrossment on August 3. *Ibid.*, III, 3,452. The final vote is found on *ibid.*, IV, 5,866.

to have an opinion, and leave the conscience to rest. (Laughter)"[54]

Mike Sollie could not ignore his conscience. A rather traditional thinker who nevertheless supported Comer's drive for railroad regulation, Sollie was oppressed by the thought that the South's "history records a grievous error. . . . It was contrary to the principles of freedom and liberty embedded deep in the American heart that slavery should exist in our midst." And Sollie feared that the South's present and future woes were growing out of this sin of the fathers. "Our prostrated and devastated South," he said, "our unequal opportunities in the race of progress and the graves of our dead heroes are all parts of the painful accounting we have thus far given for the sin committed."[55]

The uncomfortable themes of sin and retribution were suffocated under the patchwork quilt of the orthodox view of the past. This popular view gained authority from repetition, and dissent became perilous. The best of the speeches evoked all of the proper and approved historical symbols: the pernicious Yankee Slave Trader, the hallowed Founding Fathers, the Happy Slave, the glorious Lost Cause, the Faithful Retainer, Black Reconstruction, the Depraved Negro, the Blessed Redemption, the Required Corruption to maintain White Supremacy, and the Necessary Purification of the Ballot. The past was marshaled to justify the present.

The present that needed justifying was a time of racial

[54] Woodward, "The Search for Southern Identity," in *The Burden of Southern History*, Baton Rouge, La., 1960, 16-21. *Proceedings of the Convention*, III, 2,995. For other evidence of twinges of conscience see *ibid.*, II, 2,711, 2,718; III, 2,792, 2,849, 2,884, 2,969, 2,978, 2,995, 2,997, 3,001, 3,038, 3,039, 3055-3,056.
[55] *Ibid.*, III, 3,043-3,044.

proscription. In the melange of opinion four varieties of racial attitudes can be isolated. They might be called: (a) Orthodox White Supremacy, (b) Paternalism, (c) Radicalism, and (d) race-baiting Demagoguery. The orthodox white supremacy was based on what was taken to be the simple and demonstrable fact of the superiority of the white race and its inherited capacity to rule. This fact was supported by an evolutionary conception of history, but Providential rather than Darwinian evolution. In this view, "the records of history are largely narratives of man's advancement from barbarism to civilization. The great, dominant, white races of the earth have been thousands of years in reaching their present state of development."[56] Meanwhile the Negro race had been completely stationary. The turn-of-the-century euphoria about western civilization, which did so much to abet the forces of uplift, in this case contributed to the contrast between the races which justified the conclusion that "the white race must dominate because it is the superior race. . . ."[57]

The key concept in the orthodox outlook was that there should be little or no differentiation among Negroes. Every Negro should carry the value that was assigned to the race as a whole by the white community's stereotype.

By looking at Negroness in much the same way that they looked at membership in the lower class, paternalists were able to recognize differences among Negroes. They normally wanted to hold out hope to the Negro that in the future he might individually improve his status and attain some of the rights of citizenship of which he was

[56] *Ibid.*, III, 2,782. Emmet O'Neal is the speaker.
[57] *Ibid.*, III, 2,783. O'Neal again.

being denuded.[58] Where orthodox racism was based on a vague and erroneous genetics, paternalism was based on a more plastic social judgment. Some paternalists hoped that in the distant future, equal education and employment opportunities would enable the Negro to stand on his own as a full citizen.[59]

But in 1901 the Negro was not a full citizen. In fact, it seemed as if he was being pushed entirely out of society. In this atmosphere the distinctive note of paternalism was its insistence that society was an organic whole of which the Negro was an integral, although subservient, part and that the white man was charged with moral responsibility for his welfare. "The negro race is under us," argued ex-Governor Thomas G. Jones, ". . . we have shorn him of all political power. . . . In return for that, we should extend to him . . . all the civil rights that will fit him to be a decent and self-respecting, law-abiding and intelligent citizen of this state."[60]

Even more feeble in 1901 was the idealistic hope of racial cooperation. This radical point of view, extraordinary for the time, found its spokesmen among the Republicans and Populists. There was, for instance, John H. Porter from Coosa County who had in turn been a Whig, a Populist, and a Republican. Porter was not afraid to dispute the orthodox view of the past or of the present. He stated that all the Negro asked for as a citizen of the state was "to choose between two or more the one he prefers to rule over him. This right," said Porter, "in my judgment, he should have."[61]

[58] *Ibid.*, III, 3,005 and 3,056. The speaker is Dr. Russell M. Cunningham.

[59] *Ibid.*, IV, 4,297-4,299. The speaker is Leslie Brooks of Mobile.

[60] *Ibid.*, IV, 4,303.

[61] *Ibid.*, III, 3,016, 3,018-3,019.

The Republicans had been the original experimenters with biracial politics and still had obligations to their constituents. But it would be too much to say that the Populists had taken up where the Republicans left off. I. L. Brock chided O. D. Street, who was in the process of becoming a Republican, for his opposition to disfranchisement. "You know the populists always were willing and ready for the negro to be disfranchised if it could be done without disfranchising the white man, . . ." he wrote.[62] But the fact is that the foremost champion of Negro suffrage at the convention was a Populist who was also in transit to the Republican party.

Newton B. Spears was a Tennesseean and the son of a Union general. These facts do not explain his radical views on race, but perhaps they help account for his antipathy toward the Democratic Party and his freedom from its mythology. Men who were still Populists in 1901 were likely to be more unorthodox in their views on race relations than was the mass of Populists when the party was at full strength in 1894-96. Only congenital "outsiders" would cling to such an obviously dead party. In addition to this, those Populist politicians who wanted to make the shift to Republicanism had to prove they were good Republicans at heart, and standing up for Negro suffrage was one way to do this in 1901, for the lily whites had not yet taken over the party.

Spears declared that Negroes could no longer be treated as slaves. They were citizens. He challenged any delegate to stand up and "contend that the ordinance we are now considering does not abridge the privilege of voting . . ." of both black and white men. He praised the Thirteenth, Fourteenth, and Fifteenth Amendments,

[62] I. L. Brock to Oliver D. Street, September 13, 1902, Street Papers, University of Alabama.

203

characterized the proposed voter registration system as tyranny, lauded William Lloyd Garrison and Lincoln, swore by Old Hickory Jackson, called the equalitarian Jefferson the greatest Populist, and thoroughly antagonized the convention.[63]

Spears' defiance of the convention extended to thinking that Negroes should have the right to vote. He thought, in fact, that they should have justice. As the convention recovered from that idea, he asked it most prophetically if it wanted "to pursue a course and a policy that will make the negro look to Washington and not to Montgomery for protection?"[64]

Another theme, and one not at all muted, was that of strident and aggressive racism cast in terms of race conflict. This jarring chord was struck by the budding demagogue, J. Thomas Heflin. On the verge of a political career that would take him to the United States Senate, Tom Heflin was a new type in Alabama.[65] He became famous as a storyteller and spokesman for the common white man. But if his performance in the convention of 1901 is a true indication, while he was talking for the poor whites he was voting for the rich ones.[66]

The tone of Heflin's depiction of race relations, even where he was not diverging from the orthodox view, was aggressive and antagonistic. The Negro was not merely subordinate to the white race, but he was ordained by God to be the white man's servant. And Heflin did not stop at this sort of revival of the old pro-slavery argument. When, in order to rationalize its action on suffrage, the convention resorted to the theory that the ballot was

[63] *Proceedings of the Convention*, III, 2,978-2,981, 2,967-2,973.
[64] *Ibid.*, III, 2,978.
[65] Woodward, *Origins of the New South*, 340.
[66] See Appendix VII.

not a right but a privilege, Heflin went one step further and maintained that it was a natural right for the white man but a privilege for the Negro. He insisted that Negroes and whites should never be required to compete on the same level. "If you want to make a foot race," said Heflin, "let us make it with the descendants of our own tribe."[67] Tribalism and race conflict were basic to Heflin's philosophy.

Heflin thought the impending conflict rendered it mere folly to educate or otherwise equip the Negro. Consequently he supported the move (which ended in a compromise) to provide for separate Negro and white school systems, each supported by the taxes paid directly by that race. In the first place, thought Heflin, "he doesn't need encouragement. . . . Why as soon as you elevate him you ruin him."[68] But more importantly, it was dangerous. Heflin gave new clothes to the old antebellum fear of educating the slaves. "The negroes are being educated very rapidly," he told his fellow delegates who professed to think Negroes incapable of education, "and I say in the light of all the history of the past, some day when the two separate and distinct races are thrown together, some day the clash will come and the survival of the fittest, and I do not believe it is incumbent upon us to lift him up and educate him on an equal footing that he may be armed and equipped when the combat comes."[69] Heflin spoke with the voice of twentieth-century frustrations.

The shrewdness of the authors of the suffrage article, in reconciling the aims of the various racial theories, was revealed when the debates and motions to amend had

[67] *Proceedings of the Convention*, III, 2,843.
[68] *Ibid.*, III, 2,848.
[69] *Ibid.*, IV, 4,302-4,303.

run their ineffective course. The vote to approve the entire article showed an overwhelming victory, 95-19. The minority consisted of those on the right who opposed the grandfather clause and those on the left who adhered to the principle of universal manhood suffrage. Eleven of the "no" votes came from the Republicans and Populists. All of the "yes" votes were Democratic.[70] Disfranchisement was a reality after 10 years of talk and agitation.

The differential in voting between the races was immediate and marked. In 1906 there were 205,278 whites registered in Alabama, 83 percent of the male whites of voting age. Only 3,654 Negroes, 2 percent of the adult men, were registered. That has been much the ratio until the campaign to increase Negro registration in the South in the 1960s.

The effect of the new constitution on white voting is more debatable. Governor Jelks was anxious to prove that the constitution worked properly. One of the big fears of white-county delegates was that the registrars would not register white men whom they suspected of improper political leanings. Could Christ and his Disciples register under the good character clause? "That would depend entirely on which way he was going to vote," said John W. A. Sanford.[71] After the constitution was in effect, Senator Morgan became quite worried about reports that registrars in the Black Belt were registering "politically reliable" Negroes.

I think you are perhaps unnecessarily alarmed [re-

[70] McMillan, *Constitutional Development in Alabama*, 306.
[71] *Proceedings of the Convention*, III, 3,197. Discussions of white disfranchisement were too numerous to enumerate here. I have 45 notations, only a partial listing. Some of the more illuminating remarks are found in III, 3,017, 3,079, 3,180, 3,205, 3,276, 3,298, 3,367-3,368, 3,391.

sponded Jelks]. The Board of Appointment spent thirty days selecting these Registrars and in every instance we were assured positively that the appointees would carry out the spirit of the Constitution, which looks to the registration of all men not convicted of crime, and only a few negroes. . . .

What is distressing me now is the general apathy on the subject of the Payment of polls.[72]

Whether or not it resulted from apathy or poverty, Governor Jelks had cause for concern about the nonpayment of the poll tax. However, the figures for registration and for poll tax receipts might shed some light on a murky point of interpretation. Scholars are in dispute about the reasons for the rapid decline in white voting.[73] Undoubtedly both apathy and disfranchisement played a part. The question is, which should get the greater emphasis? The crux of the problem is that there is no way to measure the number of adult men who would have voted had they not been prohibited by some legal barrier.

Perhaps some rough indication can be devised to measure the effect of at least the poll tax requirement in Alabama. The separate acts of registering *and* paying poll tax *both* had to be accomplished to enable one to vote. Men over 45 years of age were exempt from the poll tax but still had to register. By assuming that everyone 45 or older actually did register, it is possible to calculate that there were at least 132,117 men registered in 1904 who were required also to pay the poll tax. Only 79,151 polls were actually paid. If we assume that registration was a declaration of interest in voting, then failure

[72] William D. Jelks to John T. Morgan, January 10, 1902, Morgan Papers, Library of Congress.

[73] Woodward, *Origins of the New South*, 342-346. Key, *Southern Politics*, 533-535.

to pay poll tax was caused by something other than apathy. On such a basis, a minimum of 35 percent of the native white males between the ages of 21 and 44 years, or 23.6 percent of the total white, male, voting-age population was disfranchised by the poll tax alone. The convention had done its job well: white voters declined, Negro voters practically ceased to exist.

Politics in the Convention

The Constitutional Convention of 1901 captured for historical analysis a brief instant in the continuous process of political change. The convention was not simply an occasion for the continuation of the bipolar conflict of the 1890s between the forces of reform and the hosts of reaction, as it is pictured in the otherwise excellent account of Malcolm C. McMillan, *Constitutional Development in Alabama, 1798-1901*. Alabama in 1901 was at a crucial midpoint in its transition from the politics of revolution to the politics of pluralistic interest groups.[1] The old configuration of conflict between highly differentiated groups and involving inevitably the fear of the breakdown of social deference was no longer salient. In 1901 no firm new pattern had emerged, but traces of the old alignment persisted and suggestions of possible new orientations could be detected in the voting patterns of the convention.

An extensive analysis of the roll calls in the convention, the methods and results of which are set forth in Appen-

[1] Robert A. Dahl, *Who Governs? Democracy and Power in an American City*, New Haven, 1961, and "A Critique of the Ruling Elite Model," *American Political Science Review*, LII (June 1958), 463-469. Nelson Polsby, *Community Power and Political Theory*, New Haven, 1963. For a differing view see C. Wright Mills, *The Power Elite*, New York, 1956.

dices V-VIII, reveals that at this moment of transition Alabama contained four broad systems of political sentiments representing a mixed breeding of circumstances with traditional American ideologies. The "Agrarians," who received their doctrine from Jefferson by way of Jackson and Populist radicalism, were disorganized and weak. Their experiences with powerlessness, frustration, and failure left them in a state of proscription and apathy from which they were to be called in the twentieth century only by the strong emotional appeals of such different men as Tom Heflin and "Big Jim" Folsom. The "Planters" acquired their Jeffersonian doctrine from John Taylor of Caroline and John C. Calhoun, a filtering process that left mainly provincialism and opposition to organized power in any form. The "Bosses" lay in the tradition that extended from Hamilton and the Whigism of Henry Clay to such spokesmen in the post-bellum South as Henry Grady. Possessing a newly emerging sensibility created by urbanism and instructed by Christian stewardship, the "Progressives" in 1901 were few in number but destined to grow to domineering proportions.

Within the assemblage of 155 men, however, the dominant force was the group of 60 Bosses. These delegates represented all parts of the state but were heavily concentrated in urban centers and the Black Belt. As the agents of the Big Mule–Black Belt alliance, which had played the leading role in state politics since 1875, the Bosses could be expected to play an influential role in the Constitutional Convention. The first clue to their control of the meeting came soon after the first session on May 21, 1901, when John B. Knox was elected president.

Knox, a railroad and corporation lawyer from the growing industrial town of Anniston in Calhoun County, wielded great power in the Convention. Aside from his position as presiding officer, he was chairman of the Rules Committee which, among other things, appointed the standing committees of the Convention. The result was predictable. Bosses controlled the key committees. T. W. Coleman of Greene County was chairman of the Committee on Suffrage and Elections, George P. Harrison headed the Committee on Corporations, Cecil Browne chaired the Committee on Taxation, and so forth. In such a large body, where most of the work was done in committee, the dice were loaded from the start. For instance, John W. A. Sanford introduced a resolution to limit the amount of land that could be held by any corporation to 1,000 acres. He asked that it be referred to the Committee on Amendment of the Constitution, but Knox thought the Committee on Corporations would be more appropriate. Sanford replied, "that Committee has not been heard from any more than the searchers for the north pole, and if referred to it [the resolution] will not be heard from any more than we do of the chariots of Pharaoh."[2] The resolution went to the Committee on Corporations and was not heard from again. The Bosses had power and they used it.

The voting performance of the Bosses announced the group's commitments. Generally they voted for lower tax rates and lower levels of governmental spending; they strongly opposed any stricter regulation of railroads or any change in the system of leasing county convicts to corporations operating outside the county; and they consistently objected to changes that might upset the established system of winning and holding office. With a few exceptions, they usually voted against any change, the chief exception being the change to a more restricted

[2] *Proceedings of the Convention*, II, 2,086.

electorate. The Bosses obviously acted for the set of interests reformers had in mind when they used the word "machine." They spoke for the officeholders and local politicians connected with the gold wing of the Democratic Party, and for the business interests associated with railroads and the new industrial segment of the economy.

There was a significant group of 37 "Planters" from the Black Belt who evidently had not made the connection after Reconstruction with the forces of the New South and as a result had remained on the fringes of the Big Mule–Black Belt coalition. The greatest differentiation between the Planters and the Bosses was that the Planters were quite willing to see stricter regulation of railroads. On this measure, they joined with the small businessmen in the cities who wanted protection against big economic powers. But on other measures they showed their reluctance to change existing patterns. They did favor the popular election of solicitors, a stand that reveals their parochialism more than their devotion to Jeffersonian principles. The Planters embodied the ethic of a class that felt no need for government. They feared others might use government for undue advantage, and thus distrusted government in direct proportion to its distance from the plantation.

There was another rural, anti-machine group in the convention, which contained 13 Democrats, all of the six Republicans in the convention, and all but one of the seven Populists there. Almost all of these "Agrarians" came from the hill counties and wiregrass region where white yeoman farmers predominated. The most distinctive characteristic of the Agrarians was their frequency of voting in the minority on questions that had the overwhelming support of the convention as a whole. They were particularly outside the mainstream on questions of suffrage restrictions that were aimed at their poor-white and Negro constituents. They differed markedly from the dominant Bosses in that they were in favor of limiting the prerogatives of local officeholders, and they bucked the prevailing powers in voting for the reform of the convict leasing system, a system that victimized Republican convicts and competed with Populist miners.

But the truly revealing thing about the Agrarian voting pattern was that it agreed with the Bosses on so many basic issues. The Agrarians were not interested in railroad reform; instead they steadfastly advocated lower limits on taxation, debt, and spending. Ignoring the realities of a modern industrial state, they remained chained to their preference for a small passive referee state.

There was one group of delegates who were aware of industrial realities but who wanted desperately to change some of them. The 32 "Progressives" in the convention represented a new set of political attitudes in Alabama, for they spoke out of their experience with the problems of the urban centers from which they generally came. Their mixture of votes was a compound of humanitarianism, concern for clean government, a felt need for governmental regulation of powerful concentrations of wealth, and a desire for increased public services. That the Progressives knew the cost of progress and were willing to pay it was reflected in their distinctive advocacy of higher debt, taxation, and spending levels. They also wanted the state government to step in and regulate railroad rates so that some of the profits of progress would stay at home rather than flowing into the coffers of Northern corporations. The moves to secure reform of the convict lease system, provide for strong anti-lynching measures, prevent the perpetuation of oligarchies of political officeholders, all found sympathetic support in

Progressive ranks. This concern with collectively sponsored progress, coupled with a concern for public and private morality, set the Progressive clearly apart from his fellows.

Perhaps a comparison of the performance of the four groups on some of the individual roll calls will help to clarify their distinctiveness.

The most active reform group within the convention was the one led by B. B. Comer, though Comer was not himself a delegate. Under its urgings, many commercial organizations and thousands of Alabamians signed petitions asking the convention for an elective railroad commission on the Georgia model. Comer sent letters, leaflets, and speakers throughout the state and hired influential men to come to Montgomery and lobby for his measure.[3] But, of course, he did not go unopposed.

The friends of the railroads, headed by President John V. Smith of the State Railroad Commission, met Comer's onslaught in the press and in the convention's lobbies. The railroads asked the convention to act quickly on the suffrage article and bring the convention to a speedy close before any great harm could be done by the reformers. They also argued that the constitution should be kept free of controversial provisions so as not to endanger its adoption in the referendum. Harrison's Committee on Corporations delayed its report so that opposition to it would not have time to build up, but, even though it was the last one considered, the article on corporations as drafted by the committee did meet vigorous opposition.

Frank S. White of Birmingham, John W. A. Sanford

[3] B. B. Comer to J. J. Willett, May 15, 1901 (two letters), and May 28, June 1, and June 5, 1901, J. J. Willett Papers, Sanford University (formerly Howard College), Birmingham, Ala.

of Montgomery, and Leslie Brooks of Mobile led the fight on the floor for an elective railroad commission in the closing days of the convention, but the convention nullified their most serious effort by a vote of 79 to 39.[4] The only roll call on the question of railroad regulation came on the compromise provision that Joel Murphree, a prominent and politically articulate merchant from Troy, had been able to wring from the Committee on Corporations of which he was a member. The convention adopted this compromise which specifically gave the legislature the power to regulate railroads. The most enthusiastic group about the compromise was the Bosses; 96 percent of them voted for it, while the other groups were split. The Agrarians cast 60 percent of their votes for it, while the Progressives and Planters, who were most in favor of regulation, contributed less than half of their votes to the compromise.

The compromise also included a section on the re-current issue of railroad passes, which prohibited rail-roads from giving free passes to judges and legislators. Railroads could still give passes to other state officials, and could even give passes to legislators if they also happened to be bona fide employees of the railroad, as many were. The six roll calls on the question of rail-road passes show a consistent pattern. Very high per-centages of the Planters and Progressives voted to do away with free passes, and very high proportions of the Bosses and Agrarians voted to retain this lucrative perquisite of office. The Agrarians were not necessarily voting for the railroads, but probably instead for the interests of local officeholders in poor counties who needed to boost their income in any way possible.[5] Pro-

[4] See Appendix VIII, roll call 66.
[5] *Ibid.*, roll calls 67-72.

gressives and Planters were voting for clean government.

Charles Beddow, the spokesman for Birmingham wage earners, not only consistently aided White in his fight for railroad reform but led a strong fight to outlaw the convict lease system. Even though he failed, he did manage to force the convention to consider the question despite the opposition of Harrison's Committee on Corporations. A combination of Bosses and Planters crushed his efforts, which were strongly supported by the Progressives and Agrarians.[6] This was a different alignment of forces than the one brought forth by railroad regulation.

A third pattern was the arrangement of forces occasioned by the needs of modern urban growth. John B. Weakley, chairman of the Committee on Municipalities and president of the League of Alabama Municipalities, struggled with limited success to release Alabama's cities from the rigid and unrealistic requirements of the constitution's limits on municipal taxing and borrowing. The convention retained the maximum tax rate of five mills for municipalities and imposed a new provision limiting their capacity to borrow to 3½ percent of the assessed value of property. The convention did provide for an additional 2½-mill tax for municipal improvements, but refused to lift the prohibition against internal improvements sponsored by the state. On the two roll calls, sounding out opinion on the proper debt ceiling for cities, Progressives and Bosses were overwhelmingly agreed that cities should have greater power to borrow money. Planters were evenly split and Agrarians were heavily opposed to higher debt limits for urban centers.[7] This arrangement appeared when the same issue

[6] *Ibid.*, roll call 129.
[7] *Ibid.*, roll calls 38-39.

came up with regard to counties, though Bosses and Progressives were not as concerned about the financial powers of the county as about the health of municipalities.[8]

The rural versus urban pattern persisted when the convention considered the financial powers of the state. Reform-minded urbanites, and to a lesser extent the town dwellers linked to railroad interests and big industry, favored a more liberally endowed government. Spokesmen for rural interests, whether "insiders" or "outsiders," opposed expensive government. On some issues there was a slight modification in the division. When the Progressives tried to raise the governor's salary from $3,000 to $5,000, they were staunchly opposed at every turn by the Agrarians. The Bosses and Planters were divided on the issue. They finally mediated a compromise that left the legislature with the authority to raise the governor's salary in the future.[9] But on the key issue of taxation, the rural-urban division remained. Cecil Browne's Committee on Taxation reported out a section that reduced the constitutional limit on the rate of taxation from 7.5 mills to 6.5 mills. Despite the opposition of such notables as Thomas G. Jones, William C. Oates, and William D. Jelks, for all of whom the governorship had been an education in the financial needs of government, the convention adopted the committee's report by a vote of 66 to 32. The Progressives wanted a higher tax limit, while the Agrarians and Planters strived to keep it low. The Bosses were willing to concede the necessity of a temporarily high tax rate, but they distrusted the taxing power enough to insist on a low permanent limit, which they got.[10]

[8] *Ibid.*, roll calls 36-37.   [9] *Ibid.*, roll calls 22-28.
[10] *Ibid.*, roll calls 29-31.

The effect of this limitation on the state's taxing power was offset by the Committee on Education's section authorizing an optional one mill tax to be levied by individual counties upon the approval of the voters of the county. John W. Abercrombie, president of both the University of Alabama and the Alabama Education Association, and backed by the Alabama Federation of Women's Clubs, urged the convention to allow each school district to levy the optional tax. The penurious convention compromised by authorizing the less satisfying county tax. Progressives gladly accepted the concession, while the Agrarians held out against any kind of special tax.[11] Friends of education also succeeded in getting the convention to earmark for educational purposes three mills of the state's revenue, provided that sufficient funds remained after the state's bonded debt had been serviced. Aided by the fact that improved educational opportunities had become a widely lauded goal, Progressives had some success in cutting through both outworn ideologies and entrenched property interests to transform rhetoric into reality.

On measures that involved political beliefs, rather than a view of the economic needs and duties of modern government, the rural-urban split was replaced by a democratic-elitist division. For instance, Progressives and Agrarians tended to favor lower property and tax qualifications for the franchise and to prefer more lenient requirements for aliens and urban workers than did the Bosses or Planters. The Progressives were not nearly so equalitarian as the Agrarians, but more so than the Bosses or Planters.[12] The Agrarians and Progressives were also much more willing to experiment with limited

[11] *Ibid.*, roll call 79.
[12] *Ibid.*, roll calls 41-61.

forms of female suffrage than were the other two groups of delegates.[13] But when it came time for the convention to honor its pledge to the Black Belt by freezing into that same fundamental law which was eliminating Negro voters the assurance that Negroes would be counted for purposes of apportionment, the Progressives deserted the Agrarians and sided with the Bosses and Planters.[14]

The primary reason for this shift in voting performance was the necessity of securing the approval of a majority of voters in the referendum, which in practice meant being wary of the special interests of important blocs of voters. The article on apportionment not only placated the Black Belt but bidded for support in north Alabama by increasing the lower house from 100 to 105 members and the upper house from 33 to 35 members and giving all of the new seats to the white counties. Even though a close student of Alabama apportionment has concluded that the apportionment of 1901 overrepresented the Black Belt slightly in both houses,[15] the new seats helped to win support for the constitution in areas of the state where it met heavy opposition.

The question of local officeholders also became very important. Since 1875 solicitors had been named by the legislature in order to minimize the influence of Republicans, and later of Populists, who might be able to carry local elections. It had come to be an integral part

[13] *Ibid.*, roll calls 63-65.
[14] *Ibid.*, roll call 62.
[15] Hallie Farmer, *The Legislative Process in Alabama*, University, Ala., 1949, Chapter 1, Maps 1, 2, 3, and 4. Also see the useful maps prepared by William Letford in *Alabama Congressional and Legislative Representation, 1819 to 1960*, Historical and Patriotic Series, Number 17, Montgomery, The Alabama Department of Archives and History, 1961.

of the political maneuvering and logrolling that centered in the legislature. The Bosses were clearly those who spoke for the maintenance of the existing system, but the other three groups managed to combine forces to wipe out this source of political payoffs and return the choice of solicitors to the people of the locality concerned.[16]

The convention became even more involved in the fate of sheriffs. The already complex situation, in which desires for political reform clashed with the need to obtain ratification of the constitution, was compounded by the race issue. It was common knowledge that many of the lynchings were carried out with the consent, if not the aid, of the sheriffs and deputies. Thomas G. Jones touched off the controversy when he proposed that the constitution grant the governor the power to suspend any sheriff charged with negligence in a lynching case pending trial in the courts. His proposal was one realistic way of providing a mild sanction against such acts. The convention quickly passed the provision giving the governor the power of suspension, along with a measure prohibiting sheriffs from succeeding themselves in office. Bosses were most solicitous of the interests of sheriffs; Planters were divided; and Progressives and Agrarians were anti-sheriff. Because Progressives were much more interested than Agrarians in other measures designed to safeguard Negro prisoners and induce sheriffs to fulfill their duties, it is fair to assume that while both groups wanted to break up the rings of local officeholders that often ruled a county for years, the Progressives were also interested in combating lynching. The Agrarians, composed of Populists, Republicans, and poor-white Democrats, were merely attacking alien authority.

[16] See Appendix VIII, roll calls 81-91.

Nothing could have more directly threatened the local cliques that formed one part of the Bosses' coalition than limiting a sheriff's tenure. Consequently it occupied the attention of the convention more than any other single issue. At the peak of the controversy late in the summer, the Sheriffs, Clerks and Registers Association convened in Montgomery for the purpose of putting pressure on the convention to rescind its two actions. The association was able to reach a settlement with Jones. They agreed that if the convention would allow sheriffs to succeed themselves, they would not oppose the provision giving the governor the power of suspension.

The Planters, who were not linked to the county machines and were anxious to clean up county government by forbidding sheriffs to succeed themselves, blocked the deal. But they were also so anti-Negro and so parochial that they opposed giving the governor the power of suspension. When the motion to allow the reelection of sheriffs came up on August 29 in the closing days of the convention, the Planters joined the Progressives and Agrarians in voting to limit the sheriffs to one term. Jones then explained the deal to the convention and said that if the sheriffs could not succeed themselves they should be freed of the threat of suspension. Under the threat of having the sheriffs oppose ratification, Progressives and Planters joined the Bosses in freeing the sheriffs from administrative action in the case of lynchings and then in granting a two-year extension to present office-holders to compensate them for the loss of their right to succeed themselves.[17] This was another instance in which

[17] *Ibid.*, roll calls 1-21. Montgomery *Advertiser*, August 13, 15, 20, 30, 1901. Mobile *Register*, August 30, 1901. *Proceedings of the Convention*, IV, 4,745.

Negro interests, in this case Negro lives, were sacrificed on the altar of Clean Government.

The convention's impulse was actually toward diminishing government rather than cleaning it up. Edward W. deGraffenreid of Hale County pointed out to his fellow delegates that they were "adopting a constitution which will curb the powers of the Legislative Department."[18] In the end, all branches of state government lost power, but the legislature lost more than any other.

The greatest innovation in the convention was the institution of quadrennial sessions of the legislature limited to 50 days, which cut legislative time in half. The Agrarians and Planters were behind this move, while the Progressives, with some help from the Bosses, voted for longer and more frequent sessions.[19]

The fact that the alignment of forces in the convention shifted as the issues changed indicated that the Bosses could be defeated if the right issue were picked. The Progressives could bid for either Agrarian votes or Planter votes. The issues on which Agrarians agreed with Progressives were those involving traditional tenets concerning how government should operate (e.g., democratic suffrage, clean government, freedom from machine rule). Johnston had been pursuing Agrarian votes with patronage and Jeffersonian rhetoric, but with the shrinkage of the Agrarian electorate, this tactic had ceased to be useful. The alternative, later chosen by B. B. Comer, was to appeal to the Planter vote by emphasizing the railroad issue. A Progressive-Planter alliance might prove unstable because the two groups had such divergent views on the role of government, but if railroad regulation held the center of the stage the players might consent to follow the same director. The Planter alliance might prove

[18] *Proceedings of the Convention*, I, 907.
[19] See Appendix VIII, roll calls 95-99.

even more compatible for the Progressives than a relationship with the Agrarians because of the powerful attraction of social similarity. Whatever differences in social origin and ambition existed between Progressives and Planters, it was much narrower than the gap between the Agrarians and the other three groups.

Available biographical data reveal the strikingly different social origins of the delegates who voted in the Agrarian pattern.[20] The Agrarian index of personal political prominence at the time of the convention was .56 while that of the other three groups was 1.0 or above.[21] More sig-

[20] Thomas McAdory Owen, *History of Alabama and Dictionary of Alabama Biography*, 4 vols., Chicago, 1921.

[21] The biographical information was analyzed in a very crude, but I think sound, way. Factors that could be used for analysis were weighted on a 3-2-1-0 scale. A delegate's most significant public office was rated on a scale granting 3 "points" for national office, 2 points for a statewide office or for the state senate, and 1 point for county or local offices or membership in the state house of representatives. The total of points accumulated by all the members of each group was divided by the number of men in the group to give an index of political prominence. The prominence of fathers of delegates was measured in the same way, except that military rank was also considered. The rank of major or above was made equivalent to a statewide political office (2 points), while the rank of lieutenant or captain was equated with local office (1 point). Only a father's single most significant status was measured. The total for each group was again divided by the number in the group to give an index figure for parental prominence. The education index was calculated in much the same way. Any man who received an A.B. and/or LL.B. degree from the University of Alabama or other public university or small college was awarded 2 points. Any degree of formal education in excess of this, or a degree from a high-status private university outside the state, was rated at three points. Any lesser amount of college education was given 1 point. The points accruing within the group were then divided by the total number in the group to arrive at the education index. Occupations and marriages to the daughters of prominent men were simply tabulated, counted, and compared.

nificantly, the education index for the Agrarians was half that for the lowest of the other three groups, and the Agrarians were similarly poor in illustrious fathers. Obviously they did not belong to the establishment.

As crude as the biographical data are, they yield highly suggestive results. The median ages of all four groups were virtually the same. The median Progressive at 47 was the oldest, while the median Populist at 42 was the youngest. Evidently the differential impact of history on separate generations was not a factor in determining the political attitudes measured by the roll calls.

Factors other than age were differentiated in an interesting pattern for the three Democratic groups. As one would suspect, there was not as much disparity among these three groups as between any one of them and the Agrarians. The Progressives showed a markedly lower education index of .81 than the Bosses' figure of 1.03 or the Planter figure of 1.16. Education was partially a measure of achieved personal status, but perhaps it was more a measure of the status of the parental family. The Planters not only led the education index but had slightly more illustrious fathers than either the Bosses or the Progressives. This supports the intuition that both of these later groups represent new men in Alabama, men with loyalties to postbellum alignments and causes.

Perhaps an even more meaningful comparison would be that between the younger halves of the three groups, men raised and educated primarily after the Civil War. Here the contrasts are even more striking. The index measuring the political and military prominence of the fathers of the younger halves of the groups is almost twice as great for the Planters as for the Progressives and Bosses. It would be fair to assume that the index also measured a degree of social status. The fact that the incidence of marriages to the daughters of prominent men was twice as great for the Planters as for the Bosses, as well as the education comparisons, supports such an assumption. Planters came from families of higher status than did the bulk of the Progressives and Bosses. Significantly, when the groups are compared for personal political prominence in 1901, the Bosses show a 10 percent advantage in the crude measurement! If the younger halves of the groups are again used for comparison of personal political prominence at the time of the convention, the superiority of the Bosses is more than twice as striking. The conclusion must be that the achievement of more significant political office before 1901, particularly among the younger Bosses, was due to their links to the ruling political and economic forces.

If this is true, then the post-convention careers of these same men should show a dramatic falling off in the ability of the Bosses to win political office because of the victory of Progressivism in the state. That is exactly what happened. By including the period after 1901 in the count of political offices held, the index of the Bosses advanced only 18 percent while the Progressive index rose 79 percent and the Planters 61 percent. The same Bosses who had occupied more significant public offices than had their contemporaries in the other two groups before 1901, did not continue to do so after 1901. It would be difficult to explain this other than by the fact that Bosses were out of fashion with the voters. At the same time, the young Planters and Progressives, combining in the Alabama Progressive movement, began to advance politically.

Occupational comparisons are also instructive. There were 90 lawyers in the convention, so it was natural that a majority of each group consisted of lawyers, but there was a slight differential distribution of the nonlawyers. Men engaged in agriculture were most highly concentrated among the Bosses and Agrarians and least represented among the Progressives. Professional men appeared twice as often among the Progressives as among the Bosses, and the Planter group contained a surprising concentration of small-town bankers. The nonlawyers among the Bosses suffered from a relative scarcity of businessmen, while the other three groups seemed devoted to the countinghouse in the same degree. Unfortunately the total instance of nonlawyers was so small that the validity of the occupational analysis is tenuous. But it conforms to the generalizations that could be made from the rest of the biographical data.

The rudimentary analysis of the membership of the four voting groups in the convention also fits a coherent view of Southern politics from Redemption in 1874 to Reform after 1890. The post-Reconstruction regime in the South was not a restoration, but instead a new order dominated by businessmen, with window-dressing allegiance from various leaders of the old order.[22] This Big Mule–Black Belt coalition flew the banner of the New South and was challenged seriously only in the last decade of the century by an uprising of rural and urban underclasses whose allegiance to the Redeemers was shattered by the economic depression of the 1890s. By 1901 only an ineffective remnant of the Populist protesters was still active. At that time, and for some time before, the solid ranks of white Democracy were feeling the growing pressure from a rising, urban, middle class group that

[22] Woodward, *Origins of the New South*, Chapter 1. Dewey Grantham, "An American Politics for the South," in Charles Grier Sellers, Jr., ed., *The Southerner as American*, Chapel Hill, 1960, 148-179.

wished to march off in the direction of reform. This group was represented in the convention by the Progressives. Some aspects of their urge to reform, particularly their desire for railroad regulation, appealed to a segment of rural and small-town men. The social status of these parochial Planters had suffered from their refusal to join forces with the Redeemer coalition following the collapse of Reconstruction. On issues directed against the usurpers of their prestige, these Planters were willing to aid their city cousins; whether they would actually do so was still an unresolved question in 1901.

The question remained unresolved even throughout the campaign for ratification of the new constitution. Governor William Dorsey Jelks (Samford had died on June 11, 1901 after a long illness) proclaimed November 11, 1901 to be election day for the referendum on the constitution. The Democratic State Executive Committee appointed Oscar W. Underwood chairman of a 14-member committee to carry out the campaign. The Democratic opposition to ratification was led by Joseph Johnston who was smarting from defeat at the hands of Senator Morgan and the Jones-Jelks wing of the party and who persisted in trying to forge a workable alliance with the old Populist electorate. He was aided by Charles M. Shelley, William H. Denson, Jesse Stallings, and Bibb Graves. Populists and Republicans were sadly disorganized. Though most Negroes were either frustrated or apathetic, a large group of prominent Negroes met in Birmingham in September to voice their protest against the proposed constitution. They resolved not to fight on election day but to carry their fight into the courts. In a fit of despair that betrayed their lack of effective power, they disclaimed any faith in either the Johnston organization or the Republican Party.[23]

At issue in the campaign for ratification was the suffrage article of the new constitution. Johnston's committee, speaking for the suspicious poor whites, attacked the powerful system of registrars which the suffrage article set up and observed that the grandfather clause was likely to be held unconstitutional, thus disfranchising all the men registered under it. Advocates of ratification continued to swear that no white man would be disfranchised by the new constitution. They declared that the issue was simply one of white supremacy, just as it had been in 1874 in the campaign for Redemption. Stallings countered that the constitution was simply the product of Black Belt bosses and corporate influences and would saddle the state with machine rule for years to come. Hilary Herbert replied that disfranchisement would allow a two-party system to develop in Alabama. Indeed, a group of genteel Republicans began to organize and work for disfranchisement on the basis of this very theory.

The Democratic committee with a massive and intensive effort carried the brunt of the campaign, however. All of the leading political figures in the state spoke for ratification. Even Senator Morgan, who had been sulking because the convention had ignored his opposition to the grandfather clause, issued a statement in favor of ratification late in the campaign. Only the little knot of Johnston politicians held out against this heavy artillery.[24]

On November 11, 1901 the new constitution was adopted by a majority of 26,879 votes out of a large

[23] The result of the legal efforts of this group was defeat in the case of *Giles v. Harris*, 189 U.S. 475.

[24] McMillan, *Constitutional Development in Alabama*, Chapter 20.

turnout of 190,347. The pattern, as Appendix IV shows, was much the same as in the heated Populist campaigns of the preceding decade. Of the 29 counties returning majorities against the new constitution, all but four had given a higher proportion of their county vote in 1896 to the Populists than the average county had. Also similar to the Populist campaigns was the fact that there was abundant evidence of fraud. Seventeen counties cast more votes for disfranchisement than the number of their potential white electorate! Again the Black Belt provided the margin of victory. The old Populist electorate, or what was left of it, was defeated one last time.[25]

[25] See Appendix IV. Key, *Southern Politics*, 545.

Progressivism Finds a Formula

Despite the defeat of Johnston's political force on the issue of ratification in November 1901, the reformers did not immediately grasp the potential of a coalition of "Planters" and "Progressives" that the convention revealed. They first had to see the impotence of the appeal to "Agrarians" demonstrated again in the gubernatorial race of 1902. Then the need for a new leader with a new issue which could bring together a winning combination of voting groups was evident. The triumphant coalition was adumbrated in the elections of 1902, showed its promise in the legislature of 1903, and proved itself in the election of the President of the Railroad Commission in 1904.

Organization of the new coalition of voters was facilitated by the persistence of bifactionalism among Alabama's politicians. Hardly had the new constitution been ratified than the Johnston politicians began to seek a candidate and allies for the gubernatorial election of 1902. Chairman Shelley sent out letters soliciting the aid and cooperation of those "who were opposed to the ratification of the new constitution,—or, are now opposed to and condemn the methods by which its ratification was accomplished,—or, are now in favor of a thorough and lasting reform of all fraudulent practices in elections and the overthrow of all political rings and cliques. . . ." Their uniting trinity was to be "good government, white supremacy and honest elections."[1]

Even before the central issues of the campaign were defined the candidates that began announcing for various offices in February 1902 fell with regular predictability into pro- and anti-Jelks categories according to old factional loyalties. When Russell M. Cunningham announced his candidacy for the new office of lieutenant governor, he pledged himself to support Jelks. Oscar W. Underwood, John Tyler Morgan, and John Bankhead added their considerable weight in Jelks' favor. The Jelks campaign committee roster abounded with the names of men who had been gold Democrats in 1896 and those who were linked to railroads and heavy industry.[2]

Meanwhile, the Johnston forces cast about for allies and a candidate. Johnston finally got going in the middle of March, at which time he was already confident there would be a primary in August to choose the Democratic gubernatorial nominee.[3] "I think our best plan," he told Stallings, "would be to call a general meeting for the next month and write all Democrats attached to the gang to come in and confer."[4]

The Johnston clan thus met for the first time on March 30 amidst rumors that Johnston would again be a candidate for the nomination. But it was not until mid-July that a conference of Johnston politicians decided he

[1] Charles M. Shelley to J.W.A. Sanford, November 19, 1901, Sanford Papers, ADAH. Persistent bifactionalism has been rare in Alabama.

[2] Birmingham *Age-Herald*, February 18, 25, July 5, 13, 24, 1902.

[3] Johnston to Stallings, March 11, 1902, Stallings Papers, University of North Carolina.

[4] *Ibid.*, Johnston to Stallings, March 17, 1902.

would again head their ticket.[5] Johnston had actually determined to run as early as the first of June, but he had waited until the state committee had made its decision on the question of the primary.

The call for a primary arose immediately after the ratification of the constitution and built up rapidly in the press until there was an almost universal cry. The *Age-Herald* announced that "such a primary is the logical outcome of the new constitution. The State is now in the hands of its best citizens, and these citizens are in no mood to longer stand the convention system." It was a "battle between the people and the politicians."[6]

There was little evidence in Alabama's immediately preceding history to suggest that the people were more powerful than the politicians, yet on July 10 the Democratic State Executive Committee acceded to popular demands for a statewide primary by a vote of 15 to 12. The committee provided that the party's candidates for statewide offices and the members of the State Executive Committee would be picked at a primary on August 25, 1902. It would, of course, be a white primary.[7] Contemporaries were a little surprised by the action of the Committee, and newspaper accounts emphasized the fact that "the judgment of the majority of the committee was opposed to a primary as inexpedient and harmful to the party. . . ."[8] It is probable that the State Executive Committee was giving in not so much to public opinion as to the wishes of their leader. Jelks had announced on June 14 that he would not oppose a primary.[9]

[5] Birmingham *Age-Herald,* July 16, 17, 1902.
[6] *Ibid.*, March 27, 28, 1902. The *Age-Herald* was anti-Progressive.
[7] *Ibid.*, July 11, 12, 1902.
[8] *Ibid.*, July 13, 1902.
[9] *Ibid.*, June 15, 1902.

The question is, why should Jelks not have viewed the primary as a threat? Many of his advisors and informants did. One local official who responded favorably to Jelks' letter announcing his candidacy told the governor frankly that he was "fearful that, if such a primary is held, it will operate against you. I believe that with a convention we can easily send for you an instructed delegation."[10]

Paradoxically Jelks' decision to permit the introduction of such a democratic device as a primary may have stemmed from his desire to prevent the advent of the two-party system, an arrangement Southern reformers repeatedly have sought as the cure for the South's political ills. The factional division in the Democracy in Alabama in 1901-1902 was so evident it was picked up by a Washington paper with the notion that it was portent of a two-party system.[11] This was far from a fanciful idea. P. C. Steagall, a member of the Johnston circle of politicos, was ready to bolt the Democratic Party. "I am in favor of calling our Committee together again and making the organization permanent and public and calling a general state primary and nominate a full ticket and we could elect it."[12]

The threatened dissolution of the Democratic Party was clearly perceived on the other side of the factional boundary. In early December a "leading East Alabamian" (who may have been Jelks himself) told the press he was in favor of a primary. He thought the Johnston-Shelley group was just looking for an opportunity to break off from the party; "they will be able to do a lot

[10] B. F. O'Connor to W. D. Jelks, April 12, 1902, Governor's Office Records, ADAH.

[11] Birmingham *Age-Herald*, December 3, 1901.

[12] P. C. Steagall to Stallings, March 6, 1902, Stallings Papers, University of North Carolina.

of devilment, too." He predicted that if a primary were ordered, "the men now in control of State affairs would prove easy winners in the primaries."[13] His confidence in the outcome was based on a perceptive appreciation of the political change the new constitution had initiated.

Whether from apathy or white disfranchisement, the electorate in 1902 had been severely pruned. Consequently, fear of the hill counties receded. "Conditions in north Alabama are such that no candidates can carry the solid vote of the various counties," observed Frank H. Miller in the summer of 1902. "The vote of north Alabama is apt to be split up, and a candidate from the black belt who develops any strength in the northern portion of the state will get the solid vote of the belt and . . . will thus stand a good chance of being elected."[14] Under these conditions there was less risk for the Bosses in a primary than in a possible two-party system. In this case, as in others, limited reform was less disruptive than trying to cling to the status quo and thereby risking a severe rupture of the system.

Such a rupture of the system was the last thing Johnston had in mind. He was not even interested in making the campaign a crusade for reform. He and Jelks toured the state debating their relative merits as "business governors." Jelks also attacked Johnston fiercely as an opponent of the constitution. Johnston denied he wanted to reenfranchise Negroes and claimed to be as much a white supremacist as Jelks, but Johnston did lash out at the men who made the constitution. He thought it was time to take the state away from men who used corrupt methods to perpetuate the machine in power and who wished to disfranchise white men. This sort of dif-

[13] Birmingham *Age-Herald*, December 6, 1901.
[14] *Ibid.*, July 13, 1902.

fuse rhetoric had not proven very successful in the past nor was its appeal to clean politics enhanced by the land scandal and the revelation of corruption in the prison system which had tarnished Johnston's reputation. That his orientation was determined by outworn political concepts was further emphasized by his appointment of Noah P. Renfro as his campaign manager. Renfro, president of the First National Bank of Opelika, had voted with the Agrarians in the constitutional convention. Nevertheless, in seeking support, Johnston enlisted not only the faithful old anti-machine men such as W. H. Denson, Sam Will John, and Jesse Stallings, but gave representation on his state campaign committee to spokesmen for labor, for prohibition, and for railroad rate reform.[15]

The signal change in this alignment of forces was the return to the Johnston coalition of the "business Progressives" who had deserted him in order to support disfranchisement. While Johnston was defending his record as a "business governor" and talking tired anti-machine terms, these Progressives changed the nature of the campaign; they made railroad rate reform the chief issue.

B. B. Comer had begun in March when he issued a long denial of the rumor that he was going to run for governor. At the same time, he said he would like for one of the candidates to be in favor of doing something about railroad "looting." "No one questions that there is railroad bossism in the state," said Comer, "when there is bossism there is loot."[16]

The railroad reformers started in earnest in June 1902. About 30 representatives of commercial groups in the state met in Birmingham and organized committees to press for an elective Railroad Commission with broad-

[15] *Ibid.*, July 22, 1902.
[16] *Ibid.*, March 2, 1902.

ened powers. Evidently they were undeterred by their failures in 1891, 1897, 1900, and 1901. The newspapers reported that "Mr. Charles Henderson, President of the Board of Trade of Troy, who is active in this movement said last night that candidates for the legislature would be asked to pledge themselves to a people's railroad committee."[17]

The merchants did not set up the people's railroad committee until July 14. After an enthusiastic local meeting in Birmingham on July 3, the reformers tried to get the convention of the Alabama Commercial and Industrial Association, meeting in Gadsden, to endorse railroad reform—and failed. The convention, evidently dominated by hostile spokesmen for heavy industry, defeated the reform resolution by a 26-13 vote.[18] It was then even more imperative that Comer establish a separate organization to agitate for the issue.

Birmingham newspapers reported that "a joint conference composed of representatives of the Board of Trade, Wholesale Grocers' Association, Retail Grocers' Association, Retail Coal Dealers' Association, Lumbermen's Association, Brokers' Association and businessmen generally of Birmingham and the Birmingham district" gathered on July 14. Frank S. White, the principal speaker, assailed J. P. Morgan and the outside railroad bosses and called upon Alabamians to assert their rights. The meeting resolved that "this fight should be made to the finish, for it ought to be determined once for all, whether the people of Alabama or J. Pierpont Morgan, through his railroads, will control the political policy of this state." White announced that they were organizing committees

[17] *Ibid.*, June 13, 1902.
[18] *Ibid.*, July 12, 1902. Montgomery *Advertiser*, April 20, 1906.

all over the state to take up the issue of economic home rule.[19]

The organization was set in motion a few days later at a meeting in Birmingham attended by Comer, White, and other movement leaders. They named men to begin traveling the state in the interests of an elective railroad commission.[20] The organization instituted at these meetings became the Farmers', Merchants' and Laborers' Association, with Frank S. White as its chairman. Over the following several years, the White Committee, as the public knew it, played an important part in state politics. It began in 1902 by waging a vigorous and comprehensive campaign to elect friends of railroad regulation to the legislature. In the most impressive effort the reformers had mounted up to that time, the White Committee covered the state with speakers, pamphlets, and circulars.

The opposition was impressive, too. Jeff Falkner, the L & N's man, told the Birmingham papers that the "Louisville and Nashville railroad will fight this movement with all the weapons that are recognized as fair in political contention. We come out into the open field."[21] Railroad men began sniping at the reform movement from all angles.[22]

The essentials of the pro-railroad argument had been set down succinctly by the Mobile *Register* on January 21, 1891 and were repeated in various forms throughout the long years of the rate reform wars. At that time the cooperative bill drafted by the joint committee of the Alliance leaders and Birmingham merchants was pending in the legislature. The first proposition set forth then was

---

[19] Birmingham *Age-Herald*, July 15, 16, 1902.
[20] *Ibid.*, July 22, 1902.
[21] *Ibid.*, July 10, 1902.
[22] *Ibid.*, July 15, 27, 30, 1902.

that the situation did not call for a radical change because the existing law gave the commission all the powers it needed. This was especially so in view of the fact that the railroads had never refused to comply with recommendations made by the Railroad Commission. In the second place, the people did not really want rate reform; it was merely a self-serving project on the part of a few politicians and Birmingham merchants. The third and more telling argument was that if Alabama managed to lower the intrastate rates, the railroads would merely compensate by raising the interstate rates over which the state had no control. In fact, ran the *Register*'s argument, the Georgia rates were not really lower than Alabama's if the through rate and the local rate to a noncompetitive point were added together. But the main thrust came in the fourth point. If the legislature passed the bill, said the *Register*, there would be bitter litigation between the railroads and the state (an accurate prediction), which would hinder rather than help the industrial and economic development of the state. Therefore the railroads should not be disturbed in their function of bringing prosperity to the state. The four arguments might conveniently be designated as "the good citizen argument," "the selfish merchant charge," "the argument from futility," and "the timid capital theory."

Friends of the railroads were not always so mild as the *Register*. In 1902 the chief defender of the railroads, Jeff Falkner, in a full-page article in the *Age-Herald*, rehearsed with minor variations the four basic arguments that the *Register* had set forth in 1891. But his key point came in rebuttal to the "absurd" assertion by Comer that railroad rates were merely public taxes; this sounded like a direct threat to private property. Falkner charged that the White Committee's "real purpose is to, if possible, induce the people of Alabama to so fix the railroad commission law as to practically take from the railroad owners the management of their own property, and put the same into a political tribunal."[23] The issue was public power versus property rights.

As potent as the appeal of property rights was, the railroads had certain disadvantages. The Alabama electorate was already sensitive to the issues of clean politics and good government, and the public linked the railroads to rule by political deals and cliques. At the height of the campaign, Alex London, a prominent Birmingham attorney, gave the public some education on this point. London had suddenly emerged in 1902 as a crusader against county political rings and the fee system on which they fed.[24] He claimed that for the past 18 years the state had been in the hands of a machine composed of Black Belt politicians and headed by the Railroad Commission, and that Johnston was the only recent governor who had not been dominated by the machine.[25] The lesson was clear. The campaign for a popularly elected railroad commission and the drive for pure government in Alabama were merely two aspects of the same thing.

Johnston attracted not only old and new anti-machine enthusiasts, in addition to the railroad reformers, but drew support from organized labor as well. The State Federation of Labor, the chief spokesman for the 40,000 organized workers in the state, was only in its second year of operation in 1902, but its constituent organizations were never healthier. The oldest was the Birmingham Trades Council, itself a federation of craft unions

[23] *Ibid.*, August 3, 1902. Doster, *Railroads in Alabama Politics*, 120-121.

[24] Birmingham *Age-Herald*, March 2, 8, 9, 16, April 3, 1902.

[25] *Ibid.*, August 7, 1902.

among which the building crafts were the highest paid and best organized. The Birmingham Trades Council alone had 50 affiliated locals and 6,000 workers in Jefferson County. At the other end of the union spectrum, District 20 of the United Mine Workers was rapidly organizing the growing mining industry. In its third year in 1902, the UMW represented 10,000 miners, approximately five out of every six miners in the state, and by 1904 the union contained 13,000 of the 19,000 miners. Labor in 1902, therefore, had reason to feel confident of their power.[26]

Through the winter of 1901-1902 labor leaders had been discussing the possibility of political action. Finally on April 27 the Birmingham Trades Council voted in favor of putting up workingmen candidates wherever it could and supporting sympathetic candidates where it was not practical for a workingman to run. At the meeting at which the White Committee was formed, J. H. Leath was present, representing the Birmingham Trades Council.[27] At the later meeting, which launched the White Committee's work, Leath was joined by two of labor's candidates for the legislature, and the three endorsed the railroad reform movement on behalf of organized labor. On Johnston's state campaign committee, labor was represented by Ed Veitch of Bessemer.[28] The aspirations of working men were thus joined with the hopes of the political reformers in the Johnston campaign, and railroad reform became increasingly the dominant issue.

Comer and the White Committee developed enough momentum to enlist many legislative candidates in their

[26] *Ibid.*, April 3, May 1, July 27, 1902, June 9, 1904.
[27] *Ibid.*, July 15, 1902.
[28] *Ibid.*, July 22, 1902.

ranks and force the two major candidates to acknowledge that railroad regulation was an important issue. Johnston's suspicion of the reformers was finally revealed in 1905 while the battle over railroads was still raging, when he said that he was aware of inequities that needed correcting, but he feared that undue hostility toward corporations would disturb business conditions.[29] In 1902, however, he was more receptive to the desires of his allies in the reform movement. W. H. Denson committed Johnston to a friendly attitude and announced that Johnston as governor would gladly sign a railroad bill if it were passed.[30] Governor Jelks declared finally that he would "promptly approve any proper bill calling for their [the railroad commissioner's] election by the people."[31] He neglected to say what he thought would be the proper sort of bill.

To the extent that it was possible, Johnston and Jelks pressed on in their private contest, ignoring the transformation of the debate that was going on around them. Nevertheless, Johnston did represent the enemies of the railroad machine. Denson put the prospects of the reformers in military metaphor when he wrote, "Of course, we will have to charge and drive the enemy from his breastworks. We fight in the open, he is protected by the fortifications of the machine. . . . The Tunstallian fleet was in the waters. . . ."[32]

The results of the election gave evidence of heavy casualties among the attackers. Johnston himself was overwhelmed. Jelks swept the state by 26,000 votes, winning all but four counties. Almost half of the quali-

[29] Johnston to DuBose, June 9, 1902, DuBose Papers, ADAH.
[30] Birmingham *Age-Herald*, August 24, 1902.
[31] *Ibid.*, August 5, 1902.
[32] W. H. Denson to DuBose, July 18, 1902, DuBose Papers, ADAH.

fied electors did not bother to go to the polls, not to mention those disfranchised by the registration and poll tax requirements, so political participation reached a new low along with Johnston's political fortunes.[33] But events in the legislature the following January showed that not all of Johnston's allies had suffered his fate. The White Committee had secured the election of a significant bloc of legislators sympathetic to reform.

When the legislature met on January 13, 1903 its choice of officers disclosed the situation. The House chose as speaker none other than A. M. Tunstall, an especially valuable attorney for the Southern Railway. His father, W. C. Tunstall, now sat on the Railroad Commission. The Senate picked as its president pro tempore Joel Goldsby of Mobile, a railroad attorney and old-line gold Democrat. To make matters worse, Governor Jelks was surrounded by advisors similar in outlook and associations to Goldsby and Tunstall.[34] It was a tough lineup for the reformers to face.

The organized rate reform movement was backing the Starr bill which provided for an elective railroad commission with real powers to set rates, examine books, and expedite appeals through the state courts. Comer's testimony before the house committee on commerce and common carriers, predictably, had little effect. The committee reported the bill adversely, and its opponents then defeated an attempt to take the bill up. Unusual tactics would be required to revive the bill.

Just such a move was made on February 12, and it caught the opponents of reform by surprise. Joel C. Du-

---

[33] Moore, *History of Alabama*, 914. Crenshaw, Elmore, Marshall, and Tallapoosa Counties were for Johnston.

[34] This can be ascertained by a perusal of the correspondence in the Governor's Office Records, ADAH.

Bose moved to amend the general election bill which was then under discussion by adding the railroad commissioners to the list of officials to be elected. The House exploded like an anthill that has suddenly been kicked. The chairman ruled that the amendment was out of order, but the House refused to sustain his ruling by a vote of 48 to 26. The friends of reform were in command. Later in the week, they agreed to a weaker compromise for fear that the resurrected Starr bill was too strong to pass the Senate. On February 19 the substitute was passed by the overwhelming vote of 81 to 12. A scale analysis of the roll calls on attempts to amend the bill reveals 69 representatives solidly for a strong bill. The disparity between the crucial vote to override the chairman's rule and the final vote on the bill indicates that the reformers had not only captured a majority of legislators in the last election, but had created an atmosphere in which those who were not for it were afraid to be overtly against it.

The same was true in the Senate, where extraordinary measures again kept the bill from being maneuvered into a pigeonhole. The crucial vote once more came on an appeal from an adverse ruling of the chair. Lieutenant Governor Cunningham had ruled that a motion to take the bill up immediately was out of order because the bill had not yet been placed on the calendar by the Senate rules committee, a committee thoroughly packed with enemies of the bill. The Senate overturned his ruling by a vote of 16 to 13; the bill then sailed through to final passage on a 20-7 roll call.[35]

The act not only made the State Railroad Commission elective, but renewed its powers to prevent "discrimina-

[35] This account of the bill's fate in the legislature is drawn from Doster, *Railroads in Alabama Politics*, 123-128.

tion" and set rates. The only restriction on the commission was that it was obligated to allow the railroad companies a "fair and just return." Unfortunately the legislators did not specify the criteria for determining what was a fair and just return. The commission and the courts were left with the rule of the *Smyth v. Ames* decision.[36] In that case the United States Supreme Court had held that the reasonableness of intrastate rates had to be determined without reference to revenue from the interstate business of the carrier. The formula for apportioning revenue and costs between interstate and intrastate traffic was biased against intrastate business.[37] But the act most importantly gave the commission the power to initiate court action against disobedient roads and put the burden of proof on the railroads.[38] In the second half of the split legislative session the following fall, the act was amended to provide for the election of the president of the Railroad Commission alone in 1906. It extended the terms of the offices from two to four years. Jelks then ignored the appeal of the Birmingham Board of Trade, which called for the appointment of at least one member of the commission who did not represent the railroads. Jelks immediately named W. C. Tunstall and W. T. Sanders. Tunstall was a long-time party fixer with two sons in the service of the railroads, and Sanders was himself a railroad attorney.[39] The railroads were therefore safe until at least 1906.

The legislature of 1903 began to respond in areas other than railroad regulation to the demands of the steadily growing and increasingly respectable forces of

[36] 169 U.S. 466 (1898).
[37] Doster, *Railroads in Alabama Politics*, 85-86.
[38] Alabama, *Acts, 1903*, 95.
[39] Birmingham *Age-Herald*, February 23, 1904.

uplift. Reformers were neither alien nor outcast at the turn of the century. That this was so was made possible in part by the fact that both the means and ends of reform were already largely a part of the accepted "American Way." It was also in part the result of the social origins of the reformers. Bolstering the prestige of the advocates of change was the national stature of such Alabamians as Julia Tutwiler, a pioneer in women's education and advocate of improved conditions in penal institutions, J.L.M. Curry, a crusader for public education from 1865 until his death in 1903 at which time he was General Agent of the philanthropic Peabody and Slater Funds, and Edgar Gardner Murphy, who began his attack on the problem of child labor in Alabama before inflating it to national scale. Some of the pressures on the legislature operated along the relatively narrow front of self-interest and appealed to the community's desire for material improvement. Others resulted from a reinvigoration and secularization of the tradition of Christian charity. Mrs. Erwin Craighead, wife of the editor of the Mobile *Register*, expressed the feeling of those traveling on this traditional avenue when she told the ladies of the Alabama Federation of Women's Clubs that "this is the 'age of movement'. The motive of the movement is the betterment of humanity: its supporting arch is organization and its keynote is education."[40] In 1903 the federation was pressing for better public education, child labor regulation, and the creation of reform schools for youthful offenders of both sexes.

The club women were not alone in their efforts to do good. They rallied behind Judge N. B. Feagin of the municipal court in Birmingham, who had become the

[40] Mobile *Register*, October 31, 1899.

leading advocate of special juvenile courts and homes for youthful offenders. The legislature of 1903 resisted their pleas in this regard but did grant increased appropriations for the Girls and Boys Industrial Schools. The legislature also responded to the urgings of the educational advocates led by John W. Abercrombie, the president of the University of Alabama, and authorized counties to levy a special one-mill tax for education as the new constitution provided. But the most significant advance in education was the passage of the uniform textbook act. Vigorous lobbying efforts by the publishers and contractors had defeated the bill in the 1901 legislature, but Abercrombie was more successful in 1903. The act he obtained set up a state textbook commission to adopt books and administer the law. The law fixed the price of books and stipulated that a title, once adopted, had to be used for at least five years.[41]

The most sensational victory for Progressivism in the 1903 legislature was the passage of the child labor law. After the legislature of 1901 had failed to pass a law regulating the hours and conditions of child labor,[42] Edgar Gardner Murphy organized the Alabama Executive Committee on Child Labor, of which he was chairman. Indicative of the way in which Murphy approached reform was the fact that he was careful to obtain the endorsement of a group of distinguished men in the state, including Thomas G. Jones. He insisted that representatives of the American Humane Association and the American Federation of Labor stay out of the state. He

[41] Alabama, *Acts, 1903*, 167. Approved March 4, 1903.
[42] Irene M. Ashby, "The Fight Against Child Labor in Alabama," Montgomery *Advertiser*, June 2, 1901. Also see the Birmingham *Age-Herald*, February 6, 1901 and the Mobile *Register*, May 9, 1901.

was convinced that he could accomplish more with the aid of powerful local men than he could with "outside agitators."[43] To the state's notables and to the public Murphy presented the question as an "issue of humanity and of business expediency."[44] This reflected Murphy's awareness that Progressivism in Alabama was powered by a combination of business expediency and humanitarian impulse.

After its organization Murphy's committee began by attacking the evil of child labor at its source in the business imperialism of New England. The committee contended that twice as many children were employed in mills owned by Northern capital than in locally owned mills. It blamed the defeat of the child labor bill in the legislature of 1901 on these alien mills. The committee published long advertisements in New England papers calling on mill owners there to give up their sinful ways.[45] These sorties drew hot replies even though they were merely diversionary.[46] Murphy knew that blaming the Yankees was no substitute for solving the problem; his main objective was a state regulatory law. That offensive got boosts from press revelations of shocking conditions of child labor in Alabama cotton mills and from the active support of the Alabama Federation of Women's Clubs.[47]

[43] Murphy to Jelks, December 22, 1902, Governor's Office Records, ADAH.

[44] Murphy to Jelks, December 16, 1902, Governor's Office Records, ADAH.

[45] Hugh C. Bailey, "Edgar Gardner Murphy and the Child Labor Movement," *The Alabama Review*, XVIII (January 1965), 47-59.

[46] Birmingham *Age-Herald*, February 23, 1902.

[47] Mrs. Emily E. Williamson, "Child Labor in Alabama," *The Annals*, XXI, March 1903, 331-332, 446. Birmingham *Age-Herald*, March 18, 1902.

The cotton mill owners bitterly fought Murphy's committee with two arguments: that cheap labor was the ingredient which made them competitive and that child labor was cheap labor; second, that the children were better off in the mills getting some manual training than they would be if left idle. Despite such appealing arguments, their resistance was only partially successful. Among the provisions that the mill owners cut out of the bill were the requirements for at least 12 weeks of schooling each year for children under 12, and the section prohibiting children under 15 from working at night.

The resistance to Murphy's drive for regulation of child labor was led by B. B. Comer and two other mill owners. They negotiated with Murphy in a room at the Exchange Hotel in Montgomery and finally agreed on the compromise bill that was passed. Murphy apparently agreed to the weakened version of his bill because he thought the railroads were supporting the cotton mill owners and that the combination was too strong to defeat totally.[48] The act of 1903 was at least a prologue to effective limits on the exploitation of child labor. It provided that no child under 12 could be employed unless a widowed mother or disabled father depended on his labor. No child under 10 could be employed for any reason. Children under 13 could not work at night and those between 13 and 16 could work at night no more than 48 hours in one week. The law also limited children under 12 years of age to a 66-hour work week. Even these modest restrictions proved ineffective because the law did not provide any special machinery for enforcement.[49]

[48] Edgar Gardner Murphy to Frank Glass, April 27, 1906, in the Montgomery *Advertiser*, June 29, 1906.
[49] Alabama, *Acts, 1903*, 68. Approved February 25, 1903.

This weakness of the child labor law resulted more from the legislature's concern for property rights than from its fear of impinging on individual rights with stringent regulations, as the passage of the Anti-Boycott Act demonstrated. This law provided criminal penalties for boycotting, blacklisting, picketing, or attempting to induce others not to have business dealings with any firm, person, or corporation.[50] Its purpose was clear. It was an effort to shackle the state's labor movement after a summer in which the unions had won several strikes. The chief sponsor of the bill was the Citizens Alliance of Birmingham whose motto was "The right to work is co-equal with the right to live." The Alliance invited the cooperation of all people interested in good citizenship and decried "class rule of any kind."[51] Labor reacted violently. The union locals in the state set up the United Labor League as a defense against the union-busting aims of the Citizens Alliance, but they could not prevent passage of the act.

The passage of the Anti-Boycott Act cast the relationship between labor and Progressivism into a new and mutually antagonistic phase. Even though the unions had the assistance of Jesse Stallings, Zell Gaston, and Frank S. White in their attempt to block passage of the bill, most Progressives voted against the unions. In the Senate, 5 of the 7 Progressives who resisted all attempts to soften the railroad commission act also were hard-core anti-boycotters. None of the opponents of the anti-boycott bill was a strong proponent of the elective railroad commission, though 5 out of 9 were weakly in favor of it. This situation alienated labor from Comer's camp.[52]

[50] *Ibid.*, 281. Approved September 26, 1903.
[51] Birmingham *Age-Herald*, October 28, 1903.
[52] Professor Doster hints on page 136 of his book, *Railroads in*

Comparisons of other roll calls in the legislature of 1903 reveal the beginnings of a focused Progressive sentiment. In the 1898-99 Senate there had been no focus. A bloc analysis based on five important roll calls in 1899 shows no tendency for senators who voted the same way on one issue to vote together on other issues. Majorities and minorities realigned on every roll call.[53] However, in 1903, a hint of order entered the picture. An analysis of 12 roll calls in the 1903 Senate discloses one faction of 14 members. These senators tended to vote on the Progressive side of the roll calls and agreed with each other at least two-thirds of the time. They were opposed on most issues by a faction of 10 senators, of which Joel Goldsby, George P. Harrison, and others of similar persuasion were members. The balance of the Senate, 11 members, was distributed in clusters of twos and threes, each showing a high percentage of agreement with one or two members of a major faction but not with all members. These floaters held the

---

Alabama Politics, that bribery may explain the *Labor Advocate*'s bitter opposition to Comer in 1904. The newspaper continued to berate Comer long after the election, indicating that the editor enjoyed the task for which he was supposedly hired. Election statistics show a tremendous increase in Comer's vote in Jefferson County between 1904 and 1906. In 1906 the *Labor Advocate* reluctantly supported Comer. This suggests that fluctuating, but natural, suspicions rather than railroad money explain the relationship between labor and Comer. The events of 1908 demonstrated that the *Labor Advocate* was correct in its suspicions of Comer.

[53] Alabama, *Senate Journal, 1898*: Constitutional Convention bill, 326; convict lease reform, 531; Jefferson County Commissioner's Court, 928; special school tax, 1,155; cotton mill tax exemption, 801. Five other major bills came up during the session but did not produce sufficient division on their roll calls to justify inclusion.

balance of power and most often floated with the Progressives.[54]

Nevertheless, in 1903 the Progressive movement was still immature. There was a slight tendency for a supporter of one form of reform to also be in favor of other reform measures. For instance, 6 of the 8 votes that opposed the legalization of certain corporate consolidations came from the 17 men who were in favor of the child labor act. But this was not yet a fixed feature. The railroad reform sentiment in particular was not yet firmly attached to other Progressive measures.

Perhaps the rate reformers thought they did not need the support of the many other groups of men coagulating around particular reforms. They seemed to think they had all they needed from the 1903 legislature. Comer and the White Committee went before the strengthened Railroad Commission in the spring of 1903 with a monster petition calling for: (a) the same classification system and rate structure as Georgia, (b) "just and reasonable" rates from points on the Tennessee River in Alabama to other points in the state, and (c) "reasonable joint rates" between boats on the Tennessee River and railroads connecting with them.[55] They argued their case with the railroads before the commission on the basis of facts, figures, profit, and the practicality of lowering intrastate freight rates in Alabama. They lost.

The White Committee then did the only thing it

[54] Alabama, *Senate Journal, 1903*: anti-boycott bill, 1,480; anti-boycott bill, 1,481; Railroad Commission bill, 562; good roads bill, 1,603; child labor bill, 407; corporation consolidation bill, 265; to protect truck farmers, 464; anti-alien resolution, 1,644; cotton and pig iron tax exemption, 593; to exempt farm tools from tax, 594; liquor tax, 631.

[55] Doster, *Railroads in Alabama Politics*, 129 and Chapter 10.

CHAPTER ELEVEN

could do. It carried the battle back into politics where words meant more than figures. The Democratic State Executive Committee met early in January and set April 11 as the day for the primary to select the nominee of the party for president of the Railroad Commission.[56] Ten days later the White Committee met and named B. B. Comer as its candidate.[57] Comer's most formidable foe was John V. Smith who was running for reelection with the backing of the railroads, and the two candidates staged a series of debates in February which added up mainly to statistical barrage and counterbombardment.[58]

The White Committee translated the difficult to comprehend numerical arguments into easily understood slogans and flooded the state with mailed circulars, each of which bore the motto: "A vote for B. B. Comer for Railroad Commissioner is a vote for cheaper local freights."[59] The counterblast from the railroads was equally to the point. One of the many anti-Comer advertisements urged electors to "VOTE AGAINST B. B. COMER, THE EXTREMIST, AND IN FAVOR OF A CONSERVATIVE CANDIDATE FOR PRESIDENT OF THE RAILROAD COMMISSION AND THUS NOT DISTURB THE PROSPERITY AND DEVELOPMENT OF ALABAMA."[60] The candidates seemed to be arguing about the best means to induce material prosperity, because for the moment the railroads had given up their argument from the Fourteenth Amendment. Walker D. Hines, first vice president of the L & N, declared, "We do not, of course deny or question the right of the state to decide what is just and fair as between the

[56] Birmingham *Age-Herald*, January 7, 1904.
[57] *Ibid.*, January 15, 17, 1904.
[58] *Ibid.*, February 20, 21, 23, 25, 1904.
[59] *Ibid.*, February 6, 1904.
[60] Montgomery *Advertiser*, April 3, 1904.

252

shippers and the railroads, and that the railroad commission has ample power to render such decisions and make them effective."[61]

Despite the agreeable tone of Hines' concession, or perhaps because of it, the campaign was the most scurrilous since 1894. Railroads used money to buy sympathetic editorial treatment as well as to gain access to the news and advertising columns.[62] Comer's charges of railroad domination were unbridled, but the railroads gave as good as they received. Comer's critics characterized him as a power-mad demagogue, and a dishonest demagogue at that. The charge that stuck the longest was that in 1892 Comer had shipped flour in meal sacks in order to get the lower rate applicable to meal.[63] Comer denied the charge.[64] In front-page cartoons, the *Age-Herald* pictured Comer as an irresponsible imitator of Theodore Roosevelt.[65] But the central theme of Comer's opposition was that he would frighten away needed capital. Capital is timid, ran this classic argument, and if it is not coaxed and coddled it will withdraw to leave Alabama an arid desert.[66] Against this emphasis on investment as the key to growth Comer preached the necessity of increasing purchasing power.

The voting public chose to follow the consumer's path to economic development. Comer won a smashing victory in the primary. He carried 57 out of 66 counties and polled 59.6 percent of the 96,078 votes counted.[67] Contemporaries felt, and the chief historian of this pe-

[61] Birmingham *Age-Herald*, February 26, 1904.
[62] Doster, *Railroads in Alabama Politics*, 136.
[63] Birmingham *Age-Herald*, March 25, 1904.
[64] Doster, *Railroads in Alabama Politics*, 137n.
[65] Birmingham *Age-Herald*, April 3, 10, 1904.
[66] *Ibid.*, James Bowron's long argument on March 31, 1904.
[67] *Ibid.*, April 21, 1904.

riod in Alabama agrees, that this election was a revolution and meant a rearrangement of political lines.[68] In fact, there was no rearrangement among the political leaders. Much the same factions had been fighting since 1894. The well-informed reporter for the *Age-Herald*, Hervey Laird, noted that at the Democratic state convention following the primary of 1904 that the old free-silver and gold-bug lines prevailed.[69] There was, however, a new arrangement among the electorate. By fixing attention on an issue that would bring together the interests of Black Belt planters, substantial farmers, town merchants, small manufacturers, and the professional men who identified with these groups, Comer had forged a winning coalition of voters. While "Agrarians" were apathetic, Comer united "Planters" and "Progressives" against the "Bosses."[70]

It remained to be seen whether Comer could translate political victory into economic reform. In his victory speech, he warned "that reforms are not made quickly, that the landslide must be followed up. . . ."[71] After his victory in the primary was duly confirmed in the general election in November 1902,[72] Comer took office on March 6, 1905 to follow it up.

[68] Doster, *Railroads in Alabama Politics*, 140.
[69] Birmingham *Age-Herald*, May 24, 1904.
[70] This will be analyzed at length in Chapter 12.
[71] Birmingham *Age-Herald*, April 20, 1904.
[72] *Ibid.*, November 20, 1904.

The Election of 1906

Braxton Bragg Comer was quite willing to shift his attack to overcome newly perceived obstacles. His enemies pictured him as a radical and unbending fanatic. To be sure, his rather shrill voice and rapid, rambling delivery when speaking, as well as the Jeffersonian rhetoric, enhanced that image. But it was misleading. As his political career progressed, he not only improved as a speaker but learned from his experiences.

Comer's first lesson as president of the Railroad Commission was that he was in a minority. He learned this immediately after taking office in the spring of 1905 when he expanded a hearing on a petition concerning a particular local fertilizer rate into a consideration of all rates on fertilizer. He was surprised when his two associates on the commission suddenly moved to consider the entire local freight rate structure in Alabama. Comer, though unprepared, did manage to show that generally local rates in Alabama were higher than those within the jurisdiction of the Georgia Railroad Commission. But his two colleagues refused to accept his argument that lower rates would not only aid shippers and consumers but stimulate traffic and boost long-term railroad revenues. To men with a static conception of society, it seemed more plausible that a reduction of rates would cause a drop in revenue. It was no surprise then that the majority decision of the commission, handed down on July 1, 1905, sustained the railroads' argument that their return on the proportion of their investment used for intrastate business was less than just and reasonable. Therefore no reduction of rates was justified.[1]

Comer saw immediately that in order to reverse the decision of the commission he would need more power, in fact, more than he could obtain simply by getting one or two of his friends elected to the commission in 1906. The arguments of the railroad attorneys warned him of this. During the hearings of 1905 a full array of railroad spokesmen took refuge in the *Smyth v. Ames* formula, the Fourteenth Amendment, and doubts as to the constitutionality of the statute delegating regulatory powers to the Railroad Commission. To combat these tactics Comer had to have control of the full resources of the state government—governor's office, administration, and legislature. "From my associates' decision against the people," he said in his dissenting opinion in July 1905, "there is no appeal except to the ballot."[2]

While the state's newspapers began to sense the impending clash of great forces, Comer announced his own candidacy for governor on October 21, 1905 and renewed his call for the election of a reform-minded slate of state officers and legislators.[3] He benefited from an extraordinary gust of popularity. Even before his formal announcement, the smart politicians began to tack to the freshening reform breeze. " 'How goodly are thy tents oh Jacob,' " quipped one Comer supporter, "when all the

[1] Montgomery *Advertiser*, July 2, 1905. Doster, *Railroads in Alabama Politics*, 140-145.

[2] Montgomery *Advertiser*, July 2, 1905 and January 16, 1906.

[3] Montgomery *Advertiser*, August 25, October 22, 1905.

boys seek shelter under their protection."[4] J. J. Willett, the behind-the-scenes politician from Anniston who had helped Comer's lobbying effort at the Constitutional Convention, advised Jesse Stallings, "if you are going to run [for the U.S. Senate], don't act the fool like Johnston did three years ago and think that your personality without any issue behind it is pleasing enough to elect you. Get on Comer's issue and ride it, ride it, ride it."[5]

The first significant political meeting of the 1906 gubernatorial race was held at Tuscaloosa on December 9, 1905, where Comer spoke to a large and enthusiastic audience. Here he set the pattern which he merely elaborated throughout the remainder of the campaign.[6] Comer's main theme was that the railroads had for years deprived the people of Alabama of their right to rule their own state and that the time had come to free the people from alien and arbitrary rule. This, with its numerous variations, was the heart of the Comer platform.

Comer's analysis began with the assertion that railroads were not private property. The Supreme Court had declared in the case of *Munn v. Illinois* that businesses clothed with the public interest were subject to public regulation.[7] The import of Comer's statement went further. He usually spoke of railroads as if they were in fact, as well as technically, "creatures of the State." In Comer's vocabulary railroad rates were "taxes."

[4] Greenville *Living Truth*, July 7, 1905.

[5] Willett to Stallings, April 16, 1906, Stallings Papers, University of North Carolina.

[6] An edited version of this speech appeared in the friendly Birmingham *News*, January 6, 1906. I quote from the stenographic transcript which appeared in the hostile Montgomery *Advertiser*, December 14, 1905.

[7] 94 U.S. 113 (1877).

The perception of railroad rates as taxes had a dual thrust. In the first place, it gave reality to the businessman's dependence on modern transportation in order to operate in a competitive world. Despite the high degree of centralization in the ownership of the railroads serving Alabama, competition did exist. Railroad attempts to set rates cooperatively through tariff and passenger associations frequently broke down into price competition. But this was irrelevant to the intrastate shipper who usually had little choice as to which railroad to use. He experienced railroad rates as arbitrarily set tariffs. More importantly, Comer's principal backers regarded railroads not as profit-making organizations but as "public service corporations" in the strictest sense of the phrase. They thought such organizations should primarily be conducted so as to benefit the business community of the state.[8]

Second, viewing railroad rates as taxes had the admirable advantage of opening to the reformers the benefits of the tradition that taxation without representation was tyranny. Comer couched his arguments less and less in terms of statistics showing that Alabamians paid rates 20 to 120 percent higher than Georgians, and more and more in terms of popular government and self-rule. Big corporations played the part of George III—Comer, of course, was Thomas Jefferson.

Like Jefferson, Comer praised farming. Certainly, no one who wanted to win an election in Alabama could ignore it or the myriad agricultural sensibilities. Comer told farmers that they were "the salvation of the state." He told them that "the rule of the farmer has never been

[8] Regularity and predictability are greatly desired by businessmen. Comer said, "what we want to do is to get all these things regulated by law." Montgomery *Advertiser*, January 9, 1906.

destructive, as the rule of capital is dangerous, as the rule of combines and trusts is dangerous. . . ."[9] But Comer denied that he was a latter-day Populist. "They say I am setting one class against another class," Comer said. "Nothing could be further from the fact, because if you take the people I mentioned (businessmen and farmers) you have got the state; all that you have left is a few mechanical politicians hanging around for graft or something else."[10] By dismissing his opponents among the business community, and by ignoring the existence of the wage-earning class, Comer was able to picture his struggle as one between a group of honest businessmen on the one hand and corruptionists on the other hand. Though Comer spoke in Jeffersonian terms, his perception of society was Whiggish.[11]

To him it was the whole of society that was hurt by railroad domination. The crucial fact, Comer said repeatedly, was that the L & N charged an average of 45 percent more on 1,600 specified items in Alabama than it did in Georgia. These high freight rates represented a loss to the state of several million dollars per year, money that should have stayed in the pockets of farmers and other producers rather than being siphoned off by out-of-state interests. Consumers were also hurt, Comer thought, by the reciprocal relationship between the rates on pig iron and agricultural products. Low rates were charged on pig iron, coal, and coke to get them to market at competitive prices and thus develop the heavy industry and bulk traffic that went with it. This subsidy was paid by the farmer. Big Mules were quite aware of their favored position and opposed Comer vehemently;

[9] Montgomery *Advertiser*, December 14, 1905.
[10] *Ibid.*, March 1, 1906.
[11] *Ibid.*, January 9, 1906.

they clung to the idea that growth was best assured by allowing outside capital to develop the state's raw materials.

Comer argued that community growth was not only damaged by draining off funds that would have meant more goods for the farmer and more profit for the merchants, but that existing railroad policy retarded the development of manufacturing enterprises which one might normally expect to flourish in the neighborhood of plentiful cotton, lumber, iron, and coal. High local rates made it more profitable to ship the raw materials out of the state with a minimum amount of processing and fabrication.

Every civic-minded townsman in Alabama felt in the depths of his ledger book that Comer was right. He offered more than the prospect of progress for the whole state. To them railroad regulation also meant uniform local freight rates, a measure of control over one of their most variable and most important cost parameters, and an equal chance against all other trading centers to make the most of their town's natural advantages. Equality of opportunity and equity were forceful appeals.

Comer and the small businessman core of Alabama Progressivism were Whigs dressed in Jacksonian clothing. They sought to accomplish Hamiltonian ends with Jeffersonian arguments. For this purpose they championed the principle of "equal rights to all and special privileges to none," but they had come to understand this in a new way. Because the nature of private property had changed since Jackson's day, a free economy could no longer sort men into their proper stations in accordance with their moral worth. Alabama Progressives were therefore determined to return to the older doctrine of governmental promotion and regulation of enterprise in the interest of the whole community. They spoke not with the defensiveness and fear of a declining class, but with the confidence of those who were a latent majority. They needed only to mobilize the community to protect itself from the ill effects of inherently privileged private economic power.[12]

Concern about insufficiently restrained use of private economic power was not peculiar to Alabama in 1906. Outward-looking and psychologically integrated with the nation as they had not been since well before the Civil War, Alabamians could easily compare state and national affairs. The struggle over the passage of the Hepburn Act to increase the regulatory powers of the Interstate Commerce Commission preoccupied the federal government. Paradoxically enough, in neighboring Georgia, Hoke Smith was running for governor on a platform promising to reduce the rates that Comer had set as the goal for Alabama. Amid the Hepburn bill debate, Roosevelt sent to Congress the Bureau of Corporations' report on the Standard Oil Company, with its documentation of secret rebate practices which also implicated the "Beef Trust" and the "Sugar Trust." Then Upton Sinclair's novel, *The Jungle*, and the government report made at Roosevelt's order, dramatically exposed conditions in the meat-packing industry. Meat, flour, coffee, and sugar were the most important purchases of the Alabama farmer. When David Graham Phillips published "The Treason of the Senate," Comer's charge that the railroads had dominated the Alabama legislature for 25 years was immediately much more plausible. At Tuscaloosa in December, Comer directed the attention of Alabamians to the effort of Charles Evans Hughes and the Armstrong investigation in New York which dis-

[12] *Ibid.*, February 18, 1906.

261

closed questionable business practices as well as political corruption in the insurance industry, a branch of commerce almost as unpopular in Alabama as the railroads.[13] State and national affairs in 1906 were beautifully harmonius. And if Alabamians were so dull that they could not appreciate this, Comer frequently emphasized the compatibility of state and national developments. "We are fighting for a law," Comer told his audience in Wedowee, "that gives every man a square deal."[14]

However, it would seem that 1906 was an inauspicious time to launch a reform movement. In most respects Alabama was at the peak of a three-year boom and an upward business trend that had gotten underway after 1898. The Southern Cotton Growers Association met in New Orleans in January and urged planters to withhold cotton until the price rose to 15 cents per pound. The current price was 10 cents, double the value of a pound of cotton in 1898. Real estate men in Montgomery reported that all sorts of real property in the city had doubled in value over the past five years, while suburban property had done even better.[15] The mineral district was also booming. In November 1906 the Commercial Club announced that Birmingham had gained a greater number of small industries in the preceding two years than in any previous five-year period. The price of TCI stock shot up from $85 to $140 a share after controlling interest was bought by John W. Gates and a syndicate that also controlled Republic Steel.[16] Don Bacon, the general

[13] Birmingham *Age-Herald*, November 23, 1905.

[14] Montgomery *Advertiser*, February 21, 1906. For further evidence that Comer identified himself with Rooseveltean Progressivism, see Comer to Michael Comer, February 3, 1908, Comer Papers, University of North Carolina.

[15] Montgomery *Advertiser*, January 13, 1906.

[16] Birmingham *Age-Herald*, November 25, December 7, 9, 13,

manager, was already in the process of raising TCI's capacity. Stimulated by purchases by the Harriman railroads, demand for TCI's steel rails was running 12 months in advance of production.[17] In addition, the number of cotton mills in Alabama had doubled since 1900, totaling 54.[18]

There were a few segments of the population that were distressed. Five thousand union miners had been on strike since July 25, 1904, and 3,800 of these were unemployed.[19] Small farmers were dissatisfied enough to respond eagerly to the organizing efforts of the Farmers Union. At the August meeting the organization claimed 53,000 members,[20] whereas in March it had claimed only 40,000 members with 70 paid organizers at work and 700 locals in existence.[21] The union, spouting the old Populist rhetoric, was weakest in the Black Belt and south Alabama, while its major strength was in northwest Alabama. Its major thrust was against the exorbitant and unrestrained prices of merchants. "We are tired of being robbed," cried one speaker. "We are tired of having men rob of us of the fruits of our toil and we are going to stop it."[22] The union had already launched an overambi-

---

14, 16, 20, 1905. John W. Gates to Oscar W. Underwood, June 1, 1906, Underwood Papers, ADAH.

[17] Birmingham *Age-Herald*, July 14, 1906.

[18] Montgomery *Advertiser*, May 25, 1906

[19] Birmingham *Age-Herald*, August 22, 1906.

[20] *Ibid.*

[21] Montgomery *Advertiser*, March 9, 1906.

[22] *Ibid.* This distrust of the merchant would seem to weigh against the hypothesis that Populism was triggered when town dwellers were finally so hurt by the depression of the 1890s that they joined the existing rural protest movement. David F. Trask, "A Note on the Politics of Populism," *Nebraska History*, XLVI, June 1965, 157-161, also suggests that town Populists were the link between Populism and Progressivism. For a discussion

tious program of cooperative warehouses, gins, and fertilizer factories, and it planned for retail stores later. These discontents, however, were not important among the people to whom the Comer forces were trying to appeal.

Comer's constituency was interested in success. But there is an endemic tension in the American mind that counters the pressure for material success with pressures to justify activity with a higher order of moral purposes.[23] Bishop Charles Betts Galloway was speaking in a long tradition of Protestant thought when he complained to the General Conference of the Methodist Episcopal Church South that the new business ways undermined the old faith. "The age has become too materialistic, too commercial," he said.[24] Because of the tension within the Protestant ethic, the alliance of humanitarian reformers, political reformers, and business reformers, antedating the advent of prosperity in Alabama, was a natural one, but the cutting edge of the Progressive movement in Alabama was primarily concerned with material progress and with changing the distribution of wealth to favor the middle range of the economic hierarchy. Consequently Progressives were readier than usual to detect in others the pathological extremes of materialistic behavior that they feared in themselves. This opened the way for a new perception of evil which was characteristic of Progressivism.

Revelations of wrongdoing had begun in 1899 when Johnston was implicated in the sale of University of Ala-

---

of the Farmers' Union see William P. Tucker, "Populism Up-to-Date: The Story of the Farmers' Union," *Agricultural History*, XXI, October 1947, 198-208.

[23] Karen Horney, *The Neurotic Personality of Our Time*, New York, 1937, 288.

[24] Montgomery *Advertiser*, May 3, 1906.

bama lands at windfall prices to industrial corporations. This was overshadowed in January 1901 when Leslie Brooks, a Progressive legislator from Mobile, foiled a special committee's efforts to whitewash the convict department. His minority report accused Johnston's administration of negligence, taxing employees for political campaigns, lax discipline, and allowing kickbacks from state contractors. John W. DuBose, an old political reformer to whom Johnston had given a job in the convict department, had an inside view of the entire affair and was shocked. "Knowing the record from daily observation of two years," DuBose wrote to a friend in 1901, "I could unfold a tale of venality the most 'calculated' that we have had in Alabama in any period. . . . But DuBose thought the legislators were guilty of rascality as great as that of the convict department.[25] He recorded that legislators in 1901 engaged in a multiplicity of corrupt practices. "Legislators stole bills that had been passed to prevent their enrollment. Legislators bribed clerks to amend bills after they had been passed. Legislators seeing the enfeebled condition of the Governor, surreptitiously amended bills that had been passed hoping yet vainly that he had not the mental force to detect the rascality."[26]

The difficulties of the state convict department had scarcely left the front pages when the most inhumane aspects of the convict lease system and the fee system were illustrated for all to see in Butler County. Innocent men, usually defenseless Negroes but sometimes itinerant whites, were being arrested, charged with unlawfully riding the trains, and sentenced to long leases in the mines

[25] DuBose to B. W. Henry, March 7, 1901, DuBose Papers, ADAH.
[26] *Ibid.*

to pay for their fine and court fees. The sheriff was paid by the railroads to be especially diligent in enforcing the railroad laws. When he made an arrest, he took the accused before the probate judge where numerous witnesses appeared to testify, at the regular witness fee, and all the court officers earned fees for their services in connection with the trial. The defendant paid for the overabundance of "due process" with cash or by a long stint in the mines. After the story came to public attention, a state examiner found that 91 men had been sentenced to the mines on the single charge of riding trains illegally in the previous three months alone.[27]

Progressives experienced afresh man's depravity.[28] At the same time, they confidently affirmed their belief that institutional reform could alleviate the results of man's propensity to sin. Reforms, whether positive or negative, are attempts to make up for the failure of unfettered human beings. Hugh S. D. Mallory expressed this somewhat anomalous phenomenon of reform based on a pessimistic perception of human nature. He spoke to a Sunday School convention in Montgomery on the subject of civic righteousness. "Untie the hands of men and see how soon disaster would overtake us," he warned in good Puritan fashion. "Ten worthy men would have been sufficient to have saved the cities," he said, referring to the story of Sodom and Gomorrah. "Take courage my friends. There are other righteous people living in the community who are working for the prevalence of right."[29] Despite the

[27] Montgomery *Advertiser*, March 8, 9, 12, 1901.

[28] For other expressions of pessimism see: R. W. Cobb to Robert McKee, July 20, 1898, McKee Papers, ADAH; W. H. Denson to John W. DuBose, December 18, 1905, DuBose Papers, ADAH; and Birmingham *Age-Herald*, November 28, 1905.

[29] Montgomery *Advertiser*, April 25, 1906. Comer used the same figure of speech, *ibid.*, January 9, 1906.

fact that the *Advertiser* attacked Comer's use of a pessimistic view of human nature,[30] he continued to paint a gloomy picture of man's inability to curb his selfish drive to accumulate wealth,[31] and balanced the picture with an appeal to Alabamians to enlist under the banner of the 10 righteous men and save their community.

To accelerate enlistment Comer ran one of the most effective campaigns in the history of the state, modeled on his masterful and successful campaign of 1904.[32] His organization was large, efficient, and well financed.[33] W. D. Nesbitt, a Birmingham warehouseman who had been active in the movement for rate reform since at least 1901, acted as campaign manager. Comer, materially assisted by Frank S. White and the Farmers', Merchants' and Laborers' Association which had been active since 1902, barnstormed the state, spoke in every county, and heavily emphasized mailing propaganda to large segments of the electorate. He enjoyed more newspaper support in this battle than in 1904, but still could count a majority of the state's weeklies and dailies against him.[34]

One of the big differences between the campaigns was that in 1906 Comer subordinated his statistical arguments to more emotional appeals to the desire for self-rule.[35] "And here was the railroads of Alabama buying

[30] *Ibid.*, March 10, 1906.

[31] *Ibid.*, February 21, 1906. This sentiment was shared by Comer's supporter, Abe Lehman, in the Greenville *Living Truth*, July 7, 1905.

[32] B. B. Comer to John A. Lusk, February 3, 1908, Governor's Office Records, ADAH. Comer reported expenditures of $8,499.96, which was less than he had spent in 1904. Cunningham spent $1,561.68. Birmingham *Age-Herald*, September 26, and 27, 1906.

[33] Montgomery *Advertiser*, August 29, 1906.

[34] Doster, *Railroads in Alabama Politics*, 149-150.

[35] Montgomery *Advertiser*, March 9, 1906.

right and left, as far as they could reach," Comer told his audiences, "with money taxed from the people. They taxed you at a higher rate and they taxed you for the purpose of buying you."[36] At Jasper, Comer pulled a sheaf of passes from his pocket and, while waving them in front of the audience, asked why it was that politicians were worth something to telegraph companies. "How can any man who is paid by the railroads serve the people?" he wanted to know.[37] He campaigned hard not only for his own election, but in order to insure the election of a majority of friendly legislators. His efforts were so effective that candidates for the legislature and lesser offices were styling themselves as official Comer candidates without the blessings of the Comer organization. Late in the campaign Nesbitt mailed throughout the state a list of candidates who carried the genuine Comer seal of approval.[38]

In his keynote speech at Tuscaloosa, Comer alluded to the fact that the railroads had announced they would take no part in the campaign. He noted triumphantly that this was in marked contrast to the open railroad opposition to the reform forces in 1902 and 1904. Comer claimed the railroads spent $500,000 to defeat him in 1904.[39] Milton H. Smith, president of the L & N, later told the Interstate Commerce Commission that his railroad occasionally made political contributions and paid political agents in order to protect the company's interests. He said he spent $15,000 in 1907 aiding an Alabama paper "which was advocating certain views upon public questions in which the Louisville and Nashville

[36] *Ibid.*, January 9, 1906.
[37] *Ibid.*, February 11, 18, 1906.
[38] *Ibid.*, August 26, 1906. Birmingham *Age-Herald*, August 26, 1906.
[39] Montgomery *Advertiser*, February 21, 1906.

concurred." Smith also admitted to spending $34,800 in "an advertising campaign to defeat Comer's schemes,"[40] but there is no direct evidence that any of this money was used in the campaign of 1906.

If railroad coffers were not open to the anti-Comer forces in 1906, "railroad environed men" (as Comer liked to call them) were active in the effort to defeat Comer and enjoyed the advantage of controlling the party machinery. They put this control to good use. In order to frustrate Comer's hopes of influencing the legislative races, a group of railroad politicians, owners, and managers met and arranged a plan of election that separated the gubernatorial primary from legislative primaries.[41] The State Executive Committee of the Democratic Party on January 9, 1906 adopted the "Whitson Plan" which set August 27 as the day for the statewide primary and left legislative races to be provided for according to the various wishes of local committees.

Even more ingenious arrangements were required to keep Comer's influence away from the process of choosing the United States senators. The next legislature would name at its only regular session two senators for terms beginning in 1907 and 1909. To unseat the incumbents —both heroes of the Civil War—was unthinkable. Yet John Tyler Morgan was 82 in 1906 and Edmund Winston Pettus was 85. There was the definite possibility that neither would live through his next term of office. The prospective passing of the two old heroes was not

[40] "Milton H. Smith Testifies Regarding Political Contributions," *Railway Age*, LXIV, March 1, 1918, 446.

[41] Montgomery *Advertiser*, January 21, 22, 25, 28, 1906. The subcommittee consisted of C. C. Whitson, T. M. Stevens, William H. Samford, Jones G. Moore, and Edward B. Almon. The last named gentleman was the only one with no known railroad connection.

to be mourned overlong if their successors could be chosen without the aid of Comer, who would probably be governor at the crucial time.

The State Executive Committee provided a solution to the problem in the "pall bearer's primary." By tacit agreement, Morgan and Pettus would be unopposed. The state committee pledged that the next governor would appoint the winners of the primary for "alternate senators" to any vacancy in Alabama's two U.S. senate seats that might occur during his administration. In this case the Big Mules felt the people were less to be feared than Comer. Thus burdened with irony, the direct election of United States senators made its appearance in Alabama.

Almost forgotten in the intricate planning based on the assumption that Comer would win the election was Comer's opponent for the governorship. From his home in Ensley, an industrial suburb of Birmingham dominated by TCI, Lieutenant Governor Russell M. Cunningham issued a long address on September 22, 1905, announcing that he would "actively enter the canvass for Governor."[42] His main problem was evident in this initial campaign document. He presented himself as a thoroughgoing reformer, but could not conceal the embarrassing identity of his supporters. Seen another way, his problem was how to convince the electorate that he was a reformer without alienating his anti-reform supporters.

Cunningham tried. He matched most of Comer's positions on issues of reform. Both candidates were in favor of increasing expenditures for education, both were for local option, both were in favor of trying to attract suitable (white) immigrants to the state, and both wanted to continue Johnston's back-tax commission. On the ques-

[42] Montgomery *Advertiser*, September 23, 1905.

tion of convict leasing, Cunningham had a legitimate claim to the title of reformer. He proposed to cease leasing convicts to private companies and instead work them in state mines. He knew the horrors of the leasing system because for a number of years he had been the physician for TCI, the state's leading consumer of convicts. In fact, he claimed that he lost this job in 1902 partly because of his activities as an advocate of penal reform. He had been chairman of the legislative investigating committee in 1897 that had looked into conditions at convict-operated mines and had supported reform then. He was also outspoken at the Constitutional Convention of 1901 and had had considerable impact on the convict policy of the Jelks administration.

The most pressing problem in 1906 with regard to the convict system was the condition of county convicts. It was an even greater political problem for Cunningham. He was depending on the support of county officeholders who in turn depended on the fine and forfeiture fund to pay the fat fees that made public service less of a sacrifice. Cunningham tried to solve his dilemma by proposing to abolish the practice of leasing county convicts while at the same time protecting the fine and forfeiture fund by devoting to it a large proportion of the income from the state convict department.[43] This would allow the wound to heal without depriving the leeches.

Cunningham also tried to undercut Comer's claim to sole possession of the issue of rate reform. He pointed out that he had voted for the Langdon bill in 1881, five years before Comer even became aware of the problem. He had also voted for the Boykin bill in 1897 and had voted to break a tie in the state senate in 1903 in favor of the rate reformers. During his year as acting governor,

[43] *Ibid.*

271

while Jelks was recuperating in the West, he had tried to prod the associate railroad commissioners into action on behalf of rate reductions. He even threatened to call a special session of the legislature if they did not act. Unfortunately Cunningham did not make the threat until the last day of his incumbency, so his sincerity in this regard was hard to gauge.

Cunningham's commitment to reform was in doubt from other sources also. Comer was an unusually dynamic man, but his activism probably represented a more general progressive attitude toward the role of government. In his speech at Tuscaloosa he had criticized his colleagues on the Alabama State Railroad Commission because they insisted that proceedings before the commission were judicial and that the commissioners should act as impartial judges. Comer thought the commissioners should be public prosecutors, while Cunningham held the traditional view.[44] Comer recognized this difference and pointed out to his audiences the passive implications of Cunningham's statement that Cunningham was "one of those who believe that the Governor should confine himself to the constitutional limitations of his office. . . ."[45] In his initial campaign document Cunningham had confirmed his distaste for governmental activism when he wrote that with regard to railroad rate reform, "all that can be done by the Executive Department of the Government has been done, and is being done by Governor Jelks and his able associates in the Executive offices."[46]

[44] Cunningham expressed this in his initial announcement, from which Comer quoted at Tuscaloosa. Cunningham repeated his opinion on other occasions. Montgomery *Advertiser*, April 24, 1906.

[45] Montgomery *Advertiser*, December 14, 1905.

[46] *Ibid.*, September 23, 1905.

Satisfaction with a minimal amount of very passive government was the chief philosophical trait of the faction of the Democratic party that Cunningham represented in 1906.[47] In 1900 William J. Samford, although an advocate of silver coinage, had voiced the same sentiment when he was running for governor. "The fundamental principle of the government," he thought, "is the protection of the citizen in the enjoyment of life, liberty and property, and when government undertakes more than that it is usurpation. The citizen is left to work out his destiny in the state."[48]

The Progressives' sharp departure from the dominant political thought of the time is thrown into bold relief against the background of Governor Jelks' attitudes toward government. Jelks was an effective administrator and did the state a great service in refunding the debt advantageously and increasing the revenue from the convict system eight-fold.[49] But he was neither an innovator nor an activist, and he made no attempt to lead the legislature.[50] Perhaps this school of thought is best illustrated in Jelks' attitude toward education. In his message to the legislature in 1903 he correctly observed that "the school spirit is alive in the State and the appropriation for the common schools which open at the door of the humbler homes should be constantly augmented, as the State Treasurer can afford it. . . ." Almost everyone was for education. As the legislatures of 1899 and 1903 showed,

[47] This theme has been touched on above in Chapter III.

[48] Mobile *Register*, January 11, 1900.

[49] The Convict Department in five years of the Jelks administration netted $937,278, while in the previous five years it had taken in only $104,278. Montgomery *Advertiser*, March 6, 1906.

[50] Moore, *History of Alabama*, 915. Wilson to Jelks, January 3, 1903, Governor's Office Records, ADAH.

273

the sheep and the goats divided on the practical question of how much money to spend and where it was to come from. Jelks was setting himself against the Progressives when he urged the legislature not to appropriate more than the treasury could afford under existing arrangements. There was also another differentiating question. What was the function of the schools? Governor Jelks observed that farm children could not afford to go to school four months a year for 9 or 10 years. They should be provided with a "healthy four year course" which would "fit him or her for the most usual demands of life." "This briefer course should not prevent the more fortunately situated children from a larger and more complete one."[51]

Jelks was not bothered by the lack of equality of opportunity because he held a static view of society. He wanted to shape institutions to fit society, but Progressives saw institutions in a more dynamic role. Few in Alabama wanted to use government or the school system transform society completely, but Progressives did want these institutions to make society function more in accordance with the success myth.

Comer was a threat to those who were satisfied with the current results of the struggle for economic supremacy and who approved of the existing rules that made those results possible. Their arguments against him came in three categories. They paradoxically insisted that Comer was not interested enough in reforms other than in railroad rates. At the same time, they tried to undermine Comer's rationale of the need for railroad rate reform. But perhaps their strongest stock-in-trade consisted of *ad hominem* attacks on Comer himself.

[51] Alabama, *Acts, 1903*, 12. The Governor's Message is found on pages 2-26.

His enemies made a persistent attempt to make it seem that Comer did not fit the genteel mold. They attacked him for being power mad, selfish, malevolent, mentally unbalanced, wild, "a howling dervish," vain, domineering, insincere, inconsistent, and generally a demagogue.[52] During one debate, after Cunningham had attacked Comer's record on child labor, which by any standard was not progressive, Comer evidently lost his temper. The hostile crowd shouted him down and refused to let him continue. Partisan papers interpreted the political impact of this incident to suit their purpose and, as was true of the whole question of Comer's character, its effect on the vote is problematical.

More basic to the point at issue were the continuous attempts to break the bludgeon of Comer's anti-railroad rhetoric. Many of the arguments reverberated with faith in limited government and the sanctity of private property.[53] The good citizenship argument was even more common. "No developing agencies in the south are doing more in the way of expansion than the railroads," declared the *Age-Herald*.[54] The theme was reiterated by the *Advertiser* and other Cunningham papers. Thomas G. Bush, an eminently successful businessman with interests in coal, iron, and railroads, as well as banking and insurance, put a final gloss on the good-citizenship argument in a pamphlet entitled "Railroads: Their Relation to the People." The effort was reminiscent of his pamphlet of 1902 arguing against the proposed change

[52] Montgomery *Advertiser*, February 6, 22, March 2, April 21, 24, 25, June 1, 6, 15-19, and 22, 1906. Birmingham *Age-Herald*, August 24, 1906.

[53] William C. Oates and John T. Morgan were among the most doctrinaire candidates in 1906. Montgomery *Advertiser*, March 13, April 10, 1906.

[54] Birmingham *Age-Herald*, November 15, December 4, 1905.

from appointive to elective railroad commissioners. "I am opposed," Bush wrote, "to disturbing in an improper way a great business interest of the country that is indissolubly connected with our prosperity."[55] At this point the reasoning is transformed into the timid-capital theory.

To guard against the failure of the timid-capital theory, Comer's opponents also advanced the argument that existing Alabama law went as far as a law could go. Both Alabama law and the *Smyth v. Ames* decision required state regulators to allow the railroads a fair and just return. The *Advertiser* gave the impression that, even if one agreed with the need to regulate railroad rates, nothing more need be done but to await the orderly enforcement of the law.[56] Comer saw clearly that laws do not enforce themselves.

One comic aspect of the campaign was that while some of Cunningham's supporters were attacking Comer for being too radical, others closer to Cunningham himself were attacking Comer for not being a real Progressive. Comer defended himself by saying that he was not a single-issue man. He supported better education, good roads, local option, and veterans' pensions. Nevertheless, he attacked Cunningham for trying to cure too many of society's ills at the same time.[57] This series of mutual recriminations became focused on the issue of child labor reform.

Comer declared he was in favor of strengthening the child labor law, but seemed far from enthusiastic about it.[58] This was the one issue that made him morally uneasy. He not only pointed out that the agitation against

[55] *Ibid.*, December 17, 1905.
[56] Montgomery *Advertiser*, March 8, 10, 1906.
[57] *Ibid.*, August 24, 1906.
[58] *Ibid.*, April 4, 20, 1906.

child labor was centered in the East and was part of a campaign to make Southern cotton mills uncompetitive with New England, also added a not so subtle appeal to race and anti-abolitionist prejudice. According to one newspaper, "He said that the same people who were responsible for the child labor agitation were responsible for the private cars that go spinning from Washington to Booker Washington's institute. . . ."[59]

The child labor debate came to a head in midsummer. It had become centered on the role Comer had played in opposing the child labor law passed in 1903.[60] The *Advertiser* asked Edgar Gardner Murphy to settle the dispute and happily printed his letter. After relating the story of the negotiations with Comer and two other cotton mill men in an effort to achieve a bill that would pass the legislature, Murphy commented: "Mr. Comer has seemed to me the most bitter opponent of child labor leigslation that I have ever known. . . ."[61] But however much Cunningham made of the child labor issue and of the need for reform of the convict lease system, he was not able to wrest the image of reformism from Comer.

Just before election day, a knowledgeable reporter noted that everyone in the capital conceded that Cunningham had the support of most of the machine.[62] As an admirer wrote to Richmond P. Hobson, who was also riding the Comer bandwagon, "if Cunningham is elected Governor of Ala. he will do the bidding of Jelks. This is sub rosa."[63] Even the *Advertiser*'s effort to create a

[59] *Ibid.*, April 24, 1906.

[60] *Ibid.*, June 29, 1906.

[61] *Ibid.*

[62] Hervey Laird in the Birmingham *Age-Herald*, August 26, 1906.

[63] Thomas Williams to Richmond P. Hobson, January 10, 1905, Hobson Papers, Library of Congress.

groundswell effect by printing enthusiastic reports of Cunningham's reception at meetings in the last few weeks of the campaign failed to help. On election day, Cunningham was crushed.

Cunningham managed to carry only seven counties, and Comer polled 61.4 percent of the total vote.[64] The election produced some superficially curious results because of the blurring effect of personalities and residences, but when closely analyzed, the election of 1906 was a resounding endorsement of Comer and Progressivism in Alabama.

One of the most important revelations of the election results is that there was no continuity between Populism and Progressivism in Alabama—Comer's movement rested on a completely different coalition of groups in society. The most obvious difference was that Comer ran up great majorities in the towns and in the Black Belt where Kolb had performed poorly. In addition, as the data in Appendix II show, there was no significant relationship between the Populist percentage of the gubernatorial vote by county in 1892, 1894, or 1896 and Comer's support in 1904 and 1906.

A comparison of the beat returns of the 1892 election and the 1906 election in the only five counties where they are available for both elections shows that in only one of the five did Kolb precincts tend to vote for Comer more than for Cunningham. By luck, the five counties (Mobile, Calhoun, Montgomery, Tuscaloosa, and Escambia) provide a moderately good representative sample of the state. Of the 78 precincts in those counties in 1906 whose

[64] Alabama State Department of Archives and History, *Alabama Official and Statistical Register, 1907*, 272. Montgomery *Advertiser*, September 8, 1906. Comer got 58,033 votes to Cunningham's 36,628.

boundaries were relatively unchanged from 1892, 64 percent followed the pattern of Jones' precincts going to Cunningham and Kolb beats going to Comer. A closer look at the returns within the counties will diminish even this slight hint of continuity.

In Calhoun County, Comer's majority of two votes out of a total 1,608 votes cast in 1906 was gained in the city of Anniston, which he carried 295-262, and in the town of Jacksonville, which he carried 54-21. Cunningham ran well in the countryside. In contrast, Kolb in 1892 lost Anniston, Jacksonville, Piedmont, and Oxford, but ran far ahead of Jones outside the towns. Of the 11 precincts likely to have been similarly constituted in 1892 and 1906, five gave Kolb a majority in 1892 and Cunningham a majority in 1906. There were also two Jones beats which voted for Comer. Only four precincts of the 11 conformed to the Jones-Cunningham and Kolb-Comer pattern.[65]

In Escambia County the vote drop between 1892 and 1906 was not quite so drastic as in Calhoun. This, plus the fact that both elections were very close, may make the comparison more valid. Jones carried the county in 1892 by 960-913 and Comer in 1906 by 436-409. This is one of the few counties in which Kolb carried the main town of the county. He led in Brewton by a vote of 411 to 276, yet lost the county by 47 votes! Comer divided Brewton almost evenly (133-131), yet ran ahead in the county by 25 votes. Of the 17 precincts existing in 1892, 10 are comparable to those in 1906. Seven of these 10 precincts follow the Kolb-Comer and Jones-Cunningham patterns. This jigger of support for Populist-Progressive continuity is diluted by the atypical fact that in this

[65] The Anniston *Republican*, August 13, 1892. *The Weekly Times*, September 6, 1906.

county Comer ran much better outside the towns than did Kolb.[66]

The precincts in Montgomery County changed so much between 1892 and 1906 that they are not comparable. City and country are distinct, however, in both races. Kolb ran only slightly better in the country than in the city and didn't do very well in either. He lost the city by a vote of 3,970 to 585 and lost the whole county by a score of 7,594 to 1,340. Under the managership of the future Progressive governor, Bibb Graves, Comer was able to win in Montgomery County by 1,252 to 1,225. He ran as far ahead of Kolb in rural Montgomery County as in the city.[67]

Mobile County was carried in 1892 by Thomas G. Jones (3,533 to 2,021) and in 1906 by Russell M. Cunningham (1,697 to 1,354), but the two candidates did not get their votes from the same places. Although over half of Kolb's Mobile votes came from the city, he polled a higher proportion of the total rural vote than of the urban votes. Comer received almost half of the city votes but was beaten by a ratio of 5-3 in the country. Furthermore, most of Kolb's city vote came from wards seven and eight which Cunningham carried in 1906! The Jones wards split evenly for Comer and Cunningham. Urban labor was not enthusiastic about Comer, as they had been for Kolb, but there were other urban men who did identify strongly with Comer. In Mobile County outside the city, 10 Jones precincts went for Cunningham and only 4 for Comer, while 3 Kolb precincts went for Cunningham and 5 for Comer. Comer polled a much smaller

---

[66] The Brewton *Standard Gauge*, August 11, 1892. *The Pine Belt News*, September 6, 1906.

[67] Montgomery *Advertiser*, August 9, 1892 and August 29, 1906.

portion of the noncity vote than did Kolb in Mobile County.[68]

Tuscaloosa yields the best evidence of continuity between Populist supporters and Progressivism. Kolb managed to carry Tuscaloosa County 2,950 votes to 2,297 for Jones. He accomplished this by running well in Tuscaloosa and Northport, then doing much better than Jones in the small towns and rural beats. Comer's pattern looked much the same. Seventeen precincts giving Kolb a majority also gave Comer a majority, while only two Kolb precincts went for Cunningham. Four Jones precincts went to Comer and 3 to Cunningham. But Comer barely carried the county, 1,074-1,036. The difference between his performance and Kolb's is that Kolb polled over two-thirds of the votes outside of Tuscaloosa and Northport while Comer polled just half of them.[69]

Conclusions must be cautious. The drop in vote was so great that all of Comer's voters could have voted for Jones in 1892 and there would still be enough Jones votes left over to account for Cunningham's total. There are also certain atypical aspects about the five representative counties. In each of them the vote was very close in 1906, whereas in the state as a whole Comer won quite easily. Comer performed much better in the Black Belt as a whole than he did in Montgomery, far better in Jefferson County (Birmingham) than in Calhoun or Mobile and better in the white counties than in Escambia. Yet it is clear that no case can be made in Alabama for the contention that Comer's Progressive movement was merely Populism with a veneer of middle class leadership.

Evidence of the lack of continuity between Populist

[68] Mobile *Register*, September 2, 1906, August 7, 1892.
[69] *Tuscaloosa Gazette*, August 18, 1892. *Times-Gazette*, September 4, 1906.

and Progressive followers can be made more certain by neutralizing the biases of the election statistics. Factors tending to distort comparisons between the election returns of 1892 and 1906 can be reduced by looking only at those counties where the distortion would be at a minimum. Considering only counties outside the Black Belt will minimize the effects of Negro disfranchisement and of the strong shift in Planter support from stand-pat candidates to Comer. Because we already know that urban labor tended to support Populism in 1892, 1894, and 1896, and that labor supported Comer in 1902, opposed him in 1904, and supported him again in 1906, nothing is lost by dropping from consideration counties containing urban centers. This will eliminate the effects of the swing of the urban, middle classes from an anti-Populist to a pro-Progressive stance. Finally, the fact that Populists who became Republicans after the 1890s probably did not participate in the Democratic primaries of 1904 and 1906 (and voted against Comer in the general elections) would inflate Comer's proportion of the vote of counties with a large Republican contingent. This can be compensated for by not considering counties that rank in the top third of all counties in Alabama with regard to their Republican vote.

Table 4 shows the trend of the vote from 1892 to 1906 in the remaining nine non-Black Belt, nonurban, non-Republican counties. The figures represent the arithmetic difference between the percentage of the county's vote and the percentage of the state's total vote that was cast against the common enemy of the Populists and Progressives. These nine counties were strongly Populist. They contributed a much higher proportion of their vote for the anti-machine candidates than did the state as a whole. But as the reformer's share of the total state vote

TABLE 4

Continuity in Nine Non-Black Belt, Non-Republican, Nonurban Counties. Arithmetic Percentage Deviation from the State Average for Anti-Boss Candidates in Each Election

Counties	1892	1894	1896	1898	1900	1904	1906
				Percent of state			
	48	43	41	31	28	60	61
Bibb	13	19	18	13	18	6	1
Conecuh	−6	17	15	23	26	15	−1
Crenshaw	14	8	12	10	10	7	11
Henry	18	2	9	11	−7	11	−1
Jackson	−7	3	4	−12	9	8	−2
Lamar	18	1	3	−11	−7	11	5
Lawrence	31	30	24	19	16	−28	−14
Limestone	27	10	6	−18	−7	−20	11
Tallapoosa	28	14	9	2	−2	3	−8
Average	15.1	11.4	11.1	4.1	6.2	1.4	.2
Median	18	10	9	11	10	7	−1

steadily decreased, and as white voter participation also fell, there was an even more rapid decline in the proportion of their vote that these nine counties gave to the anti-Boss candidates. By 1900 there was very little difference between the way the nine ex-Populist counties voted and the way the average non-Populist county voted. There was virtually no difference between Comer's performance in these counties in 1906 and his performance in the rest of the state. Every indication is that there was a reshuffling of the electorate between 1900 and 1904 so that it divided along lines completely different in 1906 from the lines of cleavage in 1892.

Comer's election signaled a new era for Alabama politics in other ways, also. New men were taking control as the ferment of Progressivism affected normally stable local political structures. In 1911 there were only 27 out of 67 counties in which either the man who was probate judge in 1907 or the man who was circuit clerk in 1907 was still in one or the other of these offices. Compared to other periods, this indicates a large turnover among officeholders. Between 1903 and 1907 there were 42 counties with continuity in these posts, and between 1919 and 1927 there were 44 counties with continuity. One would expect a high turnover rate during a depression, but even in the period 1927 to 1935 there were more counties (33) with continuity in officeholders than during the great surge of Progressivism from 1907 to 1911. There were also changes in the membership of the legislature, which reflected the nature of Alabama Progressivism. In particular, there was an increase between 1903 and 1907 in the number of members who had previous experience in municipal government. In the House the increase was 35 percent and in the Senate it was 125 percent. At the same time the Progressive movement was evidently bringing new men into state politics. The number of state senators with previous legislative experience dropped from 21 in 1903 to 16 in 1907 and to 13 in 1911—a real changing of the guard.[70]

By the time of the election on August 27, 1906 the crucial question was whether or not Comer had been able to influence enough of the local races to give him control of the legislature and of the state Democratic convention. The final word on control of the legislature could not be given until the roll calls began in January 1907. But when A. M. Tunstall announced that he would not be available for reelection as Speaker of the House

[70] The raw data for these statistics were contained in the *Alabama Official and Statistical Register* for the years 1903, 1907, 1911, 1919, 1927, 1935.

of Representatives, it was evident that those who kept a close watch on local contests knew Comer had won.[71] At the same time, the friends of railroad reform let it be known that they would control the state Democratic convention with at least 351 Comer delegates out of a total of 615.[72]

This projection proved fairly accurate. Frank S. White and the leaders of the Comer faction won control of the state convention and of the crucial executive committee on September 10 by votes of 412 to 203 and 284½ to 223½. Comer was firmly in command.[73]

Under the chairmanship of Frank S. White, the Committee on Platform and Resolutions quickly reported, and the convention quickly adopted, statements of principle and commitments to action that announced the reorientation of the Democratic and Conservative party of Alabama. In the first place, one resolution struck the word "conservative" from the party name. As if that were not enough, the preamble to the platform praised the party for at last "wrenching the political control of this state from the domination of foreign railroads." It endorsed William Jennings Bryan for the presidential nomination of the party in 1908 and hailed him as "the greatest democrat of our time." What they particularly liked about Bryan was "his arraignment of trusts, private monopolies and the abuses of public service corporations." The essential philosophy of the mood was capsulized in the credo, "We believe in equal and exact justice between man and man and between man and corporation."[74] The silver wing of Alabama Democracy was obviously back in power.

[71] Birmingham *Age-Herald*, September 9, 1906.
[72] *Ibid.*
[73] *Ibid.*, September 11, 12, 1906.
[74] *Ibid.*

As might have been anticipated, the bulk of the platform was devoted to proposals designed to bring the railroads to heel. These plants spelled out Comer's platform of lower rates, equitable car service, no discrimination, and prompt settlement of claims. Nineteen of the 36 planks were directed against railroads and corporations. To insure the justice of railroad profits, the party proposed a law requiring corporations to disclose their books so the state could see for itself just what the return was. Comer put into one plank his notion that there should be some relationship between the value of railroad property reported for tax purposes and the value reported for rate-determining purposes. The platform also proposed a law to require public service corporations to get prior approval before making any increase in their capital stock or any enlargement or expansion of their property. These and other provisions converted the discontents and desires of the friends of railroad reform into Democratic doctrine.

But other portions of the state convention's statement of goals made it clear that railroad reform was not its only interest. Among the resolutions adopted by the convention were: one in favor of seeking federal funds for better roads, one in favor of a stringent fish and game conservation law in Alabama, one to prevent members of the state board of assessment from accepting railroad passes, and another to set up a board to settle strikes. The platform also pledged the party to enact statutes limiting more severely the use of child labor, abolishing bucket shops and all forms of gambling, providing a uniform rule for local option elections on the question of how best to control the liquor traffic, prohibiting corporations from contributing to political campaigns, and requiring lobbyists to register. The platform went on to endorse more liberal expenditures for education and for pensions for veterans as well as for efforts to encourage immigrants, but not coolies, to come into the state. The convention also announced itself in favor of the direct election of the United States senators.

This formidable program revealed that Comer had become connected with men whose interests were much broader than his own narrow program of railroad rate reform, better schools, and better roads. Behind almost every plank of the platform stood an organized interest group that saw in Comer's movement a vehicle for change. Comer needed allies, so the extraneous interests were made welcome, and each new arrival brought his own pet reform along with him. Comer learned that the fisherman who fishes with a trotline may catch a wide variety of fish, not all of them palatable.

The Comer Administration

The legislature that met on January 8, 1907 was primed for railroad legislation. Comer's initial message on January 15, the day after his inauguration, renewed in familiar terms his call for railroad regulation. Special interest groups, he asserted, must give way before the demands of equity and the need to stimulate diversified industrial development.[1] Comer's picture of a unified community fighting rapacious alien corporations probably confirmed the fears of Milton H. Smith, president of the L & N. Before a New Orleans audience the previous December, Smith charged that the people were being debauched by selfish leaders who unjustly attacked the property rights of railroads. He named B. B. Comer as the most dangerous type of leader. Comer replied that Alabama had treated the railroads fairly and had been overtaxed in return,[2] a situation his legislative program was designed to correct.

Comer had his way with the legislature.[3] When it adjourned March 6 after completing 37 of the 50 legislative days allowed by the constitution, it had written the governor's program into law. Conceived in 1890, postponed by uncooperative Populists, neglected by the

[1] Alabama, *Acts, 1907*, 35-72.
[2] Montgomery *Advertiser*, December 19, 22, 1906.
[3] *Ibid.*, July 8, 1907.

diffuse Progressive forces prior to 1901, given encouragement for the first time in the Constitutional Convention, used as the cornerstone in rebuilding the old silver faction of the Democratic Party after 1901—Comer's dream of railroad rate reform was near realization. The program was designed to produce lower rates and keep the railroads out of the sanctuary of the federal courts. The first thing the legislature did was to establish the freight rates in force on January 1, 1907 as the maximum allowable rates. Then, when the railroads were ordered to abolish discriminatory rates, they would have to lower their higher rates rather than raising their lower rates.[4] The legislature then divided 110 common-use items into 22 categories and fixed the maximum charge per mile for each category.[5] The railroads in each of four classes could charge a given percentage of the fixed rate for each category of goods. In general, weaker roads could charge higher rates. One broad act regulated a wide variety of railroad services and practices,[6] while another prescribed that passenger fares would be 2½ ¢ per mile.[7] To forestall any attack on the technical validity of the 1903 act setting up the Railroad Commission, Comer had the legislature pass a new act giving the commission the power to set rates within the limits established by the legislature and granting it for the first time the power of subpoena and investigation. This same act provided that any corporation operating railroads in Alabama would lose its license if it appealed any rate made by statute or by the commission or if it withdrew a case from a state court to a federal court.[8] This "outlaw"

[4] Alabama, *Acts, 1907*, 80.
[5] *Ibid.*, 209.　　[6] *Ibid.*, 117.　　[7] *Ibid.*, 104.
[8] *Ibid.*, 135. Doster, *Railroads in Alabama Politics*, 157-163.

provision was aimed directly at the favorite defensive strategy of the railroads.

The legislature's aim was poor. The General Assembly had no sooner adjourned than the railroads operating in Alabama simultaneously on March 25 went before Judge Thomas Goode Jones of the United States Circuit Court for the Middle District of Alabama and asked him to enjoin the attorney general and the members of the Railroad Commission from enforcing any of the recently passed railroad laws. Leaving no ground for complaint uncultivated, they claimed that the passenger rate act and the commodity rate act if enforced would deprive them of equal protection of the laws, impair the obligation of contracts, deprive them of property without due process of law, and deny them a reasonable return on the value of their property. The out-of-state corporations also sought injunctions against the law that forbade their resort to the federal courts. On May 8 Judge Jones granted the temporary injunctions and also declared the outlaw act unconstitutional.[9] Outmaneuvered at the bar, the General Assembly met again on July 9 to remount its assault.

The legislature gave Comer a large appropriation to carry on the fight against the railroads, made some minor additions and amendments to the railroad statutes already passed, but did nothing substantial to give the state new weapons. By the time the legislature adjourned on August 7, however, a big break in the situation had occurred.

On August 1, Secretary of State Frank Julian, acting under a recent statute that forbade corporations in gen-

[9] Montgomery *Advertiser*, July 14, 1907.

eral from removing cases from state to federal court and which had not been included in the injunctions granted by Judge Jones, cancelled the license of the Southern Railway to conduct intrastate business in Alabama.[10] This put the Southern in a tight situation. It had just lost a war with North Carolina when that state had ignored federal court injunctions and proceeded to bring criminal proceedings against railroad officials for not abiding by state law. Governor Glenn of North Carolina finally had President W. W. Finley of the Southern arrested—which brought the railroad to terms.[11]

Now Alabama had the Southern at bay. The railroad could fight the state, but it would be a costly battle, and Comer had already let the press know that he was thinking of an extra session of the legislature to enact the North Carolina laws.[12] After a week of negotiations with Comer, J.S.B. Thompson for the Southern and E. L. Russell for the subsidiary Mobile & Ohio signed an agreement with the state. Alabama agreed to restore the railroad's license, and the Southern agreed to put the state's passenger and freight rates into effect on September 1.[13] The parties decided to let a test case on the constitutionality of the acts settle the issue. Judge Jones reluctantly granted the Southern's request that he modify his injunction accordingly. But he also took advantage of the occasion to lecture the governor for his "lawless use of state power to harrass and damage" the railroad. "It is a wicked thing," Jones declared, "to excite the

---

[10] *Ibid.*, August 2, 1907.

[11] Woodward, *Origins of the New South*, 382.

[12] Montgomery *Advertiser*, August 1, 1907.

[13] *Ibid.*, August 9, 1907. See the signed and countersigned agreement in Letterfile 108, dated August 8, 1907, Governor's Office Records, ADAH.

passions of the people against the authority of the courts. . . ."[14]

The harsh lecture from Jones did not deter Comer, for he obviously meant to force the other railroads to follow the Southern's lead. Most of them did. All the roads except the L & N, the South & North Alabama, the Western Alabama, the Central of Georgia, and the Nashville, Chattanooga & St. Louis (NC&St.L) made the same deal with the state that the Southern had made. Milton H. Smith held out.[15]

Comer's supporters greeted his victory over the Southern with exultation. Sam Will John, who was now Comer's floor manager in the lower house, wrote that it was a "Waterloo for corrupt railroad lobbyists, and hangers on around the Federal Courts. . . ."[16] "It is generally remarked around here," wrote one merchant, "that Judge Jones is making an excellent lawyer for the L & N"[17] Tom Watson, the leader of Georgia Populism who had helped Hoke Smith to win the governorship in 1906 on a Progressive platform, sent Comer his "hearty congratulations upon your courageous stand against marauding corporations and usurpatory Federal Judges."[18] Letters of approbation poured in from ordinary citizens and the barely literate, as well as from influential figures. Nevertheless, neither Judge Jones nor Milton H. Smith retreated.

Despite the war psychology that seized the Alabama

[14] Montgomery *Advertiser*, August 10, 1907.

[15] Doster, *Railroads in Alabama Politics*, Chapter 13.

[16] Sam Will John to B. B. Comer, August 10, 1907, Governor's Office Records, ADAH.

[17] Herbert E. Reynolds to Comer, August 16, 1907, Governor's Office Records, ADAH.

[18] Tom Watson to Comer, September 30, 1907, Governor's Office Records, ADAH.

public in the summer of 1907, President Smith of the L & N had reason for hope. There existed in the state a substantial fifth column on which he could depend for support. This group began a new phase of the insurgency against Comer just before the opening of the summer session of the legislature. In Selma vociferous critics of the governor dominated the meeting of the Alabama State Association of Commercial and Industrial Clubs. President A. G. Forbes told the convention, "it is not undue taxation of loan companies and other corporations, nor reduction of railroad rates that is most needed at this time, but new capital. . . . We should encourage and foster railroad extension and betterment and give every inducement to capital that is offered for investment. . . ."[19]

The desire to accommodate timid capital was a substantial barrier to Comer's program among the very group for which he spoke, the men-on-the-make. Comer's critics played on this desire throughout the railroad crisis. When John H. Bankhead appeared before the Democratic legislative caucus to make his acceptance speech after being formally designated as the successor to John T. Morgan in the United States Senate, he used the familiar argument to discredit Comer whose political ambitions he feared. "Capital is as timid as a fawn," he told the legislators, "even the shaking of a bush sends it to cover. We want and must have many millions of foreign capital."[20] As Comer was forcing the railroads into submission in August the *Advertiser* took up its old refrain—the railroads were not oversized monsters re-

[19] Montgomery *Advertiser*, July 4, 1907.
[20] *Ibid.*, July 11, 1907.

quiring regulation, but merely good citizens that brought prosperity.[21]

Consequently, when Smith began to reply to Comer in September, his audience was familiar with his favorite theme and greatly alerted by the deepening financial crisis that had begun in March. "All attempts, effectual or ineffectual, to confiscate capital invested in railroads or other enterprises," Smith informed Comer in an open letter, "discourage its investment, and the people inevitably suffer the consequence." Smith's interpretation of Comer's policies as an attack on property rights led him to the logical conclusion that Comer was unwittingly a dupe of the Socialists.[22] When disagreements reach such absolutist ground, compromise is difficult.[23]

President Finley of the Southern tried to act as a peacemaker between Comer and Smith, but failed. While the collapse of the Knickerbocker Trust Company was carrying Wall Street prices to another low stage in late October, railroad officials flocked to Montgomery to try to make peace with the state. Comer had called the legislature to meet in special session on November 7 to have another go at the railroads, and John A. Lusk, Henry C. Selheimer, and Samuel D. Weakley were hard at work drafting new legislation.[24] On October 21 the Southern

[21] *Ibid.*, August 10, September 27, 29, October 2, 6, November 12, 16, 1907.

[22] *Ibid.*, October 2, 1907.

[23] Testifying in 1915, Smith called Comer "mendacious" and "stupid" and characterized him as "an impossible man. A disordered mind. He will not be placated." U.S., Senate Documents, 64th Cong., 1st Sess., Vol. XL, No. 461, pp. 361-363. Jones was another who went beyond the bounds of propriety in criticizing Comer, and Comer replied in kind. Comer also sued several newspapers for libel.

[24] Montgomery *Advertiser*, October 10, 1907. Comer to Lusk, September 26 and October 14, 1907, Governor's Office Records, ADAH.

and the other compromising railroads made a very advantageous arrangement with Comer. The governor allowed them to raise freight and passenger rates above the statutory limit and promised them legislative immunity.[25]

This move was plotted by the state to lure the L & N into an agreement by giving its competitors substantial advantages.[26] Smith did not take the bait. He was in Montgomery and conferred with Governor Comer, but nothing came from the meeting but an exchange of insulting public letters.[27] Comer's efforts to get cooperation from Governors Hoke Smith of Georgia and Robert B. Glenn of North Carolina also came to nothing when the three met in Atlanta on November 1. Nor could Comer get anything more than professions of goodwill from President Roosevelt.[28]

When Comer's ambushes and flanking movements did

[25] Montgomery *Advertiser*, October 22, November 19, 1907.

[26] Frank Lathrop to Comer, August 19, 1907, Governor's Office Records, ADAH.

[27] Montgomery *Advertiser*, October 24, November 8, 1907.

[28] Comer met Roosevelt for the first time at the Deep Waterways Conference in early October. Montgomery *Advertiser*, October 7, 1907. Roosevelt sent Judson Clements of the ICC to investigate the situation, but never intervened. Theodore Roosevelt to Judson C. Clements, October 3, 1907, in Elting E. Morison, ed., *The Letters of Theodore Roosevelt*, Cambridge, Mass., 1952, V, 815-816. Roosevelt to Comer, November 11, 1907, *ibid.*, V, 838. Roosevelt to Charles J. Bonaparte, August 15, 1908, *ibid.*, VI, 1,174-1,176. Roosevelt to Bonaparte, August 22, 1908, *ibid.*, V, 764. See the editor's note, *ibid.*, V, 754. Horace H. Lurton to Thomas G. Jones, November 18, 1907, enclosed in Lurton to Roosevelt, November 18, 1907 [missing], Theodore Roosevelt Papers, Library of Congress. T. G. Jones to William Loeb, December 7, 1907, *ibid.* B. B. Comer to Roosevelt, December 13, 1907, *ibid.* Martin A. Knappy to Roosevelt, February 23, 1908, *ibid.* Roosevelt to Comer, August 17, 1908, Governor's Office Records, ADAH. S. D. Weakley to William E. Fort (Comer's secretary), August 11, 1908, *ibid.* Montgomery *Advertiser*, October 7, 1909.

not work, he resorted to frontal assault. He launched the legislature on a new attack. While Henry F. DeBardeleben, the entrepreneurial hero of the Alabama coal and iron industry, thundered hysterically in the press that the panic was caused by the fear of radical legislation,[29] the Alabama legislature manipulated its railroad laws to free the state from the injunctions of Judge Jones. The lawmakers repassed the commodity rate act with slightly different rates so that the old injunction would not apply. The legislature then repassed the railroad classification act and penalized the L & N by putting it in a class that was restricted to lower rates than the Southern. In order to avoid future injunctions, the lawmakers made it a crime for companies or individual employees to disobey the rate acts. This was the North Carolina formula for harassment. Enforcement was left to damage suits against ticket agents and railroad companies. These could be filed by individual passengers who were refused tickets at the low legal rate. To make matters even more difficult for Judge Jones, the new acts removed the attorney general and the Railroad Commission specifically from all responsibility for enforcing the railroad laws. This idea Comer supposedly borrowed from Arkansas. Sheriffs, solicitors, and citizens seeking criminal penalties were to enforce the law.[30] The *Nation* fulminated righteously against this array of "injunction proof" legislation.[31]

Despite the elaborate precautions, the new laws were

[29] Montgomery *Advertiser*, November 5, 1907.

[30] *Ibid.*, November 24, 1907. Doster, *Railroads in Alabama Politics*, 182-187. Alabama, *Acts, Special Session, 1907*, 23, 25, 28, 29, 43, 49, 57, 58, 59, 60, 66, 77, 91, 101, 109.

[31] "Injunction-Proof Laws Against Railroads in Alabama," *Nation*, LXXXV, December 5, 1907, 508. Also see "Lawless Legislature: Alabama and the Railroads," *Outlook*, LXXXVII, December 21, 1907, 833-835.

not invulnerable. Comer signed most of the legislation on November 23, the day the special session adjourned. Milton H. Smith, who had been in Montgomery peppering the public with public pronouncements attacking the anti-railroad legislation,[32] remained in his private car. The reason for his continued presence became evident when representatives of four railroads appeared before Judge Jones on the 27th and asked for injunctions against the injunction-proof legislation. Jones performed admirably. He not only issued injunctions against the enforcement of criminal statutes, an unusual step for a federal judge, but he enjoined everyone in the state from enforcing the acts![33] After hearing arguments in January, Jones on March 28, 1908 extended these temporary injunctions for the duration of the litigation over the merits of the case. Comer had been thwarted.

Characteristically, the governor refused to accept the existing situation. The nub of the question was the reasonableness of the rates Alabama was attempting to impose. That in turn depended on the method of assessing the value of railroad property and the method of allocating costs between interstate and intrastate business. The litigants did not settle these questions until 1914, but Comer decided to appeal the question of the preliminary injunctions, which meanwhile served the railroads as effectively as permanent injunctions, to the Fifth Circuit Court of Appeals sitting in New Orleans. This court heard the cases on March 16, 1909. It was evidently impressed by the state's attack on the gross revenue method of allocating costs between interstate and intrastate operations. Finding that the injunctions had been "improvidently issued" by Judge Jones, Judge David Shelby

[32] Montgomery *Advertiser*, November 5, 11, 13, 1907.
[33] *Ibid.*, November 28, December 1, 1907.

pointed out that railroads were not the only parties with property rights in need of protection.[34] This decision gave Comer an important victory for rate reform. The railroads put the statutory rates into effect on June 1, 1909, and then settled down for the long haul of hearings, motions, and countermotions on the constitutionality of the rate measures.

Compromise eventually broke the deadlock. Judge Jones, after more than a year of hearings before two special masters, finally issued permanent injunctions against the rate acts in 1912. The situation was radically altered, however, when the United States Supreme Court in the Minnesota Rate Case destroyed the gross-revenue method of allocating costs, which had been the rule since *Smyth v. Ames* in 1898. The state won its case before the Circuit Court of Appeals on the passenger rate of 2½¢ per mile that had been set by the state Railroad Commission and then enjoined by Judge Jones. This spurred Governor Emmet O'Neal, a political foe of Comer, to decide in December 1913 to appeal the old injunctions against the freight rates. This brought the railroads to the bargaining table. The compromise both parties accepted in February 1914, besides depriving Comer of an issue for the gubernatorial race of 1914, essentially cancelled all pending litigation. The railroad companies accepted the 2½-cent passenger rate, but retained the right to challenge the reasonableness of any future freight rate set by the Railroad Commission.[35] Essentially, the state had won its case.

The Progressives also largely won their case in the

[34] Doster, *Railroads in Alabama Politics*, 198-201.

[35] *Ibid.*, 217-220. The railroads and Governor O'Neal were getting along so well that the L & N helped Alabama float $498,000 in state bonds in 1912 and 1913. U.S., Senate Documents, 64th Cong., 1st Sess., Vol. XL, No. 461, 404.

General Assembly, where they were interested in far more than railroad regulation. The legislature of 1907, in fact, was in a mood for change. Perhaps the greatest gauge of its progressiveness was the tremendous bulk of important measures that came up for consideration, but it also contained an unusually large delegation of Progressive legislators. An analysis of 12 important roll calls in the 1903 Senate shows only five senators who voted more than 70 percent of the time on the Progressive side of these measures. In 1907 there were 11 senators who registered Progressive options on more than 70 percent of the 27 important roll calls of that session, and a hard core of 15 men who voted more than two-thirds of the time for reform. At the same time, the number of senators who voted against the Progressives more than 60 percent of the time remained at 10, just as it had been in 1903. Evidently the railroad issue precipitated some men out of their normal particularistic solution to form a healthy sediment of lawmakers who desired changes in a number of different fields. In other words, general reformers were more numerous.

The nature of the legislation of 1907 reveals much about the nature of Alabama Progressivism. In his speech at Samson in July 1908, summing up the accomplishments of his administration, Comer spoke with a Madisonian fear of unchecked power and warned that unless large concentrations of wealth were regulated they would "lead to socialism, revolution and destruction." He made Progressivism sound defensive, as if the law were being used to protect citizens from new kinds of threats from capital and labor.[36] But Progressivism was not only de-

---

[36] Birmingham *News*, July 4, 1908. Comer did not actually deliver all of this speech because of the heat, but had 102,000 copies of it printed and distributed.

fensive. In the same speech, Comer listed eight categories of laws for the benefit of particular kinds of people, four categories of new laws that benefited schools, public morals, state revenue, and general welfare, and only one category that was supposed to inhibit a particular group (railroads). So there was a positive side to Progressivism.

The important new legislation fell into four broad classes. It was designed to compel moral behavior or to provide those conditions that encouraged moral behavior and which were demanded by an advancing civilization. It prescribed rules of conduct for certain businesses and professions, but these regulations also had the purpose of providing stability to those particular segments of the economy. Ethical conduct and stable conditions were prerequisites for growth, a treasured goal. The legislature did not leave growth wholly to chance; it encouraged economic development in a number of direct ways while at the same time trying to pay for its reform program with a more equitable tax structure. Progressives sought a stable, moral order in which there would be the maximum opportunity for material and spiritual growth, both individual and collective.

Nowhere was moral conduct needed more than in the field of public service. The reason the large concentrations of wealth threatened republican institutions was that men in government had proven corruptible. There was no use preaching about the need for honesty in government, thought Comer, for "the time may never come when everything is white and pure. . . ."[37] But the government could take steps to decrease the temptation of public servants and to punish wrongdoers who were caught. The legislature of 1907 took a few of those steps.

[37] *Ibid.*

Early in the first session Comer signed a bill carrying the old fight against free passes to a successful conclusion.[38] It prohibited everyone, except a few harmless categories of people, from riding on free passes. Despite great pressures the legislature beat back attempts to exempt sheriffs and resisted pressures to allow newspapers to swap advertising (and frequently other favors) for railroad passes. Providing punishments both for the recipient and for the railroad, this law, according to Comer, unburdened the L & N of 10,000 free passes.[39]

The most obvious place for corporations and special interests to exert undue influence was in the legislature. Consequently the anti-lobby law sought to define corrupt solicitation of legislators and to make it a felony. Unfortunately the effectiveness of the bill was subverted when the legislature deleted the provision for the registration of all lobbyists and disclosure of their finances.[40] The legislators landed a slightly more substantial blow with the law that forbade corporations to use their property for partisan politics.[41]

Good government was not only in danger from the onslaughts of private interests, but from the temptation of officeholders to use their positions for profit. Existing laws merely provided criminal penalties for those who were caught participating in fraud, corruption, or boodling. A potentially more effective approach might be to change the structure that provided the opportunity for wrongdoing. As A. T. London kept reminding the state, the most fertile breeding ground for public corrup-

[38] Alabama, *Acts, 1907*, 107. It was approved on February 14, 1907. An improved version was passed later. Alabama, *Acts, Special Session, 1907*, 202.

[39] Birmingham *News*, July 4, 1908.

[40] Alabama, *Senate Journal, 1907*, 1,699.

[41] Alabama, *Acts, 1907*, 406.

tion was the fee system. This was attacked by the law that put an upper limit on an official's income from fees and by a series of laws putting various officials on salary.[42] The statute which prescribed an independent police commission for cities of over 35,000 and counties of over 125,000 population had the same purpose.[43]

Perhaps because of the brutally frank reports by Dr. Shirley Bragg, the State Convict Inspector, the legislature edged closer to the ultimate abolition of the convict lease system. The new law did not abolish the lease system, but it did bring those county convicts who were leased to work outside their own counties under the control of the state board of convict inspectors. The law also gave the governor the authority to review and cancel any county contract to lease convicts for hard labor.[44] Since the governor had no material interest in the convicts' labor, they theory went, he could be trusted to see that the judges of probate did not permit private gain to blind them to the mistreatment of convicts.

The legislature provided for moral conduct in a number of other ways. It enacted a tough vagrancy law[45] and forbade the display of nude pictures in public.[46] But the major target was liquor.

Prohibition sentiment had been growing in Alabama since the 1880s, though it was expressed only in sporadic special acts of the legislature for local areas.[47] The leg-

[42] *Ibid.*, 583, 585.
[43] *Ibid.*, 402.
[44] Alabama, *Acts, Special Session, 1907*, 179.
[45] Alabama, *Acts, 1907*, 453.
[46] *Ibid.*, 632.
[47] James B. Sellers, *The Prohibition Movement in Alabama, 1702 to 1943*, Vol. XXVI of "The James Sprunt Studies in History and Political Science," Chapel Hill, 1943, 67-68.

islature of 1898-99 passed the first general law on the subject. Sponsored by Frank S. Moody, president of the First National Bank of Tuscaloosa, the dispensary act provided legal machinery through which counties that did not have total prohibition could set up a dispensary system as a monopoly of the county, thus giving counties closer regulatory control over and the profits from the sale of liquor.[48] To the advocates of abstinence, who thought this was the first step toward prohibition, the law was imperfect in that it exempted 22 counties from its operations. Worse still, the counties were slow to utilize its provisions. Consequently, in 1907, there were still four types of counties in Alabama with respect to liquor: 21 counties under complete prohibition, 21 granting licenses to private establishments, 16 with dispensaries only, and 9 that had both dispensaries and licensed saloons.[49]

The growing pressure for stricter and more uniform controls over liquor sales was evident in the success of the Anti-Saloon League, the Alabama contingent of which was first organized in 1904. With the arrival of Reverend Brooks Lawrence fresh from temperance victories in Ohio, the League began to make rapid progress toward its initial goal of a general local option law. At the regular session of 1907 the state legislators enacted such a law, which permitted the temperance legions to force local option elections with petitions signed by one-fourth of the voters in a county. By this method counties with a dispensary system or a license system could choose total prohibition. The legislature also enacted several measures to strengthen existing prohibition provisions

[48] Alabama, *Acts, 1898*, 109.
[49] Alabama, *Acts, 1907*, 200. Sellers, *The Prohibition Movement in Alabama*, 100.

and to prescribe the time and manner of legal liquor sales.[50]

Rather than satisfying the urge for temperance, the new laws stimulated demand for stricter controls. By the end of 1907, 58 counties had exercised their option for total prohibition.[51] The Anti-Saloon League won a great victory in Jefferson County when the county voted on October 20, 1907 to go dry.[52] The league and its allies pressed their advantage, and the Birmingham *News*, Comer's chief supporter among the press, took up the cry.[53] Comer himself appeared at a rally of the Women's Christian Temperance Union wearing two white ribbons and pledged rigid enforcement of the existing prohibition laws.[54] Despite the pressure, Comer felt he could go no further than this because he was pledged to local option.[55]

The climax came in the special session in November 1907. The Anti-Saloon League's strategy was not to press for legislation beyond the manifest desires of public opinion, but their success had been so rapid and so great that in the fall they decided to try for the jackpot— total, statewide prohibition. Samuel D. Weakley took time off from fighting the railroads, a symbolic furlough from Progressivism, to draft the legislation to outlaw alcoholic beverages throughout the state. The House passed

[50] Alabama, *Acts, 1907*, 366, 784, 783, 643, 488, 518, 727, 377.

[51] Sellers, *Prohibition Movement in Alabama*, 108.

[52] Robert G. Hidden, "Prohibition in Alabama," *World To-Day*, XVIII (February 1910), 167-170. Montgomery *Advertiser*, October 29, 1907.

[53] Montgomery *Advertiser*, September 21, 1907.

[54] *Ibid.*, October 18, 1907.

[55] *Ibid.*, November 1, 1907. Comer to Reverend Francis Tappey, September 26, 1907, Governor's Office Records, ADAH.

the prohibition bill on November 17, and crowds overflowed the galleries of the Senate when the bill came up for final passage on the 19th. The swarms of people even pushed excitedly onto the Senate floor and hissed the speeches of those opposed to prohibition. When the bill passed in a dramatic roll call, they went wild.[56] Stout ladies with white ribbons pinned to their dresses and tears streaming down their faces marched through the capitol singing "Onward Christian Soldiers."[57] They did not know that the war had barely begun.

Governor Comer proudly signed the statewide prohibition bill in a special ceremony on November 23 attended by Brooks Lawrence and other prohibition leaders.[58] With a few strokes of the silver pen furnished by the WCTU for the occasion, Comer made Alabama the dryest state in the union—at least on paper. In his Thanksgiving proclamation he said everyone should "reflect with cheerful hearts upon the restoration of moral vigor everywhere apparent. . . ."[59]

Comer and others had long sought the restoration of moral vigor. This was evident not only in the regulation of individual conduct, but in the flood of concern for eleemosynary institutions and in humanitarian regulations in favor of the wards of society: women, children, the ill, elderly veterans, and convicts. The legislature provided money to establish the colony for epileptics and the tuberculosis commission Eli P. Smith, Sam Will John, and state Senator George T. McWhorter had been campaign-

[56] Alabama, *Acts, Special Session, 1907*, 71. The law was to go into effect January 1, 1909.
[57] Montgomery *Advertiser*, November 20, 1907.
[58] *Ibid.*, November 24, 1907.
[59] *Ibid.*, November 23, 1907.

ing for.[60] Greatly increased financial assistance also went to the Girls Industrial School and the Boys Industrial School, reform institutions of which the Alabama Federation of Women's Clubs had been the patron. The efforts of the club women and of Judge N. B. Feagin of Birmingham to improve the treatment of young offenders were rewarded by a law giving jurisdiction over defendants under 14 years of age to equity courts with specially assigned probation officers. Reformation was the stated goal of this special treatment.[61] In response to John W. Abercrombie, the Alabama Education Association, the Alabama Federation of Women's Clubs, and at the urging of Comer himself, the legislature doubled the usual general appropriation for common schools and provided a special fund for the repair of rural schools.[62] But the most significant step was the law providing for the first public high schools in the state. This measure set up a fund for constructing one high school building in each county as soon as the county contributed the necessary land, thus setting off a campaign to get the counties to meet the requirements that was even more furious than the campaign to get counties to vote for the special education tax.[63] A healthy appropriation also went to pay pensions to Confederate veterans.[64]

As the case of child labor shows, money was not always the answer to the problems of the wards of society. Under the continued agitation of the Alabama Child Labor Committee, the question of strengthening the 1903

[60] Smith to Comer, August 7, 1907; Rufus Rhodes to Comer, August 9, 1907; McWhorter to Comer, August 6, 1907; Governor's Office Records, ADAH. Alabama, *Acts, Special Session, 1907*, 164.
[61] Alabama, *Acts, 1907*, 442.
[62] *Ibid.*, 249, and 238.
[63] *Ibid.*, 728.   [64] *Ibid.*, 359.

statute confronted a reluctant governor. But, as on other issues, Comer could not resist the pressure to reform. During the recess in late June, he warned the cotton mill men in the state that "there will have to be some adequate child labor legislation at the approaching session of the Legislature. The party is pledged to it and it is right. You had better bestir yourself to see that reasonable, just legislation is enacted on this subject. It seems to me that you are sleeping on your rights."[65] According to Tyler Goodwyn, the ex-Populist leader of the anti-Comer forces in the House, they didn't. They participated in shaping the administration's bill, which was introduced in the House by Sam Will John.[66] The act raised the minimum legal age for working from 10 to 12, the minimum age for night work from 14 to 16, and lowered the maximum work week from 66 to 60 hours. It also required working children under 16 to attend school for at least eight weeks a year. Most important, the new law provided for the inspection of mills and factories by the State Inspector of Jails and Almshouses, who was given authority to issue orders to comply with the law and the power to levy penalties for disobedience.[67]

The fertilizer industry showed much the same pattern as child labor regulation. The pressure to reform came from farmers who were vitally interested in the price and quality of fertilizer sold in the state. This pressure was increased by the revelations made by a committee of the state Senate investigating the "Fertilizer Trust" for collusion among the manufacturers, price-fixing, and fraudulent misbranding.[68] At the same time, however, manu-

[65] Letter dated June 27, 1907, printed in Montgomery *Advertiser*, November 13, 1907.

[66] *Ibid.*, July 24, 1907.

[67] Alabama, *Acts, 1907*, 757.

[68] *Ibid.*, 400. Montgomery *Advertiser*, July 13, 1907.

facturing fertilizer and crushing cotton seed was too important an industry in Alabama for the legislature to ignore its wishes. The legislature responded by passing a law establishing minimum chemical standards for fertilizers and set up penalties for false labeling.[69] The president of the Alabama Chemical Company complained that the farmers were going to be upset at not being able to buy the customary low-grade fertilizer, but he had no other complaints.[70] The special session amended the law slightly in response to complaints from the industry.[71] Far from being annoyed at governmental intrusion into its private business, the fertilizer industry was full of praise for Comer. The president of the Alabama Cotton Seed Crushers Association wrote on behalf of his organization that he candidly believed that Comer had "acted with wisdom, and to the profit of Producer, Manufacturer and Fertilizer interests of our State."[72] The fertilizer story was repeated in other areas.

A prime example of the way in which the Comer administration acted as broker for business self-regulation was the Forest Conservation Act Comer pushed through the special session of the legislature. The act gave lumber companies a subsidy in the form of a tax exemption for every acre of denuded land they replanted in trees. It is not surprising to find that Comer included forest conservation in his program for the special session at the re-

[69] Alabama, *Acts, 1907*, 744.

[70] John W. Huger to Comer, July 27, August 23, 1907, Governor's Office Records, ADAH.

[71] Alabama, *Acts, Special Session, 1907*, 20. John W. Huger to B. B. Comer, August 23, 1907, Governor's Records, ADAH.

[72] Ernest Lamar to Comer, October 14, 1907; Comer to Lamar, October 15, 1907; Governor's Office Records, ADAH.

quest of the lumber industry and that he depended on the industry to write its own bill.[73]

The Forest Conservation Act was not the only direct encouragement to business activity. Other laws set up tax exemptions to encourage calcium cyanamid manufacturers, power companies, and cotton mills.[74] The legislature at last put public funds to work for the public, and for the favored banks, by authorizing state moneys to be deposited in certain banks and providing for the regulation of those banks.[75] It granted electric power companies easements in navigable rivers to construct dams and locks and the right of eminent domain which made their existence possible.[76] In return, the companies (in actuality, just the Alabama Power Company) were to furnish their products to the public without discrimination.[77]

As the legislation of Comer's administration illustrates, Progressive regulation of businesses was largely enlightened business self-regulation. It was not only a response to humanitarian pressure, nor was it solely an attempt of small businessmen to shackle big businessmen, though these were elements in its complex composition. It was also designed to bring stability, insure growth, and free businessmen from the necessity of acting unethically in order to compete.

Because Populists had not been interested in rationalizing the business culture from which they felt alienated, and because from the Populists' position as outsiders the

[73] Alabama, *Acts, Special Session, 1907*, 192. B. B. Comer to Hon. Thos. Powell, October 15, 1907, Governor's Office Records, ADAH.
[74] Alabama, *Acts, 1907*, 520.
[75] *Ibid.*, 280.   [76] *Ibid.*, 358.   [77] *Ibid.*, 439.

Progressives seemed as much a part of the ruling class as the Big Mules, Populists had never been enthusiastic supporters of the regulatory and promotional measures sponsored by the Progressives during the 1890s and after. Populists had been more interested in securing power for the disinherited classes—classes to whom the Progressives promised nothing special. Though the Populists had been devoted to equality and human freedom, their fear of increased taxation and distrust of the existing political order overrode whatever willingness they might have had to use government to realize their traditional goals in the new context of industrial society. For their part, the masters of the new industrial order, and the beneficiaries of the political "machine" with which it was connected, resisted all Progressive attempts to limit their privilege by changing the rules. Freed of the static conception of society shared by the Bosses and Populists, Progressives could proceed to manipulate the emerging urban environment in their own interest.

The Progressive legislature did more to foster the development of municipal corporations than any other area of life. It adopted the general municipal code drawn up under the supervision of John B. Weakley, president of the Alabama League of Municipalities.[78] In numerous additional ways it freed towns from the inhibiting fiscal restraints that the old negative-government ideology had dictated. Other new measures allowed towns to float bonds to pay for various types of improvements, including the purchase of water works.[79] Towns could now pave streets and sidewalks and lay sewers at the expense of the owners of the abutting property.[80] In response to the needs of rapidly growing communities, the legislature set up procedures to allow the orderly expansion of city

[78] *Ibid.*, 790.   [79] *Ibid.*, 586.   [80] *Ibid.*, 295.

boundaries,[81] but Birmingham required special attention.

Powerful industrial companies, as well as suburbanites seeking to avoid responsibility for the city, blocked the expansion of Birmingham's jurisdiction. By agreeing to leave the property of the Tennessee Coal, Iron and Railroad Company outside the new boundaries, the proponents of the "Greater Birmingham Bill" managed to get it through the legislature. The bill allowed city voters to participate in the referendum on incorporation and thus counterbalance the expected negative vote from the suburbs. The governor was lukewarm toward the measure, perhaps because his own factory would be incorporated into the city by the ingenious maneuver of the expansionists. But because the advocates of a greater Birmingham, such men as Jere King, Alex London, Rufus Rhodes, and N. B. Feagin, were also among Comer's foremost supporters, he finally had to sign the "Greater Birmingham Bill" into law.[82]

If Comer dragged his feet on certain Progressive measures, such as child labor legislation and the Greater Birmingham Bill, he proved himself a true Progressive on the crucial question of governmental finances. Comer observed that the best government was not always the least expensive, a revolutionary idea in itself at the time. In fact, the idea was so revolutionary that former Governor Oates thought it would lead to nothing short of plunder.[83] The Comer legislature ignored Oates' reminders about Jeffersonian principles and increased state expenses almost one and a quarter million dollars in its effort to pro-

[81] *Ibid.*, 407.
[82] Montgomery *Advertiser*, August 1, 1907. N. B. Feagin to Comer, August 5, 1907, Governor's Office Records, ADAH.
[83] Montgomery *Advertiser*, July 7, 1907.

vide modern services.[84] Comer played down the significance of the resulting deficit by blandly referring to the parable of the talents.[85]

The real test of Progressivism was tax policy. How were modern services to be financed? The objective of the Progressives was to shift the burden of taxation onto the shoulders of those most able to pay. The 1907 legislature did this in several ways. It levied a tax on the gross credits of companies who loaned money in the state; it levied a stamp tax on mortgages; and it raised the charter fees of corporations. It pursued equity by setting up a State Tax Commission to take the place of the single Tax Commissioner. The commission was not only bigger, it was more powerful and had greater direct authority over county assessors, collectors, and assessments. Its job was to raise more money and equalize assessments throughout the state.[86]

Perhaps the most typically Progressive tax measure was the franchise tax, a form of taxation Alabama had been discussing since 1896 when Johnston was governor. The 1907 legislature repealed the existing tax, enacted during the Johnston administration on gross receipts, and levied a tax on the intangible assets of foreign corporations and corporations connected with transportation. The franchise tax on foreign corporations was a graduated tax based on the actual amount of capital each one employed in the state.[87] The franchise tax on transportation companies was based on the difference between the tax-assessed value of its property and the market value

[84] *Ibid.*, September 19, 1907.
[85] Alabama, *Acts, Special Session, 1909*, Governor's Message, x.
[86] Alabama, *Acts, 1907*, 425, 318, 323, 422, 455.
[87] *Ibid.*, 418.

of its stock, plus its mortgaged debt.[88] With these two measures the tax structure was at last catching up to industrial reality.

A revealing measure of the commitment of Alabama Progressivism lies in the fact that Comer could not make all of the new taxes stick. Big Mules were already attacking his railroad policy, so the tax measures merely stoked the roaring flames of opposition. Even Comer's friends urged him to compromise when insurance companies started turning down policy applications and loans in Alabama.[89] At an acrimonious convention of the Alabama Press Association on July 18, 1907, Comer was severely criticized for "the hostility shown by the Governor towards the great developers of the State, especially the great arteries of commerce. . . ."[90] Despite the cascading expressions of popular support, and despite the fact that his whole political career had been devoted to castigating outside economic interests and championing home rule, Comer yielded to the pressures of the very forces he had been fighting.

After fierce behind-the-scenes negotiating with spokesmen for the commercial organizations of the state, Comer obtained a compromise.[91] Rather than abolish the tax on money loaned, the new law allowed a lending corporation to deduct from the figure on which its tax was based that part of its capital secured by mortgages within the state.[92] Mortgages already paid a privilege tax anyway and the compromise placated the lending companies

[88] *Ibid.*, 342.
[89] Montgomery *Advertiser*, July 1, 1907.
[90] *Ibid.*, July 18, 19, 1907.
[91] *Ibid.*, July 12, 1907.
[92] Alabama, *Acts, 1907*, 521.

whose tax bills were substantially reduced. The timid capital argument was having its effect.

In fact, the Progressive coalition in Alabama began to break up before it had exhausted the program of its most ambitious members. Even with half of the legislature committed to a broad scale of reform, the balance of power could easily be shifted by the large group of legislators who were more selective in their interests. Consequently the legislature defeated significant pieces of Progressive legislation. It left stranded at least one anti-trust bill. It hardly looked at the bill to set maximum hours for women which was sponsored by Sam Will John. The United Mine Workers failed to get an employers liability bill or a mine inspection bill. The pure food bill never reached a vote. The special session killed the compulsory school attendance bill sponsored by the Alabama Education Association. Comer's leader in the Senate, John Lusk, introduced and pushed a measure to provide for the confiscation and state operation of the property of corporations that forfeited their licenses. Not only did he fail in this, he lost his bid for Congress in 1908 despite Comer's fervent backing. By that time, Progressivism seemed to be in a rapid decline.

Yet Progressivism continued to be an effective political sentiment from time to time, and many of the unpassed reforms of 1907 slowly found their way to the statute book. The next two decades saw the achievement of compulsory school attendance in 1916, employers liability in 1919, and abolition of the convict lease system in 1927. In addition, Comer's associates in reform won the governor's chair four out of the next five times it changed occupants. But the Progressive spirit after 1907 was weak and inconsistent. For instance, the special referendum held in November 1908 approved the constitutional amendment that allowed profits from the convict system to be used to build good roads, as Comer's supporters in the Alabama Good Roads Association wanted, but at the same election, the people defeated the similarly Progressive constitutional amendment that would have provided for biennial sessions of the legislature instead of quadrennial sessions. The failure of the provision for biennial session might be blamed on the Bankhead camp which worked hard for its defeat in order to scotch Comer's possible bid for the United States Senate.[93]

No matter who was to blame, the Progressive association of interest groups was obviously breaking up. It had never been as solid as the grouping of forces that comprised Populism and it did not last as long. There was an inherent instability in Progressivism caused by the fact that a large part of its support was tied to the single issue of railroad regulation and did not share the new Progressive attitude that favored an active government. Once railroad regulation seemed accomplished, or at least when the statutory and institutional measures had been taken, Progressives with a "Planter" mentality were free to withdraw from the confederation of forces.

The cohesiveness of the coalition naturally weakened as more and more of the Progressive program became law. After its own particular reform was achieved, each constituent part of the coalition found it no longer needed the support of the other members and its enthusiasm declined. In this condition the more moderate and more satiated Progressives were vulnerable to the appeals of distracting issues. At the special session of the legislature in the summer of 1909, which repaired the battered railroad laws, the representatives of the people provided for

[93] John Hollis Bankhead to Thomas M. Owens, February 18, 1908, Bankhead Papers, ADAH.

a referendum on a constitutional amendment to make prohibition a part of the fundamental law. The people not only voted this amendment down in November 1909, but turned their backs on the prohibition forces in 1910 even though these forces were led by Comer's personal choice as his successor, H.S.D. Mallory. Instead, the people chose Emmet O'Neal, a "wet" who had the backing of some of Comer's principal lieutenants despite his gold-bug past. With such division among former allies there is reason to believe that the advent of alcohol as an issue simply dissolved Progressivism. The point to remember, however, is that the bonds had to be weakened before the solvent could work.

Another fundamental factor that weakened the bonds of Progressivism was that Comer and many of his supporters were too close to the Big Mules socially and economically not to share their basic values. In particular, they shared a common attitude toward wage labor. Most Progressives failed to see that competition was no more equitable in regulating wages and hours than in setting freight rates. When faced with the violence of the strike of 1908, Comer performed just as his Big Mule enemies would have performed in his place.

Labor in the Birmingham district had been badly demoralized by the defeat of the United Mine Workers in their strike of 1904. Since then, the big industrial companies that operated their own mines had employed some 10,000 nonunion miners, and the UMW retained approximately 4,000 members who worked for the commercial coal companies. In 1900, the last previous year for which reliable statistics are available, 54 percent of Alabama miners were Negro, a fact which provides a key to understanding the strike of 1908: a majority of both union and nonunion miners were Negro.[94]

The leading employer of miners in the state was the Tennessee Coal, Iron and Railroad Company, which had set the wage scale in Alabama mines since the early 1890s. Unfortunately for Alabama miners, TCI in 1908 was a subsidiary of United States Steel Corporation, a prize picked up during the panic of 1907 by J. P. Morgan with the blessings of Theodore Roosevelt.[95] TCI was now even less vulnerable to pressure from employees than before. There was also the fact that U.S. Steel was one of the leaders of the counterattack against organized labor that marked the period from the Homestead Strike to World War I. At contract time in 1908 big steel decreed a cut in the wages of Alabama miners from 57 to 47 cents per ton. This came on top of a cutback in operations and a reduction of the work force in the fall of 1907—a blatant example of the very type of foreign domination and exploitation that Comer professed to oppose. The miners, at least, were moved to militancy.

With no contract in sight, the International Executive Board of the UMW issued an open letter to the miners of District 20 on June 30, 1908, calling on them to cease work and make a supreme effort to organize the state.[96] A miner's wife wrote the governor that the miners had struck for higher wages and refused to be made slaves by

[94] Sterling D. Spero and Abram L. Harris, *The Black Worker: The Negro and the Labor Movement*, New York, 1931, 215, 352-357.

[95] Ethel Armes, *The Story of Coal and Iron in Alabama*, Birmingham, Ala., 1910, 515ff. Gabriel Kolko, *The Triumph of Conservatism: A Reinterpretation of American History, 1900-1916*, New York, 1963, 114-117.

[96] Birmingham *News*, July 6, 1908.

the bullying tactics of the deputy sheriffs who in fact were paid by and worked for the companies. She explained in simple language what moved the miners to revolt. "The company has not give the poor Men Worke enough to hardly Maintain his family for they sell things so high in the comasary," she wrote, "and When the Men pay house rent out of that they had but little to live on . . . our Men is not Wanting Money for Something they dont do . . . they Want their coal Weighed . . . they are tiard Working for guess Work . . . governor pleas look through this Matter and you Will see that the poor need help . . . Why isent one Man as free as a nother. . . ."[97]

The strike began on July 6, 1908. Success for the union depended on its ability to get the nonunion miners to leave the mines, so strikers bent their efforts toward convincing or coercing nonstrikers to join them. The union set up headquarters in Birmingham, and its organizers concentrated on the miners of the big companies.

Bucking big steel and the anti-boycott law was quite an order for the disorganized union; consequently the companies were confident. On July 7, the day after the strike began, they issued a statement saying they planned to maintain their open-shop policy and anticipated no trouble in being able to do so. Almost immediately the companies began firing workers who advocated unionization.[98]

After barely a week had passed, the strike situation was already dangerously taut. The union by that time had 7,000 men enrolled on its strike list, counting both Negroes and whites. Because many were homeless, the union set up whole villages of tents to house and feed the

[97] Mrs. R. H. Cox to B. B. Comer, July 18, 1908, Governor's Office Records, ADAH.
[98] Birmingham *News*, July 8, 1908.

idle workmen and their families. Heavily armed guards patrolled their grounds while crude commissaries dealt out food and mass meetings kept spirits alive. Meanwhile, violence mounted.

It is always difficult to determine which side commits the first breach of the peace during a strike. On July 14 W. R. Fairley, official organizer of District 20 of the UMW, issued a long bill of particulars against the deputy sheriffs and company guards for breaking up strike meetings, arresting men without warrants, and intimidating strikers. He charged that the coal companies were instigating a policy of aggression against the strikers.[99] Two deputies were at the time in jail on a charge of murdering a striker and another deputy was accused of shooting down a striker in his own front yard. The union had filed 25 damage suits against the Republic Iron and Steel Company alone for acts of its guards against the strikers. On the other hand, a mob of strikers had forced at least one load of strikebreakers off the train at gun point and dispersed them.[100]

Sheriff Higdon of Jefferson County, fearing that the situation might get out of hand, appealed to the governor for assistance.[101] Comer replied that he would give whatever assistance was required and stationed one company of the state militia in Birmingham ready for duty, while 2,500 additional troops were in camp at Chattanooga.[102] Fairley welcomed the calling out of the troops because he thought the strikers were the injured party.[103] He may

[99] *Ibid.*, July 14, 1908.
[100] *Ibid.*, July 16, 1908.
[101] E. L. Higdon to B. B. Comer, July 8 and 17, 1908, Governor's Office Records, ADAH.
[102] Comer to Higdon, July 15, 1908, Governor's Office Records, ADAH.
[103] Birmingham *News*, July 18, 1908.

also have been misled by Comer's reputation as an opponent of out-of-state corporations. Republic Iron and Steel showed a more perceptive grasp of the sympathies of the administration when it applied to the state for guns, but Comer refused the request with a protestation of neutrality.[104] A few days later, however, Comer announced that he was sending another company of cavalry troops to Birmingham and was making plans to send the whole Alabama National Guard if the strike was not over by July 30.[105] As if in reply, reports of skirmishes between strikers and strikebreakers increased.

By July 21, when state troops began escorting trainloads of strikebreakers brought into the state by the companies,[106] the mineral district was the scene of general bushwhacking and guerilla warfare. Dynamite exploded in the dead of night, and at least one mob lynched a Negro striker suspected of being a dynamiter. Comer came to Birmingham to stay for the duration of the strike to be near at hand in case of a great emergency, though the emergency seemed to be continuous. On July 26 the strikers held a huge rally in Birmingham to publicize their side of the story and appeal for help from the Birmingham Trades Council whose members sat on the stage during the rally. Frank S. White, Comer's old campaign manager, expressed his hearty sympathy for the cause of the union miners, but Governor Comer was chastised by the speakers as frequently as were the corporations, the troops, the sheriff, and the press.[107]

In early August Comer made it clear that Alabama

---

[104] Republic to Bibb Graves, July 15, 1908; William E. Fort to Republic, July 16, 1908; telegrams in the Governor's Office Records, ADAH.

[105] Birmingham *News*, July 20, 1908.

[106] *Ibid.*, July 21, 1908.

[107] *Ibid.*, July 27, 1908.

Progressivism was for whites only—and only for certain whites. Without declaring martial law he issued a statement which in effect said civil liberties would have to be curtailed until after the emergency. By implication, he criticized the union for dynamiting the homes of working miners and for inciting Negro strikers to violence, and pointedly reminded Negroes of Reconstruction and Redemption. Fairley retorted hotly that Comer's statement merely showed the prejudice of the governor's mind.[108]

Despite the increasingly pointed statements by the governor, the union leaders were still talking in optimistic terms on August 15. Two days later they indicated with apparent confidence that they would be willing to arbitrate and announced that they had over 18,000 strikers signed up. Although this was more strikers than there were jobs in Alabama mines, it may have been an accurate figure. The companies were importing laborers as fast as they could, and a healthy proportion of those who came as strikebreakers were soon in the ranks of the strikers. On August 22, in order to make room for more cooperative employees, the companies started dispossessing old miners who remained in company housing and two days later the union began pitching several thousand tents to house the outcast miners.[109] Comer announced the next day that the tent cities, of which there were 103, could not remain; they were a threat to health and good order, and it was clear whose health and whose good order he was protecting.

Comer's action in closing the strikers' camp broke the strike. On the 27th state troops moved into the tent cities and began tearing them down.[110] At 5 p.m. on the 29th,

[108] *Ibid.*, August 5, 1908.
[109] *Ibid.*, August 24, 1908.
[110] *Ibid.*, August 27, 1908.

after union officials had been in conference with Comer for two days, they decided they could not continue the strike, but they did not announce the news until the morning of the 31st. At the same time, the companies announced they would take back about 75 percent of the 17,000 idle miners and began hiring the more tractable men on September 3rd. By the 10th the surplus and unwanted labor began leaving the district.

In announcing the end of the strike, union officials placed the blame on the possibility of racial friction. There is no doubt that the UMW brought together Negroes, native whites, and foreigners in an intimacy that flouted the racial code of the South, and the resulting rumors of racial equality were emphasized by Comer in his public remarks. In order to avoid the growing antipathy of the community, the union at one point told Comer that it was willing to transport all of the striking Negroes out of the state in order to make the dispute one entirely between white men, but Comer refused the offer. He was not interested so much in eliminating the racial aspects of the strike as using the racial aspects to eliminate the strike.

The one thing all sides agreed on after the strike was that Comer had broken it. A. M. Shook, of the First Savings Bank and Trust Company, wrote to Comer on August 18th, well before there was any break in the strike, that "Robert Jemison of Birmingham [banker, utilities magnate, real estate developer, and opponent of Comer, as was Shook] has been spending a few days with me on the Mountain, and has told me *Confidentially* what you were doing to suppress lawlessness in the Birmingham District and I cannot refrain from writing and thanking you for the firm stand you have taken. I assure you that it is greatly appreciated by your friends and has made many new and valuable friends for you."[111] Comer's steadfast supporter, the Birmingham *News*, agreed:

The order of the governor forbidding the erection of camps was a body blow to the strike. He contended that it was against public policy to allow gatherings where sanitation could not be had and where police protection could not be afforded. Behind this there was the attitude that Alabama had never allowed a body of negroes to be maintained in idleness and his determination that the state never would.[112]

With the verdict of his friends and enemies, Comer could not quarrel. The strike had brought Comer to the limits of his urge to reform, for neither the status of the Negro nor the status of the laborer was included in Comer's mandate for change. In fact, Comer's program of reform had been fulfilled; Progressives were consequently free to divide over prohibition. Though many Progressives disagreed, Comer tended to see the whiskey men as new recruits to the army of railroad men and politicians and therefore as a new threat to home rule. Home rule for Comer meant the rule of men very much like himself in status, position, and outlook, and such men would desire humanitarian, regulatory, and promotional activity that would enhance their own role in society. As the strike of 1908 emphasized, however, new advances for other social groups in Alabama would have to await new champions.

[111] A. M. Shook to B. B. Comer, August 18, 1908, Governor's Office Records, ADAH.

[112] Birmingham *News*, August 31, 1908. On the story of the strike see Woodward, *Origins of the New South*, 362-64.

The Crocheted Design

The continuing argument about the nature of political conflict in the United States might be put into better perspective by the realization that between 1890 and 1910 Alabama experienced the two major varieties in turn. Populism was an attempt to create a mass political party. It was led by men with little claim to elite status and was supported by a following normally unorganized and in some cases socially disorganized. Faced with such a disruption in the natural order of society, those who identified their own welfare with the continuation of the existing status structure refused to join. The various elites within the state, the advocates of change as well as the defenders of the status quo, cooperated sufficiently to defeat Populism. But they did not cease their own pluralistic squabbles, and, with the demise of Populism and the disfranchisement of the Negro, the community was free to reorient its politics around the seething contentions of elite-led interest groups. The Progressive movement, then, was a loose federation of the leadership and membership of different associations and informal groups interested in short-term reform. Contrary to Robert Wiebe's stimulating thesis in his book, *The Search for Order, 1877-1920*, Populism was a protest of the alienated against the established community, and the Progressives were the true spokesmen for the local community against the forces linking Alabama to the outside world: the low-down thieving Yankees and their tyrannical railroads.

The alienated on whom Populism drew for support came mainly from the section of the social spectrum that included tenant and yeoman farmers of both races, urban labor, and thwarted merchants and professional men from small towns. The Progressives got less enthusiastic and less constant help from organized labor in the cities than did the Populists, but they received much more substantial support from merchants and professional men of more secure status. The Bosses naturally drew support from the industrial managers and those, of whatever class, who linked their identities to the fate of the economic elites. But the greatest reservoir of power was the Black Belt.

The support of the Black Belt was the key to victory in Alabama. Without it, the Populists could come close but could never win. With it, the Bosses controlled the state except for the four-year period after 1896 when the emergent Progressive movement, benefitting from Joseph Johnston's personal connections in the Black Belt, gained enough Black Belt backing in the Democratic primaries to secure possession of the party. This was but an interim; the Big Mule-Black Belt alliance was back in power in 1900 when Johnston's attempt to maintain power by attracting political immigrants from the moribund Populist party failed repeatedly. As the Populist party declined, its leaders dispersed along many political and ideological paths ranging from socialism to fascism. Similarly the membership scattered. The politically homeless Populist masses did not inflate Democratic ranks; most withdrew from politics or voted Republican. In order for the Progressive faction of the Democratic party to achieve real ascendancy it had to find support among the politically active Democrats, and this meant Black Belt Planters.

An analysis of the voting in the Constitutional Convention of 1901 shows there was a potential pool of support in the Black Belt for some Progressive measures, particularly railroad regulation. The Progressive urge there was inhibited by anti-Negro fixations among the Planters and by the fact that Negro suffrage was used by the machine to maintain itself in power. Disfranchisement, therefore, was a prerequisite of Progressivism in Alabama. The melange of motives that made disfranchisement a reality in Alabama, against the wishes of Populists and poor whites, included both the desire to make reform possible and the wish to make it impossible. Progressives, and Populists too for that matter, were no less racist or prejudiced than their fellow Alabamians, but among the proponents of Negro disfranchisement the majority and the moving spirit were composed of the opponents of reform. The disfranchisers thought they could cleanse their consciences, retain their power, and prevent a further recurrence of Populism all at the same time. They were wrong. Once the political aspect of the Negro problem had been solved by abolishing the Negro's political rights, and the rights of plenty of poor whites in the bargain, the way was open for the Progressives to assemble from the purged electorate a winning coalition, a coalition that owed little to Populist antecedents.

The Populists were neither backward-looking nor revolutionary; they were merely provincial. Though they were anxious to modernize their own farms to increase their leverage in the marketplace, they were not interested in the modernization of their region. Though they saw clearly what was happening to the yeoman farmer in America, they did not know what to do about it. They distrusted middle class reformers, so they could not cooperate with the budding Progressive movement. They had not rejected the outmoded tenets of Jeffersonianism, so they repeatedly voted against measures to equalize taxes, curb corporations, and provide the services needed by an industrial society. In fact, the Populists resembled primitive rebels. Unlike the issue-oriented Progressives, the Populist program was symbolic of a more basic urge for power that in turn grew from feelings of distrust, betrayal, frustration, and impotence. Unable to create a new, more appropriate system of values for their situation, and hampered by the lack of leaders drawn from traditional sources, the Populists were also unable to stimulate the sort of commitment in the electorate that could withstand adversity. They failed because they were neither revolutionaries nor reformers.

Revolutions are made possible by the perceptions of gaps between expectations and reality, gaps caused by the structure of society. The Populist experience suggests that when the gap between aspiration and achievement is caused by the deterioration of real conditions, the insurgents may reject traditional rulers but will find it difficult to substitute new values for the old, to focus discontent on common goals, or to sustain motivation among the following. However, reformers such as the Progressives are motivated by the dissonance between conflicting cultural commandments. For them the problem was to institutionalize the older ethical mandates while at the same time providing for stability and progress. The contradictory values of Christian brotherhood and American competitive success were thus rationalized, and the result was a powerful force that was restricted in its operation by the Progressives' sense of class loyalty and notions of a conflict-free society. In contrast to Populism, Progressivism's narrow commitment excluded any but the most traditional humanitarian concern for the working classes.

On one thing the two movements could agree: equality of opportunity was a good thing. The problem was, their views of the nature of reality differed sharply. In action, if not in words, the Populists clung to their traditional idea that the way to insure equality of opportunity was to keep taxes low and government small. For most of them the barrier to opportunity came from too much of the wrong kind of government interference and the barrier could be removed simply by returning government to the hands of the people and by abolishing privilege. The Populists had a static conception of social reality, an outlook they shared with their enemy, the Bosses.

The Progressives viewed reality in dynamic terms. For them, abolishing privilege was not enough. Greater equality of opportunity could only come through greater economic growth to multiply the chances of success, and such a goal could only be realized through increased governmental services to stimulate growth and enable individuals to take advantage of the greater opportunity. With such a commitment it was obvious that, even though they honored the myths of the Southern past, the Progressives were earnestly interested in changing Southern society.

There is a great deal more than irony in the fact that the myth of the Old South was created and sponsored by the groups in the post-Reconstruction South that were doing the most to alter the nature of Southern life. The new facts of defeat and poverty successfully challenged the assumptions that had supported the plantation-centered culture of the antebellum South, and the new men who "redeemed" the ex-Confederate states from the regimes of Reconstruction neither sprang from the old ruling class nor adhered to its ideology. Instead they championed industrialization or at least allied themselves with the capitalists of the North who wished to exploit the South's great natural and human resources. At the same time, however, the Redeemers and their heirs, the Bosses, masked their break with the past by defending the existing institutional structure of society and celebrating the virtues of the Old South and the Lost Cause. Though it is not unusual for revolutionaries to stress their agreement with traditional values, the truth is that the Redeemers were not the modernizing elite that students of modernization see as a prerequisite of substantial change in the social structure. They did not propose the creation of new institutions and they advocated no change of function for any existing institution. Retrenchment in governmental services and opposition to an expansion of the regulatory functions of government lay at the heart of their program. In fact, the Redeemers were so intent on exploitation that they were more analogous to colonialists than to a nationalistic leadership eager to adjust society to the needs of development. The Progressives, however, did resemble an innovating elite dedicated to rational growth.

Southern Progressivism, of course, was not all of a piece, but Alabama's divergence from the norm, if there was one, exceeded even the most generous limits previously recognized. In its program and accomplishments, Alabama Progressivism resembled more the Eastern, urban, Roosevelt brand than the Western, rural, Bryan variety. Perhaps the reason for this is that the movement early came under the influence of B. B. Comer, an urban businessman who differed markedly from the stereotype of the Western or the Southern Progressive leader who had to rely on emotionalism to motivate the electorate, as Robert Wiebe has pointed out in *The Search for Order*. Alabama's early Progressivism is also at variance with Wiebe's observation that Southern and Western Progressivism lagged behind the national movement.

If the profile of national Progressivism created by George Mowry in his book, *The Era of Theodore Roosevelt*, is accurate, then Alabama was not completely harmonious with national trends, and one suspects that the phenomenon in Alabama was more truly national than the ideal type sketched by Mowry. In some characteristics there was agreement between Alabama and the Mowry model. According to both conceptions, the reformers were young, well educated, with a fundamental faith in the soundness of the American system, and with a distrust of organized labor. It is not surprising that Alabama Progressives held a restricted definition of "the people," a belief in a leadership elite, an insistent belief in the compatibility and mutual dependence of all classes within society, and a faith in individualism. As Robert Wiebe points out in his book, *Businessmen and Reform*, these were tenets shared by comfortable Americans everywhere.

Strikingly like the reform-minded businessmen in Wiebe's study, and in contrast to Mowry's Progressives, Alabama's Progressives were not optimistic about human nature. They were confident of the future and believed in manmade progress, but they also thought a crucial function of law was to restrain the human propensity for evil. Far from wishing to extend democracy, Progressives in Alabama wanted to purify it and actually assisted in restricting it. Though Alabama Progressives in cases may have boasted of family backgrounds superior to those of their enemies, the biographical data of the Constitutional Convention show that it was not status anxiety, or a rejection of materialism, but rather their new role as upwardly-mobile businessmen that led Comer and his cohorts to Progressivism. Comer's campaign rhetoric was overwhelmingly economic and political rather than moral. It is true that the character of the movement was deeply influenced by reformers whose projects did not stem directly from economic self-interest, but those men and women might more logically be seen as responding to the urgent commands of traditional anti-machine politics and humanitarianism than to a status squeeze. Nostalgia for old rural virtues and distrust of the city were absent from Alabama Progressivism. Unlike the version of Progressivism portrayed by Mowry, the Alabama variety was realistically concerned with the problems of an urbanizing and industrializing society.

Alabama Progressivism was not dominated by producer values such as Mowry attributes to the national Progressives. Along with the Populists, Alabama Progressives shared in a value system derived from the Puritan ethic and the American success myth, but while the Populists emphasized the work ethic in hopes that laborers and farmers who did their own manual work could get a larger share of America's unequally distributed wealth, the Progressives stressed the code of ethical business practices that was a part of the success myth. They wanted the state to enforce these ethical commandments primarily by promoting growth with stability. The chaos and corrupting competition could then be abolished through state regulation and state-sanctioned self-regulation by business. In this way men of character would properly get a larger share of the community's wealth while other classes would benefit from the resulting economic growth as the enlarged fund of wealth radiated through society from the middle class.

The final way in which Alabama Progressives differed from the Mowry portrait of Progressivism is that the Alabama Progressives were not opposed to reform in the 1890s and their views underwent little change after the turn of the century. It was merely opportunity that was altered. That Populism was too radical for them does not negate the fact that while the Populists were calling for the people to take control of government, Progressive leaders were advocating free silver and moderate reform. As the old silver faction slowly came to power in Alabama after 1902, Populism withered. But it did not disappear, because the evils that called it forth did not disappear. Just as the Progressives unsuccessfully offered a moderate alternative in the 1890s, such organizations as the Farmers Union and political leaders of various accents from time to time in this century have offered the dispossessed and powerless a semblance of the radical alternative Populism might have been. That Progressivism was the path chosen is a significant fact in the recent history of the United States.

Appendices

Notes on Sources

Index

APPENDIX I

Negro percent of total male voting age population, Alabama, 1900

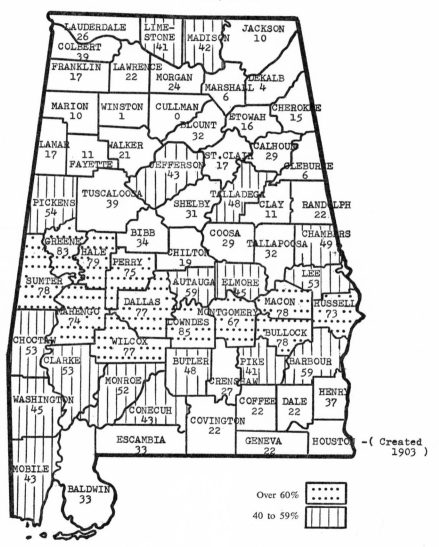

Over 60%

40 to 59%

APPENDIX II

Pearson Product Moment Coefficients of Correlation Among Political and Social Indicators, All 66 Alabama Counties

Variable	A	B	C	D
a. Populist percent of gubernatorial vote, 1892	1.00	0.22	−0.59	−0.35
b. Comer's percent (Progressive) of gub. vote, 1906	0.22	1.00	−0.31	−0.26
c. Negro percent of total pop.	−0.59	−0.31	1.00	0.13
d. Percent pop. living in towns of 2,500	−0.35	−0.26	0.13	1.00
e. Percent farms operated by owners	0.42	0.09	−0.76	−0.04
f. Total value annual farm product	−0.35	−0.16	0.33	0.62
g. Total dollar value added by manufacturing	−0.29	−0.29	0.06	0.79
h. Percent pop. employed as wageearners	−0.07	−0.21	−0.07	0.35
i. Republican percent 1902 gub. general election	0.54	0.27	−0.85	−0.20
j. Populist percent 1894 gub. vote	0.79	0.11	−0.72	−0.17
k. Populist percent 1896 gub. vote	0.80	0.14	−0.68	−0.20
l. Comer's percent (Progressive) of 1904 vote for pres. state Railroad Comm.	0.22	0.36	−0.22	−0.29
m. Republican percent of 1888 vote for president	−0.16	−0.28	0.14	0.23

E	F	G	H	I	J	K	L	M
0.42	−0.35	−0.29	−0.07	0.54	0.79	0.80	0.22	0.16
0.09	−0.16	−0.29	−0.21	0.27	0.11	0.14	0.36	−0.28
−0.76	0.33	0.06	−0.07	−0.85	−0.72	−0.68	−0.22	0.14
−0.04	0.62	0.79	0.35	−0.20	−0.17	−0.20	−0.29	0.23
1.00	−0.48	0.15	0.02	0.60	0.58	0.53	−0.00	−0.06
−0.48	1.00	0.51	0.29	−0.27	−0.33	−0.31	−0.20	0.33
0.15	0.51	1.00	0.30	−0.09	−0.08	−0.11	−0.31	0.19
0.02	0.29	0.30	1.00	0.04	0.01	0.05	−0.03	0.01
0.60	−0.27	−0.09	0.04	1.00	0.70	0.64	0.32	−0.12
0.58	−0.33	−0.08	0.01	0.70	1.00	0.91	0.22	−0.04
0.53	−0.31	−0.11	0.05	0.64	0.91	1.00	0.25	−0.19
−0.00	−0.20	−0.31	−0.03	0.32	0.22	0.25	1.00	−0.41
−0.06	0.33	0.19	0.01	−0.12	−0.04	−0.19	−0.41	1.00

Pearson Product Moment Coefficients of Correlation Among Political
and Social Indicators, 30 Alabama Counties Outside the Black Belt
With No Significant Urban Population

Variable	A	B	C	D
a. Populist percent of gubernatorial vote, 1892	1.00	−0.01	0.07	0.08
b. Comer's percent (Progressive) of gub. vote, 1906	−0.01	1.00	−0.38	−0.29
c. Negro percent of total pop.	0.07	−0.38	1.00	−0.04
d. Percent pop. living in towns of 2,500	0.08	−0.29	−0.04	1.00
e. Percent farms operated by owners	−0.52	−0.11	−0.13	0.18
f. Total value annual farm product	0.35	0.11	0.12	−0.11
g. Total dollar value added by manufacturing	−0.40	−0.42	0.40	0.27
h. Percent pop. employed as wageearners	−0.34	−0.41	0.47	0.32
i. Republican percent 1902 gub. general election	0.20	0.25	−0.74	0.17
j. Populist percent 1894 gub. vote	0.66	0.01	0.01	0.01
k. Populist percent 1896 gub. vote	0.48	0.04	0.17	0.18
l. Comer's percent (Progressive) of 1904 vote for pres. state Railroad Comm.	0.01	0.33	−0.43	0.10
m. Republican percent of 1888 vote for president	−0.02	−0.16	0.16	−0.36

E	F	G	H	I	J	K	L	M
−0.52	0.35	−0.40	−0.34	0.20	0.66	0.48	0.01	−0.02
−0.11	0.11	−0.42	−0.41	0.25	0.01	0.04	0.33	−0.16
−0.13	0.12	0.40	0.47	−0.74	0.01	0.17	−0.43	0.16
0.18	−0.11	0.27	0.32	0.17	0.09	0.18	0.10	−0.36
1.00	−0.70	0.48	0.57	0.04	−0.37	−0.39	−0.16	0.04
−0.70	1.00	−0.07	−0.25	−0.12	0.23	0.27	0.06	0.09
0.48	−0.07	1.00	0.85	−0.40	−0.32	−0.23	−0.18	−0.05
0.57	−0.25	0.85	1.00	−0.43	−0.29	−0.10	−0.37	−0.21
0.04	−0.12	−0.40	−0.43	1.00	0.52	0.29	0.48	−0.02
−0.37	0.23	−0.32	−0.29	0.52	1.00	0.74	0.22	0.13
−0.39	0.27	−0.23	−0.10	0.29	0.74	1.00	0.32	−0.31
−0.16	0.06	−0.18	−0.37	0.48	0.22	0.32	1.00	−0.38
0.04	0.09	−0.05	−0.21	−0.02	0.13	−0.31	−0.38	1.00

Some Political and Ecological Correlations

		Correlations with same counties ranked as to:		
	Which of the 66 counties were selected and what factor determined their rank	*Popu-lism*	*Progres-sivism*	*White Republi-canism*
1.	66 counties ranked according to the Populist percent of their total vote in 1892	1.0	.18	.57
2.	66 counties ranked according to Comer's percent of their total vote in 1906 primary	.18	1.0	.16
3.	66 counties ranked according to the Republican percent of their total vote in the 1902 election for governor.	.57	.16	1.0
4.	66 counties ranked according to proportion of Negroes in their total pop. in 1900	−.53	−.22	−.80
5.	66 counties ranked according to percent of total number of their farms operated by owners	.35	.08	.73
6.	66 counties ranked according to percent of their total pop. employed as wage-earners in 1900	.14	.30	.13
7.	Those 44 counties ranking lowest in percent of total pop. Negro, in rank order according to their Populist vote in 1892	1.0	—	.29
8.	Those 22 counties ranking lowest in percent of total pop. Negro, ranked according to their Populist vote in 1892	1.0	—	.35
9.	Those 22 counties ranking between no. 23 and no. 44 in percent of pop. Negro, ranked according to their Populist vote in 1892	1.0	—	−.07
10.	Those 22 counties ranking between no. 23 and no. 44 in percent of pop. Negro, ranked according to percent of their pop. Negro	−.37	—	—
11.	Those 22 counties ranking between no. 45 and no. 66 in percent of total pop. Negro, in rank order according to percent Negro	.13	—	—

Some Political and Ecological Correlations (*continued*)

	Which of the 66 counties were selected and what factor determined their rank	Popu- lism	Progres- sivism	White Republi- canism
		\multicolumn{3}{c}{*Correlations with same counties ranked as to:*}		
12.	Those 22 counties ranking between no. 23 and no. 44 in percent of their total vote that was Populist in 1892, ranked according to percent Negro	—.03	—	—
13.	Those 24 counties ranking in the bottom two-thirds of counties in percent Negro and in the bottom one-half of counties by percent urban in 1900 and in bottom two-thirds in percent wageearners, ranked according to percent Negro	.24	—	—
14.	Those 14 counties ranking highest in percent urban, ranked according to percent Negro	—.50	—	—
15.	Those 12 counties outside the Black Belt ranking highest in percent urban, ranked according to percent Negro	—.20	—	—
16.	Those 9 counties that do not rank in the top one-third of all counties with regard to percent Negro, percent wageearners, nor percent of white Republican vote; ranked as to the value of an acre of farmland	.12	—	—
17.	The same 9 rural, white, non-Republican counties, ranked according to percent Negro	—.05	—	—
18.	The same 9 counties ranked according to their percent of owner-operated farms	—.53	—	—
19.	Those 23 counties ranking in the top third of all counties with regard to neither their percent Negro nor their percent Republican, ranked according to their percent of owner-operated farms	—.37	—	—
20.	The same 23 non-Black Belt and nonwhite-Republican counties, ranked according to their percent Negro	—.29	—	—
21.	The same 23 counties ranked according to the value of their farmland per acre	—.27	—	—

Some Political and Ecological Correlations (*continued*)

	Correlations with same counties ranked as to:		
Which of the 66 counties were selected and what factor determined their rank	Popu-lism	Progres-sivism	White Republi-canism
22. Those 22 counties ranking in the top third of all counties in percent Populist, ranked according to percent owner-operated farms	−.06	—	—
23. Those 12 counties outside the Black Belt ranking highest in percent of owner-operated farms, ranked as to percent of owner-operated farms	.05	—	—
24. Those 22 counties ranking highest in percent of wageearners, ranked as to percent of wageearners	−.20	—	—
25. Those 17 counties outside the Black Belt ranking highest in percent urban, ranked as to percent urban	.10	—	—
26. Those 22 counties ranking highest in white Republicanism, ranked as to percent of owner-operated farms	—	—	.53
27. Those 23 counties ranking in the top third of all counties with regard to neither percent Negro nor percent white Republican, ranked as to percent Populist	—	.23	—
28. Those 9 counties not ranking in the top third of all counties with regard to percent wageearners, percent white Republican, nor percent Negro, ranked as to percent Populist	—	.20	—

APPENDIX III

The Pattern of Populism: The Alabama
House of Representatives, 1894

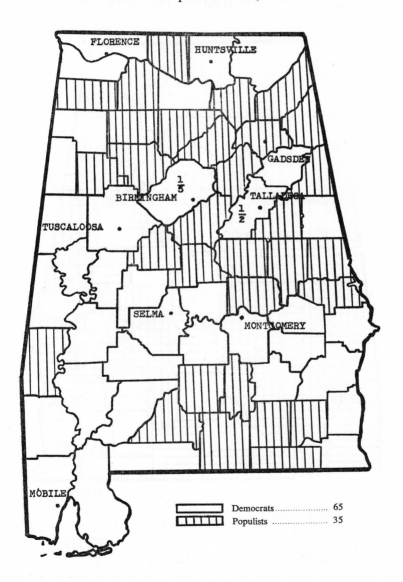

Democrats...................... 65
Populists 35

APPENDIX IV

The Results of Elections of April 23, 1901 Calling the Constitutional Convention, and of November 11, 1901 Ratifying the New Constitution

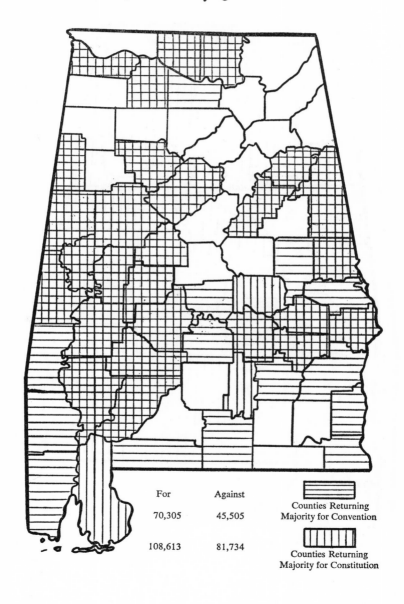

For	Against	
70,305	45,505	Counties Returning Majority for Convention
108,613	81,734	Counties Returning Majority for Constitution

APPENDIX V

Home Counties of Convention Delegates of 1901 Indicating Membership in Political Pattern

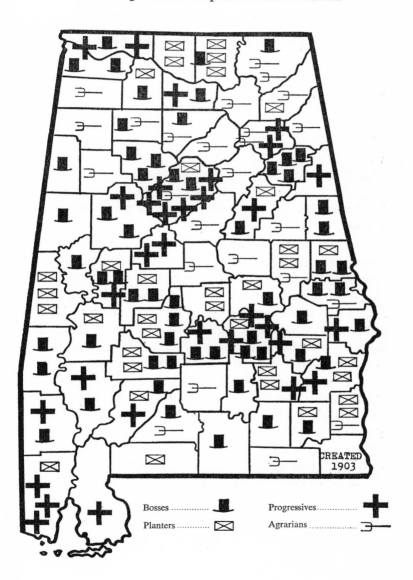

Bosses .... 🎩 Progressives .... ✚

Planters .... ⊠ Agrarians .... ϶—

APPENDIX VI

Method

THERE are only two ways to vote on a roll call, yes and no. But as soon as a second roll call is added, there are four possible ways of voting or kinds of voting patterns. If, for instance, one considered 133 roll calls, there would be 17,558 possible combinations of yes and no votes. In a convention of 155 delegates there could easily be as many voting patterns as voters. The most accurate way of proceeding would be to describe each individual's voting behavior, but such a mass of unrelated events would be almost meaningless and certainly useless as a way of thinking about what went on in the convention. To be meaningful, the voting behavior must be generalized.

The problem in the case of the Alabama Constitutional Convention of 1901 was to find or construct a number of voting patterns with one of which each but the most idiosyncratic voter would agree a significant proportion of the time, so that the least number of patterns possible would be needed. Before arriving at a final solution, the meaning of "most idiosyncratic" and "significant proportion" must be made explicit.

One pattern readily available was that described by the majority of all voters on each roll call. When each delegate was compared to the majority, it was found that the average delegate voted with the majority 63.1 percent of the time. It was then arbitrarily specified that an acceptable set of patterns would engage the agreement of 90 percent of the delegates more than 63 percent of the time and 75 percent of the delegates at least 70 percent of the time.

Because voting patterns to fill these specifications would most likely approximate one or more of the patterns actually found in the convention, the first step in what was really a trial and error search for the most satisfactory patterns was to compute the percentage of agreement of each possible pair of delegates in the convention. With the aid of a high-speed computer this was not difficult. There were 170 roll calls in the convention, but only those roll calls were used on which there was a minority of at least 10 percent of those voting. There were 133 such significant roll calls.

With this mass of data in hand it was easy to sift through the percentages of agreement of each delegate and note with whom he agreed most highly. If one were interested in isolating factions within a convention, he would merely assemble into groups those delegates who show a mutual percentage of agreement in excess of a chosen standard.* Even though the problem at hand was defined differently, this was a good way to start.

One group of delegates stood out immediately as mutually cohesive and different from other delegates. This group was composed of Populists and Republicans and a few hill-county delegates. Another distinctive group, though less obviously so than the Agrarians, centered on Frank S. White, C. P. Beddow, Leslie Brooks, B. B. Boone and a few other delegates, most of whom shared being from an urban center. It was known that White was the spokesman at the convention for the men around B. B. Comer primarily interested in getting a stronger railroad

* David B. Truman, *The Congressional Party, A Case Study*, New York, 1959, 45. A significant recent contribution to roll-call analysis, which also serves as a convenient entry into the literature, is Duncan MacRae, Jr., "A Method for Identifying Issues and Factions from Legislative Votes," *The American Political Science Review*, LIX (December 1965), 909-926.

commission. Other urban delegates, notably the leading railroad attorney James Weatherly, conspicuously did not agree with White a high proportion of the time.

Difficulties arose when a large number of delegates did not agree a high percentage of the time with the way in which the majority of the remaining (non-Populist and nonurban-reformer) delegates voted. Further analysis was possible by dividing the roll calls into groups composed of related issues. By computing the percentage of agreement for each pair of delegates on each one of the issue groups, we could discern where sharp cleavages between groups of delegates occurred.

For each set of roll calls a list was made for each delegate consisting of the other delegates with whom he agreed 70 percent of the time or more often. This could be done by computer. The significance of the delegates who were absent more than one-third of the time was discounted in analyzing the results. A perusal of these lists revealed that there was a group of delegates who agreed with White on the railroad questions but who did not agree with him on the tax questions. The suspicion that this was the nucleus of another distinctive group was confirmed by the fact that many of its members also agreed with White and company on the matter of solicitors.

At this point four possible groups were evident. One group followed the lead of the non-Democrats, a second centered on the reformers, a third was composed of delegates like Merrill of Barbour County and Miller of Wilcox who were interested in curbing the power of railroads and officeholders, but not in spending money for Progressive measures, and a fourth group that followed James Weatherly in a pattern of voting that would have been dictated by a Big Mule-railroad-officeholder-Black

Belt machine if such a thing really existed. Sensitivity to these categories was certainly sharpened by being aware of the nature of the conflicts and the character of some of the key delegates. This arrangement of forces made sense.

The next step was to test the hypothesis and see if the patterns of the four groups satisfied the requirements. A representative was chosen for each of the four groups (Reynolds of Chilton County for the Agrarians, White of Jefferson for the Progressives, Weatherly of Jefferson for the Bosses, and Merrill of Barbour for the Planters) and each delegate was assigned tentatively to the group with whose representative he most agreed. Then a composite voting pattern was assembled for each of these groups, using the majority vote of the group on each of the 133 roll calls. Then each of the 154 delegates (one delegate who died during the convention after voting only three times was dropped from the analysis) was compared to the four composite patterns. Each delegate was then reassigned to the group with whose composite pattern he most nearly agreed. A final composite pattern was then assembled for each group and the percentage of agreement of each delegate with each of the four composite patterns was recomputed for the final time. See Appendix VII for the results, and see Appendix VIII for an indication of the cohesiveness of each group. For mechanical reasons, the proportion of each group which voted Yes on each question was computed. In all the computations, only votes were considered and not absences.

The average cohesiveness of the groups ranged from 71.1 to 75.8 percent. In addition, for the least distinctive two groups the average agreement of the members with their own group's voting pattern exceeded their average agreement with the other group by 11 percent. Almost two-thirds of the delegates showed a percentage of agreement with their own group more than 10 percent greater than with any other group. The voting patterns themselves are distinctive enough so that the most similar two patterns coincide only 66 percent of the time. Only 10 delegates did not agree with at least one of the patterns in excess of 63 percent of the time. Forty-two delegates, only slightly more than 25 percent of the convention, did not agree with at least one of the patterns at least 70 percent of the time. Furthermore, a "chi square" test of statistical significance indicated that the chances were much less than 1 in 1,000 that the voting behavior of a random selection of four groups from the convention as a whole would have deviated as much as these four particular groups from the way in which the majority of the convention voted on each roll call. It would seem that real differences and agreements were being measured.

Percent Agreement Among Voting Patterns

	Boss	Planter	Progressive	Agrarian	Convention
Boss	100	66	45	39	78
Planter	66	100	62	43	75
Progressive	45	62	100	49	68
Agrarian	39	43	49	100	47
Convention	78	75	68	47	100

The Percent of Agreement of Each Delegate with the Majority of Each Group and with the Majority of the Convention on 133 Roll Calls

Delegates	*Boss*	*Planter*	*Progres-sive*	*Agrar-ian*	*Conven-tion*
(Bosses N=60)					
D. C. Almon (Lawrence Co.)	85	54	43	50	72
J. H. Barefield (Monroe)	74	59	54	44	69
Cecil Browne (Talladega)	77	57	43	59	69
John P. Burnett (Conecuh)	73	51	61	52	68
John F. Burns (Callas)	71	62	55	43	69
A. H. Carmichael (Colbert)	71	44	48	42	59
M. S. Carmichael (Coffee)	58	36	48	51	53
G. H. Carnathan (Choctaw)	73	63	39	43	62
J. E. Cobb (Macon)	72	65	53	31	65
E. W. Coleman (Walker)	79	73	40	30	66
T. W. Coleman (Greene)	76	71	48	39	74
J. B. Duke (Chambers)	61	50	59	44	62
B. T. Eley (Bullock)	65	58	55	44	72
J. C. Eyster (Morgan)	77	55	56	34	68
C. W. Ferguson (Jefferson)	76	63	53	37	75
J. M. Foster (Tuscaloosa)	80	59	61	50	75
W. F. Glover (Choctaw)	70	63	44	39	64
E. A. Graham (Montgomery)	68	51	55	44	66
L. W. Grant (Calhoun)	73	63	58	50	73
J. W. Grayson (Madison)	64	50	50	43	59
C. H. Greer (Perry)	78	65	52	33	79
L. F. Greer (Calhoun)	78	57	45	56	65
C. L. Haley (Winston)	70	43	51	56	62
W. A. Handley (Randolph)	71	67	49	37	62
G. P. Harrison (Lee)	67	50	48	57	63
J. T. Heflin (Randolph)	70	49	46	45	55
J. T. Heflin (Chambers)	75	54	44	45	67
Evans Hinson (Lowndes)	70	54	57	53	72
W. B. Inge (Hale)	80	68	48	36	68
E. C. Jackson (Lee)	65	57	53	54	69
S. C. Jenkins (Wilcox)	68	50	55	47	65
R. C. Jones (Wilcox)	75	68	61	41	78
J. T. Kirk (Colbert)	63	60	48	41	62
W. W. Kirkland (Dale)	66	45	47	55	55
W. N. Knight (Hale)	76	61	55	47	72
J. B. Knox (Calhoun)	71	60	54	53	73
T. Lomax (Montgomery)	66	51	62	29	63

Delegates	Boss	Planter	Progres-sive	Agrar-ian	Conven-tion
T. L. Long (Walker)	69	41	45	50	60
G. MacDonald (Montgomery)	66	54	50	42	64
J. T. Martin (Calhoun)	66	57	59	53	66
C. C. Nesmith (Lamar)	75	65	62	59	65
E. O'Neal (Lauderdale)	66	58	62	34	64
H. Opp (Covington)	79	63	50	27	68
R. A. O'Rear (Walker)	81	59	39	49	68
G. H. Parker (Cullman)	80	58	55	43	73
J. F. Proctor (Jackson)	76	46	44	53	66
H. F. Reese (Dallas)	79	63	55	43	75
C. J. Rogers (Lowndes)	72	56	63	40	70
G. A. Searcy (Tuscaloosa)	82	57	50	53	75
J. O. Sentell (Crenshaw)	78	48	45	61	66
J. H. Stewart (Perry)	71	69	54	43	72
W. M. Vaughan (Dallas)	67	65	57	40	70
B. deG. Waddell (Russell)	63	54	56	50	60
J. Weatherly (Jefferson)	88	62	48	46	79
E. D. Willett (Pickens)	78	41	59	59	62
A. E. Williams (Elmore)	65	46	48	51	62
G. W. Williams (Marengo)	75	55	54	43	69
J. N. Williams (Barbour)	64	62	49	43	59
E. P. Wilson (Washington)	72	46	44	48	66
M. Wilson (Clarke)	71	51	52	44	66
Averages	72.2	56.3	51.6	45.4	
(Planters N=37)					
W. A. Altman (Sumter)	57	83	60	57	66
D. S. Bethune (Bullock)	64	76	63	45	66
T. L. Bulger (Tallapoosa)	63	64	54	64	59
R. Chapman (Sumter)	57	76	55	53	62
B. H. Craig (Dallas)	59	73	60	56	66
J. A. Davis (DeKalb)	56	69	52	66	56
T. M. Espy (Henry)	50	80	71	56	67
A. S. Fletcher (Madison)	59	80	57	51	67
J. C. Henderson (Pike)	46	63	60	61	50
A. C. Howze (Jefferson)	66	67	57	38	67
J. M. Jones (Hale)	63	90	65	48	73
E. W. Ledbetter (Talladega)	62	68	68	46	63
N. R. Leigh (Escambia)	58	68	67	49	62
L. W. Locklin (Monroe)	63	69	52	39	71
W. T. Lowe (Lawrence)	51	73	55	62	54
L. McMillan (Wilcox)	59	67	66	59	68
G. H. Malone (Henry)	49	70	67	57	61

Delegates	Boss	Planter	Progres-sive	Agrar-ian	Conven-tion
J. C. Maxwell (Tallapoosa)	62	78	74	61	73
A. H. Merrill (Barbour)	61	81	65	41	68
C. H. Miller (Marengo)	59	69	56	64	66
J. N. Miller (Wilcox)	69	85	66	48	74
J. H. Parker (Elmore)	57	70	70	61	66
E. Pettus (Limestone)	54	62	59	59	62
P. H. Pitts (Dallas)	62	77	66	51	72
J. J. Robinson (Chambers)	52	69	57	45	58
J. A. Rogers (Sumter)	55	70	50	54	62
W. A. Samford (Pike)	68	71	59	36	71
W. T. Sanders (Limestone)	59	71	63	53	64
J.W.A. Sanford (Montgomery)	52	58	54	48	58
G. L. Smith (Mobile)	70	79	66	47	72
M. A. Smith (Autauga)	47	64	60	61	56
M. M. Smith (Autauga)	57	66	51	49	61
M. Sollie (Dale)	41	50	41	39	47
R. E. Spragins (Madison)	53	75	58	56	60
W. H. Tayloe (Perry)	60	74	65	47	70
R. W. Walker (Madison)	62	84	59	49	65
J. J. Winn (Barbour)	57	70	64	52	69
Averages	57.9	71.6	60.4	50.2	
(Progressives N=32)					
J. T. Ashcraft (Lauderdale)	53	69	77	54	67
W. H. Banks (Russell)	42	61	80	53	56
C. P. Beddow (Jefferson)	40	57	76	60	53
S. Blackwell (Morgan)	53	62	73	62	64
B. B. Boone (Mobile)	57	71	79	52	67
L. E. Brooks (Mobile)	49	55	78	53	56
R. M. Cunningham (Jefferson)	64	71	77	54	74
S. H. Dent (Barbour)	47	73	77	53	60
E. W. deGraffenreid (Hale)	61	57	68	29	62
W. C. Fitts (Tuscaloosa)	36	65	74	69	61
J. A. Gilmore (Clarke)	41	62	72	65	62
J. B. Graham (Talladega)	51	67	76	49	63
O. R. Hood (Etowah)	61	72	71	50	69
W. P. Howell (Cleburne)	55	56	78	64	61
J. C. Jones (Bibb)	50	64	71	56	53
T. G. Jones (Montgomery)	53	51	70	39	62
R. B. Kyle (Etowah)	51	62	70	67	62
R. J. Lowe (Jefferson)	60	46	62	39	61
B. F. McMillan (Baldwin)	53	75	80	60	65

Delegates	Boss	Planter	Progres-sive	Agrar-ian	Conven-tion
E. R. Morrisette (Monroe)	59	67	82	30	65
J. D. Murphree (Pike)	41	59	70	66	57
J. D. Norman (Bullock)	54	68	80	51	68
J. Norwood (Lowndes)	59	64	74	39	71
W. C. Oates (Montgomery)	40	58	62	54	50
J. W. O'Neil (Jefferson)	66	47	68	44	67
D. Palmer (Washington)	58	67	69	55	69
H. Pillans (Mobile)	67	68	72	57	76
H. C. Selheimer (Jefferson)	57	49	70	35	57
J. F. Thompson (Bibb)	53	55	66	62	61
T. H. Watts (Montgomery)	56	63	70	49	60
J. B. Weakley (Lauderdale)	56	63	74	57	63
F. S. White (Jefferson)	37	54	79	58	53
Averages	52.5	61.8	73.3	52.7	
(Agrarians N=25)					
W. H. Bartlett (Marshall)	44	46	47	85	49
J. R. Beavers (Shelby)	60	53	53	67	64
J. A. Byars (Franklin)	37	42	48	83	44
H. W. Cardon (Cherokee)	55	51	45	59	44
D. C. Case (DeKalb)	54	40	50	81	51
W.T.L. Cofer (Cullman)	38	53	50	76	51
T. J. Cornwell (Jefferson)	59	58	55	68	68
H. T. Davis (Etowah)	53	56	61	75	60
J. M. Foshee (Conecuh)	31	42	56	77	39
N. H. Freeman (Winston)	33	52	63	81	50
P. W. Hodges (Jackson)	46	56	61	72	56
J. L. Long (Butler)	67	40	31	76	50
M. Moody (Jackson)	44	56	48	62	41
W. D. Mulkey (Geneva)	33	52	70	81	53
J. P. Pearce (Marion)	61	69	47	70	58
E. A. Phillips (Clay)	38	57	56	75	44
J. H. Porter (Coosa)	35	45	56	80	47
N. P. Renfro (Lee)	67	63	44	78	69
L. H. Reynolds (Chilton)	38	42	52	81	45
R. I. Reynolds (Henry)	55	54	38	57	53
J. B. Sloan (Blount)	47	49	54	85	49
G. A. Sorrell (Tallapoosa)	64	60	51	77	67
N. B. Spears (St. Clair)	33	53	59	76	44
S. L. Studdard (Fayette)	48	49	43	87	53
W. W. Whiteside (Calhoun)	48	48	53	77	55
Averages	45.9	51.0	51.6	75.4	

APPENDIX VIII

The Proportion of Voting Delegates of Each Group Who Voted Yes on Each of the 133 Roll Calls

Page Sequence		Boss	Planter	Progres- sive	Agrar- ian	Conven- tion	A Yes Vote was . . .
1670-	1	71	69	25	77	62	against special rapid trials where lynching threatens
901-	2	52	30	80	53	54	to prevent an impeached sheriff from holding other office
913-	3	83	87	65	50	75	to allow sheriff to succeed himself or hold other office
989-	4	61	37	92	77	63	for pensions for sheriff and posse killed in line of duty
992-	5	36	58	12	31	36	against pensions for sheriff and posse
1004-	6	41	21	82	47	45	for mandatory provision for pensions
1006-	7	51	73	15	28	46	for leaving constitution silent on pensions
1028-	8	57	76	21	44	53	for a permissive provision for pensions for sheriffs
4018-	9	32	46	95	82	55	for trial of impeached sheriff before Supreme Court vice Cir. Court
4025-	10	28	47	53	78	43	opposed to allowing sheriffs to succeed themselves
4029-	11	38	45	65	78	49	for giving governor power to suspend impeached sheriff
4033-	12	53	52	29	22	44	against governor keeping power to suspend impeached sheriff
4144-	13	31	39	75	93	50	for giving governor power to suspend sheriff pending impeachment
4148-	14	60	32	21	07	39	for allowing sheriff to succeed himself
4156-	15	51	70	85	87	67	for limiting sheriff to one term in office
4161-	16	76	80	29	33	62	against governor's power to suspend pending impeach- ment

| Page Sequence | | Percent | | | | A Yes Vote was . . . |
	Boss	Planter	Progressive	Agrarian	Convention	
4376- 17	92	96	64	54	82	for abolishing governor's power to suspend sheriff
4738- 18	37	56	65	53	50	against sheriff's immunity and succession rights
4743- 19	59	46	31	20	49	for allowing sheriff to succeed himself. Compromise.
4746- 20	06	00	08	44	10	for giving governor power of suspension. Compromise failed.
4850- 21	75	77	42	24	61	for extending present sheriff terms for 2 years
930- 22	69	57	91	14	63	for whole Executive Dept. Article with permissive pay raise
1405- 23	81	90	100	60	84	for final passage of Executive Article
581- 24	20	24	70	0	29	for $2,000 salary increase for governor
591- 25	78	74	30	100	69	for eliminating salary increase for governor
767- 26	44	23	04	76	37	against governor's pay raise even if no tax needed
775- 27	47	57	85	05	50	for higher salary for governor written into constitution
803- 28	42	39	11	90	42	for tabling amendment to leave governor's pay to legislature
1243- 29	75	79	22	88	68	for lower property tax rate limit
1247- 30	68	90	50	94	74	opposed to even temporary higher limit on tax rate
1364- 31	29	23	71	14	33	for higher tax rate limit
1471- 32	89	84	91	56	84	for denying per diem pay to delegates if convention adjourned
1476- 33	54	69	75	35	59	for denying per diem pay to delegates absent without leave
1979- 34	36	22	19	12	26	opposed firing convention employes for economy
4647- 35	75	59	60	18	62	for spending $100 to index convention proceedings

Page Sequence	Boss	Planter	Percent Progres-sive	Agrar-ian	Conven-tion	A Yes Vote was . . .
1494- 36	62	19	50	29	45	for higher limit on county borrowing capacity
1501- 37	54	87	46	83	65	opposed to higher debt limit for larger counties
1591- 38	16	52	08	41	26	opposed higher debt limits for cities
1595- 39	71	56	89	31	67	for higher debt limit for cities
2642- 40	89	89	65	45	79	opposed to giving state power to spend for internal improvement
3188- 41	57	63	41	06	48	for disqualifying strikers from right to vote
2736- 42	92	74	68	43	76	for denying vote to aliens who remain aliens longer than need
2738- 43	73	41	60	46	59	for allowing aliens to vote who have taken first papers
3224- 44	49	35	46	40	44	for allowing first paper aliens to register to vote
3238- 45	48	55	36	44	47	opposed to allowing aliens to register
3099- 46	91	97	61	40	79	in favor of fighting grand-father clause
3450- 47	83	82	96	31	79	opposed to making grandfather clause permanent
3125- 48	66	59	50	14	55	for allowing 18-21-year-olds to register under temporary plan
3141- 49	63	60	70	0	56	adoption of Section I of Suffrage Article
3291- 50	74	67	37	28	59	opposed to making Board of Registrars multi-party
3382- 51	67	54	59	0	53	opposed to starting poll tax exemption at lower age
3402- 52	59	55	59	0	52	opposed to letting legislature decide age to begin exemption
3405- 53	70	54	82	71	69	for compromise on poll tax exemption age
3409- 54	49	43	21	67	44	for compromise on poll tax exemption age

Page Sequence	Percent					A Yes Vote was . . .
	Boss	Planter	Progressive	Agrarian	Convention	
3411- 55	44	44	73	13	46	for whole Section containing poll tax compromise
3272- 56	86	77	77	06	71	opposed to leaving property & education standards to legislature
4804- 57	41	23	13	05	25	opposed to lowering the property qualification
4865- 58	22	30	57	95	42	for lower property qualification for suffrage
4872- 59	73	64	44	11	57	for higher property qualification for suffrage
4877- 60	70	69	42	06	55	for higher property qualification
3848- 61	96	100	70	31	83	final passage of Suffrage Art.
3922- 62	17	11	26	91	25	against making total pop. basis of apportionment
3820- 63	53	48	38	25	45	opposed to female property owner vote for bond issues
3823- 64	50	54	72	79	60	for female property owner suffrage
3873- 65	87	86	62	50	78	opposed to female suffrage on reconsideration
4597- 66	96	43	46	60	68	opposed compromise on elective Railroad Comm.
2323- 67	51	21	14	60	37	for allowing legislators with RR passes to collect mileage too
2337- 68	15	80	78	13	42	for outlawing use of RR passes to all public officials
2340- 69	32	81	78	31	52	for RR-pass prohibition to apply only to legislators
2354- 70	78	19	14	81	53	opposed to prohibiting only legislators from using free passes
2541- 71	54	19	0	71	33	opposed to considering RR pass question again
2546- 72	45	89	88	40	66	for forcing anti-free pass ordinance out of committee
2661- 73	69	50	61	25	58	opposed Brooks' strong anti-trust amendment

Page Sequence	Percent					A Yes Vote was . . .
	Boss	Planter	Progres-sive	Agrar-ian	Conven-tion	
4545- 74	73	67	83	27	67	opposed harsh regulation of Bldg. & Loan Co. interest rate
3679- 75	64	70	72	43	64	opposed supporting agriculture schools from general fund
4221- 76	86	71	67	92	79	compromise on education taxes
4265- 77	10	18	05	20	13	opposed to co-opting Board of Trustees for Univ. Ala.
4309- 78	75	72	77	73	74	opposed to dividing school funds by race
4316- 79	30	35	08	65	31	opposed to compromise giving counties (not cities) option-al 1 mill tax for education
4408- 80	82	75	83	30	76	for large increase in annual funds for Univ. Ala.
3581- 81	80	04	19	12	39	opposed to popular election of Circuit Solicitors
4057- 82	93	28	21	06	51	opposed to popular election of Circuit Solicitors
4063- 83	05	77	83	100	49	for popular election of Circuit Solicitors
4066- 84	98	22	22	06	52	for popular election of Circuit Solicitors
4105- 85	94	19	24	06	50	for election of Solicitors by legislature
4247- 86	53	07	09	0	23	for Legislative election of Solicitors
4325- 87	88	13	22	06	47	opposed to popular election of Solicitors
4353- 88	08	78	78	95	50	opposed reconsideration of popular election of Solicitors
4355- 89	93	22	22	10	51	opposed popular election of Solicitors
4359- 90	95	27	2	05	51	same as no. 89
719- 91	44	75	60	25	52	for prohibiting legislators from holding appointive office
723- 92	54	22	27	68	43	for allowing dual office holding
752- 93	67	32	30	75	53	same as no. 92

Page Sequence	Boss	Planter	Progres-sive	Agrar-ian	Conven-tion	A Yes Vote was . . .
			Percent			
754- 94	66	27	32	76	52	same as no. 92
2252- 95	22	09	32	15	19	for 2-year terms for legislature
2280- 96	36	29	62	39	39	for biennial sessions of legislature
2281- 97	45	67	38	71	53	for quadrennial sessions of legislature
2299- 98	50	72	41	56	55	same as no. 97
4712- 99	81	90	58	58	75	same as no. 97
2426-100	88	78	52	67	76	for strict limit on legislature's power of appropriation
2483-101	61	41	76	57	58	opposed to limiting legislature to governor's est. of revenue
2510-102	71	68	57	30	64	opposed to binding legislature to governor's revenue bill
857-103	68	71	50	24	58	prohibited legislature from going behind county election returns
1812-104	41	36	25	56	39	opposed to local legislation
1830-105	29	37	63	29	38	opposed to prohibiting legislature granting special privileges
1841-106	50	47	24	69	46	opposed to local option and dispensary system
1970-107	65	70	62	39	62	for compromise giving precedence to general laws
2467-108	88	90	87	82	88	for comprehensive article prohibiting local legislation
2089-109	75	73	79	25	68	opposed easy creation of new counties
2112-110	31	48	53	73	46	opposed giving legislature sole power to change boundaries
2118-111	68	54	62	27	57	inverse of no. 110
2171-112	61	77	68	79	70	to table tough new county rules
2178-113	46	35	65	29	44	to retain tough rules about moving county courthouses
2470-114	96	94	91	53	89	for compromise on new counties
4687-115	53	50	68	33	52	opposed to splitting Jefferson

360

Page Sequence	Boss	Planter	*Percent*			A Yes Vote was . . .
			Progres-sive	Agrar-ian	Conven-tion	
1687-116	63	56	33	40	51	opposed to allowing ¾ jury render verdict in civil case
1724-117	10	03	21	0	10	for allowing ¾ jury verdict except in case of tort
1726-118	16	20	50	33	27	for allowing ¾ jury verdict
3499-119	73	68	45	20	56	for continuing equity juris-diction in Chancery Courts
3621-120	55	57	27	27	46	opposed to providing verbatim records in Circuit Court
3624-121	33	28	58	55	39	for big section of Judicial Article
3674-122	13	69	77	83	48	for elective county solicitors instead of Circuit Solicitors
3750-123	90	17	21	19	50	opposed to county solicitors
3753-124	94	13	19	25	50	same as no. 123
4754-125	20	96	86	80	59	for giving legislature option of method of choosing solicitors
1109-126	66	46	67	06	53	opposed to lowering the fertilizer tax
1179-127	74	50	74	24	61	for maintaining right to tax manufactured articles
4427-128	70	82	67	87	74	for making permissive the command to lower the guano tag tax
4908-129	61	68	27	29	51	opposed to reform of county convict leasing system
4389-130	77	84	88	31	76	for allowing Mobile to keep special liquor tax for schools
4454-131	16	33	16	20	20	for leaving fate of Negro militia company to legislature
31-132	65	76	74	89	72	for choosing convention seats by lottery
1472-133	29	27	38	41	32	for adjourning to celebrate the Fourth of July
Average Cohesion	71.1	72.3	72.8	75.8	63.1	

M anuscript sources relevant to an understanding of
Alabama politics between 1890 and 1910 are
more abundant than one would expect. The Alabama
State Department of Archives and History (abbreviated
"ADAH" in the footnotes) contains especially valuable
collections. The papers of Alabama's two foremost jour-
nalists, Robert McKee and John W. DuBose, were rich
far beyond anticipation. Both had wide acquaintanceships
among important men and both were in the habit of cor-
responding about public affairs. The papers of Chappell
Cory and John W. A. Sanford are not numerous but contain a few interesting items, particularly in the case of
Cory who was Joseph F. Johnston's personal secretary
for a short time. All of these men were connected with
what became the Progressive wing of the Democratic
Party. An important member of the opposing faction,
Russell M. Cunningham, left no correspondence of value
to the historian; his papers contain mostly speeches and
clippings. This is all too frequently the case with defenders of the established order. The correspondence of
Oscar W. Underwood is useful in this regard because
Underwood was firmly connected to Alabama industrialists. Though Congressional politics are fully illuminated here, Underwood was little concerned with the
day-to-day functioning of state politics and tried to keep
the two separate. The papers of John H. Bankhead, Sr.
help to document the fact that one aspect of the conservative mind can be a nonideological approach to poli-

tics. His papers are skimpy for the period before 1910, with the exception of their full and interesting documentation of the political campaigns of 1906. The personal papers of Thomas Goode Jones therefore offer a rare opportunity. They are full and they cover the entire period. The incoming and outgoing correspondence of the Governor's Office, where the Jones correspondence for his years as governor will be found, contains much significant and under-utilized material amid a great deal of trivia. These official Governor's Office Records provide the only good source of information for Governors Joseph F. Johnston (1896-1900), William J. Samford (1900-1901), William D. Jelks (1901-1906), and for Russell M. Cunningham who was acting governor when Jelks suffered a lengthy illness. The official correspondence is also the best source for the intimate thinking of Braxton Bragg Comer before 1908.

The Comer papers in the Southern Historical Collection of the University of North Carolina begin only in 1908 and contain few important letters. By far the most valuable collection at Chapel Hill for the purposes of this study was the Jesse Stallings Papers. Stallings was a Congressman and was active in Alabama politics, generally on the side of the Progressives, from the mid-1890s on. His correspondence was particularly useful after 1900. Frederick G. Bromberg's papers contain almost nothing of political importance after 1890. The diary of William J. Samford reveals him to have been a deeply religious man who evidently thought much more about the weather than politics. Thomas D. Samford continued the diary after his father's death in 1901. His entries reveal factional ties at the county level and the intricate linkage between the county level and Governor Jelks. Hilary Herbert's papers reveal little about state politics but do contain some interesting correspondence with national leaders on matters of race and politics.

Available in the library of the University of Alabama are the papers of Oliver Day Street, the only existing collection of the correspondence of an Alabama Populist. Street was more interested in the mechanics of politics than in ideas, but his letters are most revealing as to those mechanics, especially so because he became Alabama's leading Republican and remained active into the 1930s. The Henry D. Clayton papers, also at Tuscaloosa, contain no correspondence of political importance for the period prior to 1910.

The library of Samford University (formerly Howard College) in Birmingham, Alabama contains the large and as yet unorganized collection of the correspondence of Joseph J. Willett. Most of the correspondence concerns Willett's law practice, but there are also some interesting letters to and from Comer in the years 1901, 1904, and 1908.

The papers of Senator John Tyler Morgan in the Library of Congress are full, but they are mostly concerned with the isthmian canal question in the 1890s. State politics are most illuminated when Morgan was being challenged by Governor Johnston in the period 1898 through 1902. Except for the important matter of patronage, congressmen paid little attention in their correspondence to the operations of politics within the state. The effort of Richmond P. Hobson to identify himself with Comer's forces and with Progressivism in general is a partial exception to this rule. Hobson's extensive correspondence could tell an interesting story about the rise and stagnation of a national hero, particularly because much that remains is of a personal nature. Even so, his letters written during the campaigns of 1904 and 1906 (when he defeated John H. Bankhead, Sr. for a seat in the U.S. House of Representatives) are interesting and revealing. The Library of Congress also houses the papers of Booker T. Washington, whose efforts to influence the course of political events in Alabama around the turn of the century are unfortunately not fully documented in his surviving correspondence. In the same depository are the papers of Presidents Cleveland, McKinley, and Theodore Roosevelt. The Cleveland and McKinley papers are available on microfilm and are indexed so that the presidents' dealings with significant men may be followed conveniently. Easy access to the Roosevelt correspondence is provided by Elting E. Morison and John M. Blum, eds., *The Letters of Theodore Roosevelt*, Cambridge, Mass., 1951-54. Those interested in obscure issues of state politics must still consult the manuscripts themselves, however.

The excellent newspaper collection in the Alabama State Department of Archives and History was especially rewarding. I found the Montgomery *Advertiser*, despite its right-wing bias, to contain the most complete coverage of state politics. I also relied heavily on the Mobile *Register* which had a similar ideological slant throughout the 20-year period. The Birmingham *News* reflected the outlook of Comer Progressivism fairly consistently, while the Birmingham *Age-Herald* changed hands and ideological orientation twice. In 1895 and 1896 the *Age-Herald* was owned by Joseph F. Johnston. Before that time it had been sympathetic to agrarian grievances but not to Populism, and after the Johnston regime it developed into an anti-Progressive paper, though not so intransigent as the *Advertiser* and *Register*.

The availability of Populist papers was a pleasant surprise. Though many Populist papers are lost to historical research, enough survive to justify confidence in the portrait that emerges from them. There are a few that exist in relatively long runs: The *Ozark Banner*, the Randolph *Toiler*, and the Troy *Jeffersonian* in the period before 1896. After 1896 the Ozark *Free Press* and the Greenville *Living Truth* were particularly useful, while the *Choctaw Alliance* is available through both periods (1893-1901). There are numerous other Populist papers which are represented by less extensive files. The footnotes will provide the best guide to these and other weekly newspapers.

Existing Negro newspapers from Alabama are even more fractional. The Huntsville *Gazette* (1881-1894), the Huntsville *Journal* (1899-1905), and the Mobile *Southern Watchman* (1899-1902) were the most revealing. Scattered issues of other Negro Republican papers also exist. The *Tuscaloosa Chronicle* (1898-1899) is a Negro Democratic paper, and the *Baptist Leader* (1900-1905), the organ of the Alabama Colored Baptist Convention, devoted itself to the concerns of the church. See Warren Brown, *Check List of Negro Newspapers in the United States, 1827-1946*, "Lincoln University Journalism Series," No. 2, Jefferson City, Missouri, 1946; and Armistead Scott Pride, *Negro Newspapers on Microfilm; A Selected List*, Washington, D.C., 1953.

Newspaper sources for other shades of opinion are less plentiful. The Birmingham *Times* was the chief organ of the lily-white Republicans. The *Southern Republican,* The *Alabama Home*, The Anniston *Republican*, and the Huntsville *Republican* were also white-Republican papers. The *Labor Advocate* and the *Bessemerite* reflected the viewpoint of organized labor. For other Alabama papers, Rhoda Coleman Ellison's *History and Bibliography of Alabama Newspapers in the Nineteenth Century*, University, Ala., 1954, is a very useful but by no means exhaustive guide.

Statistics revealing the contours of Alabama's society and economy were gleaned from numerous sources. The *Eleventh Census of the United States* and the two succeeding censuses published by the Bureau of the Census yielded figures for population, agriculture, mining, and manufacturing. Much of this information, tabulated by county, city, and other divisions, is conveniently located in a pamphlet issued by the Bureau of the Census, *Statistics for Alabama*, Washington, D.C.: Government Printing Office, 1913. The *Alabama Official and Statistical Register*, published by the Alabama State Department of Archives and History in 1901, 1903, and quadrennially thereafter, contains election returns, biographical data on state officials, names of county officers, and numerous tables of useful figures. An earlier analog is Saffold Berney's *Handbook of Alabama*, Birmingham, 1892. The *Auditor's Office Annual Report* gives a breakdown of state finances, with tax receipts and expenditures by county, and the *Tax Commission Report* for 1907 and 1909 yields abundant information about the tax structure and about individual businesses in the state. The *Department of Insurance Annual Report*, 1895, 1901, 1903, and 1906, could be used to measure gross business activity but it also presents a good view of an area of continuing grievance to Alabama businessmen.

The state's inactivity in the area of greatest concern to businessmen is disclosed in the *Annual Reports of the Railroad Commission*. The railroad problem is illuminated by various documents from the Interstate Commerce Commission: *Railways in the United States in 1902*, Sixteenth Annual Report, App. G, Part II, IV-V; Washington, D.C., 1904; *Intercorporate Relationships of Railways in the United States as of June 30, 1906,* Washington, D.C., 1908; and *Hearings Relative to the Financial Relations, Rates, and Practices of the Louisville and Nashville Railroad Co . . . ,* Senate Documents, 64th Cong., 1st Sess., No. 461. A framework for understanding these technical reports is provided by several historical studies: William H. Joubert, *Southern Freight Rates in Transition,* Gainesville, 1949; John F. Stover, *The Railroads of the South, 1865-1900: A Study of Finance and Control,* Chapel Hill, 1955; David Potter, "The Historical Development of Eastern-Southern Freight Rate Relationships," *Law and Contemporary Problems,* XII, No. 3 (1947), 416-448; and Jean E. Keith, "The Role of the Louisville and Nashville Railroad in the Early Development of Alabama Coal and Iron," *Bulletin of the Business Historical Society,* XXVI, No. 3 (September 1952), 165-174.

The more general problem of monopoly also engaged the interest of Alabama Progressives. B. B. Comer headed the Alabama delegation to the famous gathering in September 1899 whose proceedings were published by The Civic Federation of Chicago in 1900 as the *Chicago Conference on Trusts.* The other standard source of information and opinion on the monopoly problem of the period is the Commission on Industrial Relation's *Report of the Industrial Commission,* 8 vols., Washington, D.C.: Government Printing Office, 1900-1901. The most notable invasion of a trust or monopoly into Alabama was the acquisition of the state's largest mining and manufacturing concern in 1907 by the United States Steel Corporation. This was investigated by the United States Senate Judiciary Committee in hearings published in 1911 under the title, *Absorption of the Tennessee Coal, Iron and Railroad Co.,* Senate Documents, 62nd Cong., 1st Sess., Vol. XXVIII, No. 44. Because the episode became involved in the political feud between Theodore Roosevelt and William Howard Taft, it has received frequent attention in secondary works. The most recent scholarly account is found in Gabriel Kolko, *The Triumph of Conservatism: A Reinterpretation of American History, 1900-1916*, New York, 1963. A contemporary account that is surprisingly full and accurate is found in Ethel Armes, *The Story of Coal and Iron in Alabama*, Birmingham, 1910. Despite the fact that it was published under the auspices of the Birmingham Chamber of Commerce and has the bias which that implies, *Coal and Iron in Alabama* is a mine of otherwise unavailable information about the new and dynamic sector of the state's economy and the men who managed it.

Some of the social costs imposed on Alabama by these men and the businesses they controlled are investigated in the *Report of the Joint Committee to Examine the Convict System*, 1888-1889 and 1901. More regular but less honest reports of conditions are found in the *Board of Inspectors of Convicts Quadrennial Reports* and the *Annual Report of the Factory Inspector*, 1912. A full account of one of the most violent disturbances in the mining industry in Alabama is William Warren Rogers and Robert David Ward, *Labor Revolt in Alabama: The Great Strike of 1894*, "Southern Historical Publication Number 9," University, Ala., 1965. Southern response to the evils of child labor is treated in Elizabeth H. Davidson, *Child Labor Legislation in the Southern Textile States*, Chapel Hill, 1939. The foremost reformer in this field is the subject of two articles: Hugh C. Bailey, "Edgar Gardner Murphy and the Child Labor Movement," *The Alabama Review*, XVIII (January 1965), 47-59; and Daniel Levine, "Edgar Gardner Murphy: Conservative Reformer," *The Alabama Review*, XV (April 1962). A contemporary report is Emily E. Williamson, "Child Labor in Alabama," *The Annals of the American Academy of Political and Social Science*, XXI (March 1903), 331-332. The report of the joint legislative committee, headed by Russell M. Cunningham, on the conditions and operation of the convict leasing system will be found in the *Journal of the Senate of the General Assembly of the State of Alabama for the Regular Session Commencing . . . 1898.*

The *Senate Journal* and the *House Journal* for each session of the legislature are indispensable sources which are too frequently overlooked. Interpreting roll call votes is dangerous business, but it is better to err than to ignore. Those bills that survived the legislative process and received the governor's signature appear in the *General Laws and Joint Resolutions Passed by the General Assembly of the State of Alabama* (cited in the footnotes as *Acts*) for each session of the legislature. The legislature and the power of the governor in the twentieth century in Alabama have been skillfully analyzed by Hallie Farmer in the book, *The Legislative Process in Alabama*, Bureau of Public Administration of the University of Alabama, 1949. The Constitutional Convention of 1901 was another instance of reality being tested with roll call votes. The Constitutional Convention can most directly be studied through its own verbatim record, whose importance is enhanced by the fact that Virginia was the only other state to keep such a record of a disfranchising convention: *Official Proceedings of the Constitutional Convention of the State of Alabama, May 21st, 1901, to September 3rd, 1901*, Wetumpka, Ala., 1941. This convention received thorough treatment at the hands of Malcolm Cook McMillan in his study, *Constitutional Development in Alabama, 1798-1901: A Study in Politics, the*

Negro, and Sectionalism, "The James Sprunt Studies in History and Political Science," Vol. XXXVII; Chapel Hill, 1955. Various misconceptions about disfranchisement must be avoided. Joseph B. Taylor's article, "Populism and Disfranchisement in Alabama," *Journal of Negro History,* XXXIV (October 1949), is clearly wrong in saying that Populists favored disfranchisement in Alabama. I think Alabamians and other Southerners were very aware of the disfranchising possibilities of a poll tax at least as early as 1890, when Mississippi used it, but an argument to the contrary is contained in an article by Frank B. Williams, Jr. "The Poll Tax as a Suffrage Requirement in the South, 1870-1901," *Journal of Southern History,* XVIII (November 1952), 469-496.

The problem of race was as salient for contemporary observers as it has been for historians. *Race Problems of the South,* the report of the conference held in Montgomery in 1900 under the auspices of the Southern Society for the Promotion of the Study of Race Conditions and Problems in the South, further documents this point. That a wider audience was interested is attested to by the fact that this conference attracted national attention. See Samuel M. Lindsay, ed., "The Race Problem: A Southern Conference," *The Annals of the American Academy of Political and Social Science,* XV (March 1900), 307-310; Booker T. Washington, "The Montgomery Race Conference," *Century Magazine,* LX (August 1900), 630-632; and Hilary Herbert, "The Race Problem at the South," *The Annals of the American Academy of Political and Social Science,* XVIII (July 1901), 95-101. E. L. Godkin disclosed the theft of Negro votes in Alabama as the basis of Redeemer strength in his report, "Politics and the Race Question in Alabama," *The Nation,* LIX (September 20, 1894), 211-212. *The Forum* aired the opinions of two prominent Alabamians, Negro educator William H. Councill and Congressman Oscar W. Underwood. See Councill, "The Future of the Negro," XXVII (July 1899), 570-577; Charles Henry Grosvenor, "The Negro Problem in the South," XXIX (August 1900), 720-725; and the reply by Underwood, "The Negro Problem in the South," XXX (October 1900), 215-219. Edgar Gardner Murphy, who originated the idea of the Montgomery race conference, expressed his opinions in his article, "The Freedman's Progress in the South," *The Outlook*, LXVIII (July 1901), 721-724.

The best place to start for an account of racial matters in historical perspective is C. Vann Woodward's book, *The Strange Career of Jim Crow*, 2nd rev. edn., New York, 1966. Useful also is Charles S. Mangum, Jr.'s work, *The Legal Status of the Negro*, Chapel Hill, 1940. An excellent recent survey of Negro thought in this period is August Meier, *Negro Thought in America, 1880-1915: Racial Ideologies in the Age of Booker T. Washington*, Ann Arbor, 1963. The variety of thought among whites is illuminated by Guion G. Johnson, "The Ideology of White Supremacy, 1876-1910," in Fletcher M. Green, ed., *Essays in Southern History Presented to Joseph Gregoire deRoulhac Hamilton*, "The James Sprunt Studies in History and Political Science," Vol. XXXI, Chapel Hill, 1949, 124-156. Horace Mann Bond's study, *Negro Education in Alabama: A Study in Cotton and Steel*, Washington, D.C., 1939, has an importance that goes beyond what the title would indicate, though its most striking interpretations pertain to periods prior to 1890. Considerable attention by others was paid to the problem of lynching before 1940; consequently the subject is well documented. Some of the figures were brought together by the National Association for the Advancement of Colored People in *Thirty Years of Lynching in the United States, 1889-1919*, New York, 1919, and by The Southern Commission on the Study of Lynching, *Lynchings and What They Mean*, Atlanta, 1931. More figures and analyses are found in James H. Chadbourn, *Lynching and the Law*, Chapel Hill, 1933, and Arthur F. Raper, *The Tragedy of Lynching*, Chapel Hill, 1933. The Negro's role in the agrarian revolt is discussed and probably overemphasized in two articles by Jack Abramowitz: "The Negro in the Agrarian Revolt," *Agricultural History*, XXIV (January 1950), 89-95; and "The Negro in the Populist Movement," *The Journal of Negro History*, XXXVIII (July 1953).

Populism has attracted the attention of numerous scholars interested in Alabama history. The standard account is by John B. Clark, *Populism in Alabama*, Auburn, Ala., 1927. Subsequent additions to this body of knowledge have been large. Allen J. Going looks at one crucial election in his article, "Critical Months in Alabama Politics, 1895-96," *The Alabama Review*, V (October 1952), 269-281, while Charles G. Summersell looks at another in "The Alabama Governor's Race in 1892," *The Alabama Review*, IX (January 1955), 5-35. Summersell provides a survey of opinion in another article, "Kolb and the Populist Revolt as Viewed by Newspapers," *The Alabama Historical Quarterly*, XIX (Fall 1957), 375-394; and James F. Doster questions Populism's anti-railroad feelings in a note entitled, "Were the Populists Against Railroad Corporations? The Case of Alabama," *The Journal of Southern History*, XX (August 1954), 395-399. Thomas Goode Jones defended himself in an essay written toward the end of his life and reprinted as "The 1890-92 Campaigns for Governor of Alabama," *The Alabama Historical Quarterly*, XX (Winter 1958), 656-683. Another participant in the battles, John Tyler Morgan, justified his position even before the outbreak of the third party movement: "The Danger of the Farmers' Alliance," *The Forum*, XII (November 1891), 399-409. Two unpublished studies shed light on the principal actor of Alabama Populism: Luther Lister Hill, "Reuben Kolb and the Populist Revolt in Alabama," unpub. senior thesis, Princeton University, 1957; and Charles G. Summersell, "Life of Reuben F. Kolb," unpub. master's thesis, University of Alabama, 1930.

The most recent scholar to make a thorough survey of Populism and its background is William Warren Rogers. Much of the information in his study, "Agrarianism in Alabama, 1865-1896" unpub. Ph.D. diss., University of North Carolina, 1959, he has made available in article form: "The Alabama State Grange," *The Alabama Review*, VIII (April 1955), 104-118; "Alabama's Reform Press: Militant Spokesman for Agrarian Revolt," *Agricultural History*, XXXIV (April 1960), 62-70; and "Reuben F. Kolb: Agricultural Leader of the New South," *Agricultural History*, XXXII (April 1958), 109-119.

The period of Alabama history falling between Redemption and the outbreak of Populism is best covered in Allen Johnston Going, *Bourbon Democracy in Alabama, 1874-1890*, University, Alabama, 1951. More information on this same period is provided by several articles. Justin Fuller sketches and analyzes the new breed of businessmen in a two-part study, "Alabama Business Leaders: 1865-1900," appearing in *The Alabama Review*, XVI (October 1963), 279-286 and *The Alabama Review*, XVII (January 1964), 63-75. Frances Roberts treats the chief pre-Populist leader of agricultural discontent in Alabama in "William Manning Lowe and the

Greenback Party in Alabama," *The Alabama Review*, V (April 1952), 100-121. Various aspects of a most important section of the state are reviewed sympathetically and somewhat nostalgically by Glenn Sisk in a series of articles: "Social Aspects of the Alabama Black Belt, 1875-1917," *Mid-America*, XXXVII (January 1955), 31-47; "Town Business in the Alabama Black Belt, 1875-1917," *Mid-America*, XXXVIII (January 1956), 47-55; "Towns of the Alabama Black Belt," *Mid-America*, XXXIX (April 1957), 85-95; "Crime and Justice in the Alabama Black Belt, 1875-1917," *Mid-America*, XL (April 1958), 106-113; "Social Classes in the Alabama Black Belt, 1870-1910," *The Alabama Historical Quarterly*, XX (Winter 1958), 653-655. Five elusive Alabamians are scrutinized by Hugh C. Davis, "An Analysis of the Rationale of Representative Conservative Alabamians, 1874-1914," unpub. Ph.D. diss., Vanderbilt University, 1964. Davis considerably stretches the meaning of conservatism by including in his interesting study men who flirted with Populism and embraced Progressivism.

Of course, Populism in Alabama was part of a more general national, but chiefly Southern and Western, phenomenon. The classic explanations of the discontent out of which it arose were penned by Benjamin B. Kendrick, "Agrarian Discontent in the South, 1880-1900," *Annual Report of the American Historical Association for the Year 1920*, 265-272, and by Solon J. Buck, *The Agrarian Crusade: A Chronicle of the Farmer in Politics*, New Haven, 1920. In elaborating this explanation, Hallie Farmer treats Populism as the outburst of dispossessed yeomen farmers who resented urban prosperity and the economic power of the town merchants, "The Economic Background of Southern Populism," *South Atlantic Quarterly*, XXIX (January 1930), 77-91; while Herman C.

Nixon emphasized the economic differences between the South and the New West on the one hand and the Middle West on the other hand, "The Cleavage Within the Farmers' Alliance Movement," *Mississippi Valley Historical Review*, XV (June 1928), 22-33. Subsequent authors have played similar tunes around the theme of these economic ills: John D. Hicks, *The Populist Revolt*, Minneapolis, 1931; C. Vann Woodward, *Tom Watson, Agrarian Rebel*, New York, 1938, and *Origins of the New South*, Baton Rouge, 1951; Thomas D. Clark, "The Furnishing and Supply System in Southern Agriculture Since 1865," *The Journal of Southern History*, XII (February 1946), 24-44; Chester McArthur Destler, "Agricultural Readjustment and Agrarian Unrest in Illinois, 1880-1896," *Agricultural History*, XXI (April 1947), 104-116; Carl C. Taylor, *The Farmers' Movement*, 1620-1920, New York,1953; and Theodore Saloutos, *Farmer Movements in the South, 1865-1933*, Berkeley, 1960.

Fred A. Shannon injected a new idea into the discussion of the conditions that made Populism possible when he suggested that the Turnerian safety-valve theory might be turned on its head: cities might have been safety valves for rural unrest. This idea is developed as part of an explanation for the coming of Populism in his book, *The Farmer's Last Frontier: Agriculture, 1860-1897*, New York, 1945. This possibility is now part of the ongoing consideration of Turner's original idea, which receives an intelligent review in Norman J. Simler, "The Safety-Valve Doctrine Re-Evaluated," *Agricultural History*, XXXII (October 1958), 250-257. Evidence that the issue is still alive is found in the discussion in Henry M. Littlefield, "Has the Safety Valve Come Back to Life?" *Agricultural History*, XXXVIII (January 1964), 47-49. The analyses of the economy in the late 19th century by

Rendigs Fels, *American Business Cycles, 1865-1897*, Chapel Hill, 1959, unfortunately offers little evidence to support the possibility that urban stagnation might have played a part in timing the outbreak of rural discontent. Yet the existing explanations of the rise of Populism do not completely explain why it occurred when it did, nor is the existing literature specific enough about who the Populists were and what motivated them. David F. Trask in a recent article, "A Note on the Politics of Populism," *Nebraska History*, XLVI (June 1965), 157-161, suggests that it was the defection of town merchants from the old parties that finally ignited the rural discontent. In view of the farmer's resentment of middlemen, it is hard to see how this could be so. But in testing such a theory in local settings we may get a better understanding of Populism. This hypothesis also puts forward the notion that town Populists might prove to be the (missing?) link between Populism and Progressivism.

Since Arthur Link wrote his seminal article, "The Progressive Movement in the South, 1870-1914," *The North Carolina Historical Review*, XXIII (April 1946), 172-195, the skeleton of Southern Progressivism he discovered has taken on considerable body, and the movement in Alabama has received gratifying attention. Railroads were the chief target of Alabama Progressives from Redemption on. Allen J. Going discusses the first fruits of this concern in his article, "The Establishment of the Alabama Railroad Commission," *The Journal of Southern History*, XII (August 1946), 366-385. But James F. Doster has been the chief historian of the movement for railroad regulation. His book, *Railroads in Alabama Politics, 1875-1914*, University, Ala. 1957, and his four articles soundly cover the subject. See Doster, "Alabama's Gubernatorial Election of 1906," *The Alabama Review*,

VIII (July 1955), 163-178; "Alabama's Political Revolution of 1904," *The Alabama Review*, VII (April 1954), 85-98; "Comer, Smith, and Jones: Alabama's Railroad War of 1907-1914," *The Alabama Review*, X (April 1957), 83-95; and "Railroad Domination in Alabama, 1885-1905," *The Alabama Review*, VII (July 1954), 186-198. Allen J. Going was the first student to look at the accomplishments of Comer's tour as governor. See "The Governorship of B. B. Comer," unpub. master's thesis, University of Alabama, 1940. Some Progressive Alabama congressmen emerge from Anne Firor Scott's studies, "The Southern Progressives in National Politics," (unpub. Ph.D. diss., Radcliffe College, 1957; and "A Progressive Wind from the South, 1906-13," *The Journal of Southern History*, XXIX (February 1963), 53-70. One of these politicians is the subject of two articles by Evans C. Johnson: "Oscar W. Underwood: A Fledgling Politician," *The Alabama Review*, XIII (April 1960), 109-126; and "Oscar W. Underwood: An Aristocrat from the Bluegrass," *The Alabama Review*, X (July 1957), 184-203.

Several monographs have illuminated special aspects of Alabama history in the period 1890 to 1910. Allen Woodrow Jones follows the changes in the electoral machinery in his essay, "A History of the Direct Primary in Alabama, 1840-1903," unpub. Ph.D. diss., University of Alabama, 1964. Martha Carolyn Mitchell focuses on an important new city in "Birmingham: Biography of a City of the New South," unpub. Ph.D. diss., University of Chicago, 1946. An older study proved to be helpful in understanding the real resistance to the idea of using state funds for internal improvements: William E. Martin, *Internal Improvements in Alabama*, "Johns Hopkins University Studies in Historical and Political Science," Series

XX, No. 4, Baltimore, 1902. The untiring efforts of some Alabamians to ban alcoholic beverages within the state are traced by James B. Sellers, *The Prohibition Movement in Alabama, 1702 to 1943*, "The James Sprunt Studies in History and Political Science," Vol. XXVI, No. 1, Chapel Hill, 1943. Lee N. Allen looks at another side of the Progressive movement in "The Woman Suffrage Movement in Alabama, 1910-1920," *The Alabama Review*, XI (April 1958), 83-99.

The best general history of Alabama is by Albert Burton Moore, *History of Alabama*, Tuscaloosa, 1951, which was first published in 1927 as part of a three-volume history and biographical dictionary. *The History of Alabama and Dictionary of Alabama Biography*, 4 vols., Chicago, 1921, by the first state archivist, Thomas McAdory Owen, is an excellent source of biographical and other sorts of data. *Origins of the New South*, Baton Rouge, 1951, by C. Vann Woodward must be consulted in order to put Alabama history in perspective. Three other histories of the South are useful: Francis Butler Simkins, *A History of the South*, 3rd edn.; New York, 1963; John Samuel Ezell, *The South Since 1865*, New York, 1963; and Thomas D. Clark and Albert D. Kirwan, *The South Since Appomattox: A Century of Regional Change*, New York, 1967.

Nothing can compare with letting the Alabamians of the period speak for themselves. Insight into the Populist mentality can be gained from a reading of the books produced by three of Alabama's Populist leaders. See Milford W. Howard, *If Christ Came to Congress*, Washington, D.C., 1894, and *Fascism: A Challenge to Democracy*, New York, 1928; Joseph C. Manning, *Fadeout of Populism: Presenting, in Connection, the Political Combat Between the Pot and the Kettle*, New York, 1928;

and William H. Skaggs, *The Southern Oligarchy: An Appeal in Behalf of the Silent Masses of Our Country Against the Despotic Rule of the Few*, New York, 1924. Edgar Gardner Murphy was probably not a typical Alabama Progressive, but he was the only one who wrote books. See for instance *The Basis of Ascendancy: A Discussion of Certain Principles of Public Policy Involved in the Development of the Southern States*, New York, 1909, and *Problems of the Present South: A Discussion of Certain of the Educational, Industrial and Political Issues in the Southern States*, New York, 1904. Joseph B. Graham disclosed some of the concerns of Progressives when he discussed education in his article, "Current Problems in Alabama," *The Annals of the American Academy of Political and Social Science*, XXII, September, 1903, 280-283. William Garrott Brown revealed much about himself in his history, *The Lower South in American History*, New York, 1902, and in an article, "The South and the Saloon," *Century Magazine*, LXXVI (July 1908), 462-466. A much more orthodox mind was disclosed when Benjamin F. Riley discussed The Question in his book, *The White Man's Burden, A Discussion of the Interracial Question with Special Reference to the Responsibility of the White Race to the Negro Problem*, Birmingham, 1910, a book that is interesting precisely because it was much closer to orthodoxy than to Populism or Progressivism.

White Committee, 237, 240
 251-52, 267
White, Frank S., 167, 173, 175,
 195, 214, 237, 249, 267,
 285, 320
Whitehead, James M., 27, 84,
 97, 98
white primary, 47. *See also*
 segregation
white supremacy, 40. *See also*
 segregation
White, William Allen, ix
Whitney, William C., 100
Wiebe, Robert H., xii note,
 xiii note, 324, 329-32

Willett, J. J., 257
Williams *v*. Mississippi, 160
Wilson, Massie, 158
Wiley, Ariosto A., 136, 145,
 152
Women's Christian Temperance
 Union, 304-305
Wood, William J., 131-32
Woodward, C. Vann, x, xi note,
 xiii-xiv, 15n, 98n, 199
work ethic, 81-82
Wormely House Conference,
 15

Young, E. B., 60